AUTOBIOGRAPHICAL CULTURES IN POST-WAR ITALY

AUTOBIOGRAPHICAL CULTURES IN POST-WAR ITALY

Life-Writing, Communism and Feminism

Walter S. Baroni

BLOOMSBURY ACADEMIC
LONDON • NEW YORK • OXFORD • NEW DELHI • SYDNEY

BLOOMSBURY ACADEMIC
Bloomsbury Publishing Plc
50 Bedford Square, London, WC1B 3DP, UK
1385 Broadway, New York, NY 10018, USA
29 Earlsfort Terrace, Dublin 2, Ireland

BLOOMSBURY, BLOOMSBURY ACADEMIC and the Diana logo
are trademarks of Bloomsbury Publishing Plc

First published in Great Britain 2021
This paperback edition published in 2022

Copyright © Walter S. Baroni, 2021

Walter S. Baroni has asserted his right under the Copyright, Designs
and Patents Act, 1988, to be identified as Author of this work.

Series design by Adriana Brioso

All rights reserved. No part of this publication may be reproduced or transmitted
in any form or by any means, electronic or mechanical, including photocopying,
recording, or any information storage or retrieval system, without prior
permission in writing from the publishers.

Bloomsbury Publishing Plc does not have any control over, or responsibility for,
any third-party websites referred to or in this book. All internet addresses given in
this book were correct at the time of going to press. The author and publisher
regret any inconvenience caused if addresses have changed or sites have
ceased to exist, but can accept no responsibility for any such changes.

A catalogue record for this book is available from the British Library.

A catalog record for this book is available from the Library of Congress.

ISBN:	HB:	978-1-7883-1337-7
	PB:	978-0-7556-3611-2
	ePDF:	978-1-3501-9073-3
	eBook:	978-1-3501-9074-0

Typeset by Integra Software Services Pvt. Ltd.

To find out more about our authors and books visit www.bloomsbury.com
and sign up for our newsletters.

CONTENTS

INTRODUCTION   1

Chapter 1
INSTITUTIONAL COMMUNIST AUTOBIOGRAPHIES, 1944–1956:
ADMINISTRATIVE IDENTIFICATION AND NARRATIVE IDENTITY   11
   Communist autobiographies: Origins   11
   The Italian way to autobiographical control: Elements of context   19
   The communist autobiography: Plot and story   30

Chapter 2
FEMINIST SELF-ENUNCIATION: BETWEEN SILENCE AND
INFINITE SPEECH   47
   The paradox of emancipation and its autobiographical strategies   47
   Paranoia: The infinite discourse   60
   Schizophrenia and catatonia: Poetry, dreams and discursive hesitations   74

Chapter 3
THE REMAINS OF TWO TRADITIONS: INSTITUTIONAL MONUMENTS
AND IMPOSSIBLE MOURNING   89
   After the end: The collapse of communism and the self-narrative   89
   Late feminist autobiographies: The journey towards legitimacy and
      normality   104
   Echoes of the origins: The autobiographies of Giorgio Napolitano
      and Laura Lepetit   121
         Giorgio Napolitano: The man who made himself an institution 121
         Laura Lepetit: Feminism as distraction   127

CONCLUSIONS   135

Notes   142
Bibliography   167
Index   177

INTRODUCTION

This book presents an analysis of communist and neo-feminist autobiographies produced in Italy after the Second World War. It focuses on the narrative techniques used to recount the self, regarding them as a means of responding to a paradoxical injunction – similar to the command to 'be spontaneous' – underpinning the operation of such autobiographical forms of enunciation. Its aim is to provide a description of those political traditions from an original point of view, that is, the autobiographical cultures that they developed to emancipate the selves of militants and activists.

It first considers the practice that required new communist party recruits to prepare a free-form autobiography, to be included in their personal file, managed by the cadre division. Members' autobiographical duties did not end with their acceptance into the Italian Communist Party (PCI), however. They were also required to repeat the process as part of courses run by the party schools and in the event of promotion, in the case of officials. In the Italian neo-feminist context, meanwhile, the text examines the set of self-enunciation practices that emerged from consciousness-raising groups, where women recounted and analysed their personal experiences.[1]

At first glance, the comparison proposed here may seem historically questionable. The golden age of communist autobiographical writing as an institutional tool applied to militants spanned the fifteen years following the Second World War. Feminist self-enunciation, meanwhile, emerged later between the end of the 1960s and the beginning of the 1970s. Though relatively short in chronological terms, the distance between these two experiences is marked by the historical watershed represented by the 1968 movement, which separated the old left from new.[2] The risk, then, is comparing two things that, in historical terms, are incomparable.

An initial response to such an objection might be offered simply by considering the facts. From 1956 onwards, the autobiographical obligation incumbent on PCI militants slowly began to ease, gradually losing its organizational and political significance.[3] As such, the chronological parameters of this project are largely dictated by historical events. This presents at least one advantage, enabling us to consider communist and feminist employment of autobiographical writing, respectively, at their most prolific points.

In the communist case, this means examining the autobiographical practice in the context of the enormous pedagogical effort engaged in by the PCI in relation to its militants. The political schooling of the latter began with the emergence of Togliatti's 'new party' in 1944, and, like the autobiographical activities, fell into decline following the 1956 crisis that saw the PCI caught between the destalinization process in the Soviet Union and the invasion of Hungary.[4] This gives us an insight not only into the negative side of this practice – represented by a desire to control the militants – but also into its positive aspects, specifically the active establishment of communist subjectivity. Such considerations were no longer relevant by the 1970s, when the party imported cadres from elsewhere into its organization. This bypassed the need to attend party schools and produce a wholly communist biography.[5] In the feminist context, meanwhile, autobiographical practice was first associated with the consciousness-raising experience, which emerged in the first half of the 1970s and continued, albeit with less momentum, into the second half of that decade.[6] My work focuses mainly on feminist self-discourse produced in Milan. A pole of attraction for the multifaceted Italian neo-feminist scene – thanks to its proximity to other European capitals and its economic power[7] – it is here that the neo-feminists sought to erect theoretical scaffolding to support feminist self-enunciation practices, with a view to contributing to the Italian feminist debate.[8]

Such chronological considerations aside, however, it should be noted that *this is not a history book*. Rather, it is a book that examines the forms of self-enunciation that emerged in the context of a single political tradition – the twentieth-century left – before and after 1968. The historical distance between the self-narrative experiences explored here gives the comparative analysis its significance, enabling me to highlight how a practice such as recounting the self, which is seemingly so generic, can be transformed so completely in the hands of communist militants or feminist activists respectively. This work, then, might be defined as an exercise in 'constructive comparativism',[9] involving the selection of two historical subjects for comparison and examining them through the innovative lens of the political self-narrative strategies that emerged in each context.

As regards the general positioning of my research, while it shares common ground with the 'biographical turn' approach popular in recent studies on the international communist movement, it does not belong in that category.[10] The self-narrative is not analysed here as an innovative means of accessing the communist – or feminist – universe, privileging the perspective of the subject over that of the movement. Nor is it approached, in more general terms, as an ego-document, revealing the true self of the historical figure and the latter's means of interpreting his or her world.[11] The text is not an exploration of how the individual subject reflects upon, represents, presents, appropriates or creatively repurposes communism or feminism in their daily lives. To put it simply, I am not concerned with what Goffman defines as the 'problem of expression',[12] that is, how the individual performs his or her communist or feminist role and the complicated dance of moving closer to, and drawing away from, one's political identity.

My work has more in common with the studies that approach communist autobiography as a form of Foucauldian self-improvement, that is, as a technology of the self.[13] Here, however, more so than in the self, I am interested in the technological apparatus used by the communist militants and feminist activists to prepare their autobiographies. The issue at the heart of my work resembles the challenges of following coding instructions discussed by Garfinkel. Moving between the sources of information underpinning the research – clinic folders, in his case – and codification by the coders, who transformed those materials into items on a coding sheet, raised a number of questions: 'Via what practices had actual folder contents been assigned the status of answers to the researcher's questions? What actual activities made up those coders' practices called "following coding instructions"?'[14]

Garfinkel sought to highlight the implicit procedures according to which his researchers moved from a set of unordered documents to the final text on which the work was based. This book seeks to shed light on the narrative technologies – similar to Garfinkel's procedures – by way of which communists and feminists imposed the stable form of a self-narrative on the set of unordered events that made up their lives. The scope of my investigation, then, is not defined by the distance between the individual subject and communism or feminism, but rather by the much shorter gap separating that individual subject from his or her own self-narrative. It is that 'seen, but unnoticed'[15] space within which the narrative order of the communist and feminist autobiographies takes shape, which is generally taken for granted, considered undeserving of specific attention.

To examine such technologies, we must avail of a definition of autobiography that enables their identification and allows us to highlight their operation. The classic definition offered by Lejeune is perfectly apt in this regard.[16] The French scholar suggests that an autobiography is characterized by the shared identity of the author, narrator and character, with the same proper noun being used in the paratext – the domain of the author[17] – and the text, inhabited by the narrator and character. Just as the paratext is responsible for the text becoming a book and acquiring a social existence, so too is the author of the autobiography the textual function that ensures that the account refers, in the extra-textual world, to a self that actually exists. Together with the shared identity, another key feature of the autobiography is the specific reading contract – or 'autobiographical pact' – that distinguishes the text from a novel – characterized by a 'fictional pact' – and from a biography – governed by a 'referential pact'.

Some further observations in relation to Lejeune's theory are useful for the purposes of this work. First, the three figures to whom he refers – author, narrator and character – are not inert roles but instead engage in power relations within the text. In other words, their relationship within the autobiographical field is variable. What happens, then, if the author overpowers the narrator and character to the point of their elimination? Or, on the contrary, if the character and narrator break free and somehow subjugate the author figure? The first scenario is the most interesting. Is there such a thing as a *purely authorial autobiography*, where the character and narrator disappear in favour of the author? This may seem like a ridiculous question, as it alludes to an impossible object, that is, a paratext without a text, situated in a sort of non-Euclidean textual space.

An example of such a bizarre textual configuration does, however, exist in the form of a generic identity document that records the personal details of the subject. Such a document even holds specific autobiographical power: it states that I am me. From a narrative perspective, of course, the story recounted is not particularly compelling. In a certain sense, it sees the subject of the statement merging with the autobiographical subject of the enunciation, just as the autobiographical text elides into the autobiographical act. This is represented, for example, by an individual showing their passport to various airport officials, repeating the assertion that they are themselves. In any case, this assertion – that I am me – is the driving force behind any autobiography. We are presented, then, with the most basic model underpinning any autobiography, an affirmation of the shared identity of the three figures involved – even if, in this case, the narrator and character are essentially invisible.

At the extreme opposite end of the scale are texts in which the latter figures prevail over the author. Once the paratext threshold has been crossed, the author merely serves as the condition for the unfolding of an account with the narrator and character at its centre. The extreme example of this configuration is once again somewhat bizarre. It would involve a self-narrative in which the narrator and character are forced, in the name of autobiographical truth, to dissociate themselves from – and even cut ties with – the author as referential function. To quote Lejeune, 'accuracy' and 'information' would be entirely sacrificed in favour of 'fidelity' and 'meaning'.[18] It is far more difficult here, than in the case of the identity document, to imagine the form such a textual arrangement would take. It would manifest as a non-referential, yet authentic, text, of absolute autobiographical significance.

By limiting ourselves to material considered in this study, however, we can identify at least one example of such an object: the transcription of dreams, rather commonly practiced – as we will see – by Italian neo-feminists. In feminist dream-like reports, in fact, the object of reference is, strictly speaking, absent. Not so much because it is impossible to verify – as historians or good journalists would seek to do – that the dreamer actually dreamed, and reported their dream correctly, but rather because a dream is the expression of an object that, in itself, is beyond reach and evades expression, that is, the unconscious.

Feminist dream transcripts – such as those that abound in Carla Lonzi's *Taci, anzi parla* (*Shut Up, Actually Speak*)[19] – are textual artefacts wherein what matters is not so much the act of dreaming, but what one dreamed about, even if the reality (the referent) of the dream only exists within the text that recounts it. The eradication of the author's power is obtained, here, by relegating the latter to the role of mere notary attesting to the fact that the narrator and character of the self-narrative dreamed. The latter figures are released from the requirement of reality, generally upheld by the author, by way of the dream, which by its nature, evades reference.

Taking this logic to its extreme conclusion, we might imagine an autobiographical text that takes the abused metaphor of 'life as a dream' literally, transforming the self-narrative into a presentation of all dreams dreamed by the author, thus transforming one's story into a single big dream. The result would be a sort of autobiography of the unconscious, in which the subject of the enunciation is asleep and the subject of the statement is entirely released from the shackles of reference. As strange as this may seem, one text comes very close to doing just this: Lea Melandri's dream notebooks, kept by the Milanese feminist from the second half of the 1960s.[20] Admittedly, the writings are much closer in form to a diary than a proper dream-like autobiography, and the dreams are often accompanied by attempts at analysis and brief notes. Nevertheless, these notebooks offer a good approximation of how the second extreme version of autobiographical enunciation might manifest.

At one end of the continuum of autobiographical expression, then, is the identity document, defined by identification and verification of the personal details of the subject, while the other end sees the subject being liberated from the confines of reference imposed by the author figure, pushing the account into the realm of a dream-like self-narrative. It is clear, then, that the different power dynamics between author, narrator and character produce a range of autobiographical effects; likewise, the 'autobiographical pact' between writer and reader gives rise to very distinct textual results depending on its slant.

The concept of a contract proposed by Lejeune is somewhat liberal in nature. The writer enters into a contract, guaranteed by his or her signature, with a reader who freely accepts it, according to a model of equivalent exchange: the time and money of the latter in exchange for the life, in written form, of the former. And so the 'autobiographical pact' functions, in legal terms, on the assumption that the relevant agents operate on an equal footing in a universe based on trade. This is no surprise, given that the point of reference for the French scholar's definition of autobiography is the publishing market and its various transactions.

Removed from that context, however, the liberalist notion of a contract no longer works, because the writer and reader of the autobiography cannot be compared to economic subjects exchanging an asset by way of a deed freely signed by both parties. Instead, the balance of power may be tipped in favour of the reader or the writer. In the first instance, the autobiography inevitably assumes the tone of a confession. It places the reader in a position of superiority compared to the writer. The former may, therefore, judge the adequacy of the self-narrative presented, as in the case of the confession provided by Augustine to the ultimate reader, that is, God, humbly offering him a report of his death and spiritual rebirth.

In the second instance, the autobiography would take the form of an exemplary account of the self. This does not necessarily equate to a sort of self-hagiography. Such accounts may, in fact, be presented in anti-hagiographical terms, yet still be classified as exemplary. Indeed, positive or negative, an example involves the expression of an independent system of standards that is not confined to the existing legal context. Exemplary behaviour does not involve complying perfectly with the law, but rather going beyond it, to establish superior legality.[21] In our case, tipping the balance of power in favour of the autobiographical writer results in a text that violates the reader's legitimate expectations, leaving the latter with no choice but to accept such violence. Refusal to do so would mean to stop reading, at which point the 'autobiographical pact' would cease to apply.

My approach to communist and neo-feminist autobiographies, then, involves examining the 'technical' management of the distance and power relations among the author, narrator and character, starting with the different autobiographical pacts governing the two distinct systems of production of the self-narrative. This, in turn, makes my decision to investigate the work pertaining to these two movements together easier to understand. The two strands of my research are, in fact, situated at the two far ends of the continuum of contemporary autobiographical enunciation. The communist autobiography largely involves presentation of the self for disciplinary purposes. It is closer to a curriculum vitae than an autobiography. Though intended to meet party disciplinary requirements, the communist militant self-narrative does not limit itself to performing a merely referential function. Instead, though the latter serves as an inalienable backdrop, such texts nevertheless involve a complicated game between narrator and character that I will examine later. Even in the communist case, then, the autobiographer is never merely a biographer of the self or a historian of his or her own life, but rather continues to serve as a first-person self-narrator. As such, the communist autobiography is never simply a detached document about the self, but always resembles a sort of confession. The militants do not write for God, as Augustine did, but they are, nevertheless, subordinate to their reader, in this case the party.

The neo-feminist self-narrative, on the other hand, moves in the opposite direction, producing the narrativization, to the point of paradox, of the self. This does not always involve placing the author function in parenthesis, as in the extreme case of the dream-like autobiography. Instead, the referential function is relegated to a secondary role, without being eliminated completely, in favour of complex textual games essentially aimed at granting it exemplary power. The power embodied by the neo-feminist example, in turn, is directed towards curtailing the supremacy of male law. The feminist activists' self-narrative, then, works in the opposite direction to that produced by communist militants. It does not involve submitting to a control figure (represented by the party) but instead seeks to establish a new form of legality by way of one's story, which inevitably manifests as anti-legality with regard to the status quo. As such, Italian communism and neo-feminism also serve as case studies on the various modes of use of autobiographical discourse. They enable such discourse to be considered in light of the increasing social control exercised in the twentieth century and the subjective strategies that emerged to circumvent that control. The former phenomenon is best expressed by communist autobiographies, the latter by their feminist counterparts.

A discussion of the technological mechanism by way of which the author, narrator and character blend together, however, would be incomplete without a description of the main discursive device that drives the autobiographical machines examined here. This book seeks to demonstrate that the autobiographical performances considered herein operate according to the 'paradoxical injunction' mechanism.[22] The distinguishing feature of such a command is that it 'must be disobeyed to be obeyed; if it is a definition of the self or the other, the person thereby defined is the kind of person only if he is not, and is not if he is'.[23] A paradoxical injunction only works if the subject to whom the command is addressed is subordinate to the person issuing the command, and must comply with the order given to him or her, thus being forced to perform an act of obedience that is always also an act of disobedience. This is the double-bind situation in which the subject to whom the paradoxical injunction is addressed finds himself or herself.[24]

From this perspective, communist and feminist autobiographical enunciations may be regarded as products of the command to 'be yourself', which might also be translated as 'be what you are'.[25] Naturally, being oneself means being one's communist or feminist self. Though, in logical terms, we might consider the self that acts as separate to the self that is the object of that action – similar to William James' distinction between the I as the pure subject of knowledge and action and the Me as the object of that I[26] – this becomes impossible in a double-bind situation, and we remain trapped in the paradox.[27]

If I am myself, I do not become myself, and, therefore, I disobey the injunction, but if I become myself does it mean that I was not truly me – otherwise, why would I have to become myself? – and, therefore, that it is not me who becomes myself, but another. And if this is so, I am violating the command addressed to me. In the first instance, I comply with the substance of the injunction, but violate its form. In the second instance, I comply with the form of the injunction – I obey the command – but violate its substance because, in a certain sense, the I to whom the order is addressed disappears and it is no longer clear who the subject is that should become himself or herself. In simpler terms, the imperative to 'be (the communist or feminist) yourself' is an instruction that can only be complied with by disregarding the rule on which it is based; the command places the subject to whom it is addressed in an essentially passive condition, because the origin of his or her action is the will of another.

As we will see, the real issue, in the contexts of enunciation examined here, is posed not so much by the former form of violation, but by the latter, whereby becoming who one is always means not knowing what one has become, giving rise to a constant doubt as to whether one truly is a communist or feminist. On this point, let me pre-emptively address an objection that may be raised in relation to the application of the paradoxical injunction and double-bind concepts to the feminist self-narrative. One might argue that communists were forced to present their self-narratives by a master reader, in the form of the party, whereas feminists recounted theirs freely. This is not a valid criticism, however, for one simple reason. A paradoxical injunction may operate in the objective sphere of an institution, as in the communist case, or in the subjective sphere of an individual not subject to institutional demands, as in the case of neo-feminists writing as part of the feminist consciousness-raising collectives. In other words, it does not matter whether a paradoxical injunction is imposed by an external or internal force, it remains a paradoxical injunction. What changes, as I will seek to demonstrate later, are the effects produced on the autobiographical enunciation depending on whether the undertaking is a response to external or internal demands.

To summarize, then, this book explores the self-narrative – in the communist and feminist contexts – as a product of the injunction to be oneself politically. It considers the autobiography as an autobiographical act governed by a paradoxical injunction, wherein different dynamics emerge between the textual figures whose shared identity defines the self-narrative: author, narrator and character. In the case of communism, the resulting autobiographical technology relies on the primacy of the author and narrator pair over the character, while in the feminist context the character functions as a pole of attraction for the narrator and author.

Having laid the theoretical foundations, let me now provide some details on the historical materials considered here. My analysis of communist texts draws on the autobiographies contained in the *Partito Comunista Italiano (PCI), Federazione di Bologna* archive, *Commissione Quadri* subseries, held by the Fondazione Gramsci Emilia Romagna di Bologna.[28] I looked at sixty-three individual folders, with details of eight women and fifty-five men. In four cases, no autobiography was included in the file, leaving only the pre-filled biographical sheet. Eleven folders contained two different autobiographies for the same militant, and three contained three different autobiographies. In one instance, there were four versions. Twenty-four autobiographies were undated: the remaining documents were written between 1949 and 1959. The oldest militant was born in 1897, the youngest in 1933. The documents are still being inventoried, meaning that no exact archive location can be provided. For privacy reasons, all sensitive information contained in the autobiographies has been omitted, and the original names have been replaced with pseudonyms.

My examination of feminist autobiographies, meanwhile, considers texts included in Italian neo-feminist publications – such as *Sottosopra* [*Upside Down*] – and makes ample reference to the self-narrative work of Carla Lonzi, founder of the Rivolta femminista group and author of the aforementioned *Taci, anzi parla*, which I regard as a sort of encyclopaedia of the possible forms of feminist self-narrative. I also refer to materials contained in the *Maddalena (Lea) Melandri* archive, held by Fondazione Elvira Badaracco in Milan, focusing on the *Quaderni di appunti* subseries, and specifically on the personal diaries, written between 1966 and 1976, containing transcriptions of dreams, self-analysis, travel notes and consciousness-raising reports. I chose this archive due to the radical continuity with which Melandri approaches the issue of speaking of oneself in the first person from a feminist perspective. These writings enable an in-depth examination of the relationship between feminist self-enunciation and the paradoxical injunction.

This book, however, also considers the question of what remains of that autobiographical mobilization movement, of what is left when the machine stops. To this end, I examine a *corpus* of autobiographies written *après le déluge*, in the wake of the historical experiences of communism and neo-feminism. These include the works of well-known academics such as Luisa Passerini and Rosi Braidotti, together with former president of the Italian Republic, Giorgio Napolitano. These are texts published after the millennium, in which the protagonists of those historical periods recount and take stock of their political past. The autobiographical act is thus removed from the political context to which it refers, losing its pragmatic power and being reduced to the story of a life: the sepulchral monument to an era of mobilization that is gone forever. Whereas the self-enunciation artefacts produced in the height of the communist and feminist struggles demonstrate the full power of the relevant autobiographical techniques, they manifest in the later works as malfunctioning wrecks or jammed mechanisms, the value of which lies in their capacity to evoke the magnificence of days past, rather than in any potential use. I explore the communist autobiography in the first chapter and neo-feminist autobiographical writing in the second. The third chapter, meanwhile, looks at the issue of autobiographical commemoration of the communist and feminist past.

All that remains at this point of the introduction is to make some final observations. Does this work represent a comprehensive survey of communist and feminist autobiographical documents from the historical period that I consider? Or does it at least present samples of autobiographical materials that accurately represent that age? The answer to both questions is no. Not only due to the specific focus of the research engaged in, as already discussed, but also because the materials analysed here have been selected for their significance and not their representative nature.[29] Howard Becker referred to this issue as the problem of the good synecdoche[30]: are the portions of communism and feminism examined capable of representing all (Italian) communism and feminism? My response to that question echoes Becker's own: the purpose of this work is not to adequately represent the phenomenon in question, but to provide an unexpected representation, which approaches the topic from an innovative perspective. The issue of 'poor sampling' can also be seen from another perspective, which somewhat complements Becker's approach. Undoubtedly, this work provides a picture of the political and social phenomena in question that exaggerates certain aspects to the detriment of others. As Günther Anders notes, however, in such cases the distortion – *Entstellung* – has a methodical value: the alterations it makes shed light on certain things that would otherwise go unnoticed.[31]

These methodological considerations lead me to the final thanks and acknowledgements required in an introduction. A particular thank you to the Fondazione Badaracco in Milan and Laura Milani, who manages that archive, for her help in unravelling the maze of Milanese feminism. A collective thanks to the Fondazione Gramsci in Bologna and Rome, who rigidly guards the documentary heritage represented by the communist autobiographies. These texts are yet to be introduced to a wider public beyond the usual handful of students and specialists who enjoy the privilege of consulting those files.

And finally, this work has been made possible thanks to funding from the European Union's Horizon 2020 Research and Innovation Programme (Marie Skłodoska-Curie Actions) under Grant Number 658297.

Chapter 1

INSTITUTIONAL COMMUNIST AUTOBIOGRAPHIES, 1944–1956: ADMINISTRATIVE IDENTIFICATION AND NARRATIVE IDENTITY

Communist autobiographies: Origins

The issue of biography was central to the new society produced by the October Revolution.[1] As the period that began with the outbreak of the First World War in 1914 and ended with the Red Army's victory over the White movement in 1921 – marking the conclusion of the civil war – drew to a close, the Bolshevik social interpretation model was in tatters. The long years of war had erased the social identities used by Bolshevism to understand the Russian context and drive the revolution. Military clashes had eradicated the working class in whose name the 1917 revolution had been conducted, with workers scattering to rural areas following the closure of industrial plants.[2]

Faced with such a situation, the victors undertook the complicated task of modelling the biographical identities of the revolutionary society's citizens. The Bolshevik experiment required a radical reinvention of the forms traditionally used by subjects to narrate their personal stories: 'noble ancestry, social success achieved through "hard graft", academic merit, creative genius or business prowess (the "captains of industry", "merchant adventurers", "conquerors of new worlds")'.[3] The communist revolution had eroded the objective status of such biographical narratives, revealing them to be cultural products, the apparent inherence of which was dependent on stable cooperation among the various social actors.

A natural point of reference was offered by the proletarian biographical model. People scrambled to demonstrate their working-class provenance, as proof of such a background gave rise to a series of benefits in terms of accommodation, food rations, work and academic opportunities.[4] The competition to prove working-class biographical origins in the newly established revolutionary society was accompanied by progressive use, in the 1920s, of the biographical machine as an organizational tool by the Bolshevik party.

Biography was used, on the one hand, in a rather traditional way to erect a celebratory monument to the ruling Bolshevik class that had led the revolution and emerged victorious. To this end, volume 41 of the Granat Encyclopaedia – published in 1927 to mark the tenth anniversary of Red October – contained three books featuring 246 biographies and autobiographies of Bolsheviks who had participated in the revolution. For the purposes of the collection, this covered the period from the inception of the Bolshevik movement right through to the civil war.[5] It was a work of Bolshevik self-celebration; in presenting a public account of their achievements, it sought to atone for years of pre-revolutionary silence, characterized by the muteness of exile, illegal conspiracy and imprisonment.

On the other hand, biographical control became necessary to manage a party that had undergone a profound change in its nature in the wake of the revolution. It was no longer an organization made up of a few thousand activists engaged in avant-garde revolutionary action, in accordance with Lenin's model. From 1917, membership began to increase at a relentless rate, making careful consideration of the identity and background of new party members essential.[6] As such, cadres and activists were subject to periodic 'purges', consisting of inspection and assessment activities aimed at ridding the organization of any members deemed politically unworthy of party membership.

The first of these internal cleansing operations took place during the civil war. At the eighth congress of the party in 1919, members were required to reregister. The purpose of this procedure was to expel those with an obscure political past and those whose conversion to Bolshevism was deemed opportunistic. Purges of this kind took place throughout the 1920s, with little procedural variation. A committee of high-ranking, trusted comrades was established to ascertain the political background of militants within the party cell. The committee collected reports on the cell in question, before meeting and hearing from members individually, both in private and in the presence of others, without any standard protocol. Finally, decisions regarding the subject's future in the party were made public.[7] The inspection committee, therefore, served as a mechanism for the production of oral and written biographical and autobiographical accounts, based on the Bolshevik modes of expression and narrative canons.

As the 1920s gave way to the 1930s, the biographical framework came increasingly to serve as an organizational management tool. Periodic party purges were accompanied by an extension of the autobiographical assessment of militants; previously a procedure reserved for adult members of the party, it began to be applied to the Komsomol (the All-Union Leninist Young Communist League) and later to the various administrative bodies of the state. The practice of writing and orally presenting one's self-narrative became quite common within party schools.[8] This increasing obligation to engage in autobiographical practices coincided with a gradual shift in the methodologies used to interpret the narrative materials produced by militants and relied upon during purges.

No longer purely significant as a form of 'genealogy of social origin', such accounts evolved into devices for 'revelation by deeds', according to the interpretation presented by Oleg Kharkhordin.[9] The procedures used to individualize communist subjects in the pre-Stalin era had focused on the reconstruction of that subject's social origins: their proletariat ancestry, professional background, political past and conduct during the civil war. Only later did the biographical assessment begin to consider positions held within the party at the time of the purge and any problematic conduct during their time with the organization. The new interpretative model introduced under Stalin, however, saw party members being judged on their revolutionary zeal and most recent political performance.

In a speech at the February–March Plenum in 1937,[10] Stalin himself identified the fundamental criteria underpinning the new parameters for assessing party cadres. The new communist society faced a different enemy, the double-dealer, whose opaque nature could not be revealed through simple career background checks. A more subtle hermeneutic approach was instead required to investigate the subject's performance as a party member and Soviet citizen. This new approach, which characterizes the mature forms of self-narratives in the Stalinist era, is not solely defined by a shift in analytical focus from the communist subject's past to her present. Rather, with reference to the analytical categories outlined above, it involved a reformulation of the autobiographical pact imposed by the reader upon the author of the self-narrative. This variation to the reading contract saw the narrator take priority over the character in the autobiographical material.

A 'genealogical' reading focuses on what the subject who is recounting her life has achieved as the protagonist of his own story. As such, the central position is occupied by the character, complete with her ascribed and acquired characteristics, established by way of the events recounted by the narrator. The specific twist that, in this case, distinguishes the autobiographical pact reduces the narrative to a *historia res gestae*, that is, a simple collection of events. The latter, attributed to the character on a textual level, are subsequently linked, by way of the author function, to the individual subject that exists in the extra-textual world, confirming the reliability of what the author has recounted.

The 'revelation by deeds', on the other hand, occurs within the sphere of *historia rerum gestarum*. Of significance, here, is not so much what the character has done, but rather the way in which they have done it, demonstrating their 'zeal' or ability to be active. Naturally, a mere account of the events of one's life is inadequate for the purposes of such an assessment. Here the reader is seeking a reflexive relationship between the self as character and the self as narrator that, though presented by way of a series of occurrences, goes beyond the linear nature of a chronicle. In other words, what matters is no longer simply the *story* used to organize the events of one's life in a linear fashion, but rather the *plot* underpinning that *story*. In order to pinpoint that elusive 'zeal', then, and expose any deceptive double-crossing enemies – capable of feigning the 'zeal' of a true revolutionary – an assessment of the relationship between narrator and character is required. This involves examining the setting in which the narrator places the protagonist of the life story and analysing the complicated links between the narrator's present and the past inhabited by the character.

To summarize, the new processes of constructing the communist subject through self-narrative focused not so much on the 'deeds' as on their 'revelation', that is, the ways in which the actions of the social and political actor manifest in the account. This is confirmed by the fact that, during Stalin's reign of terror, self-enunciation in response to an accusation became a deciding element in determining whether a person was a true Bolshevik or an enemy of the revolution.

A significant semantic short-circuit, then, saw the 'revelation by deeds' occur via 'deeds of revelation', which were critical to determining the individual's salvation or condemnation, thus highlighting the primacy of the form of self-narrative over its content.[11]

The very centrality of the act of narrating the self explains the significance of the act of confession as an element of proof within Soviet law. Nikolai Krilenko, the Commissar for Justice, believed that a judicial investigation was redundant if the accused had confessed. Likewise, Andrei Vyshinskii, Stalin's grand inquisitor, affirmed that half a confession written in the accused's own hand was equivalent to a full confession drafted by the accuser and signed by the accused.[12]

Krilenko and Vyshinskii's perspectives provide an insight into the specific curvature of the act of narrating the self in the Stalinist era, revealing its confessional form. The latter, as stated previously, is characterized by the primacy of the reader – or the listener, in the case of an oral confession – over the person presenting the truth about themselves. This asymmetry in the autobiographical contract gives shape, in turn, to the essential content of the act of telling the truth about oneself: the very act of confessing implies confessing to a fault. An act of confession, by definition, always inculpates because, even if one has not committed a morally or legally reprehensible act, communication of a confession is characterized by its subsequence to that which is being confessed. A confession cannot precede that which is confessed: the act of telling the truth about oneself in the future tense takes the form of a promise, a commitment made by the subject to itself with regard to something. And nor can a confession be simultaneous to the act that is confessed. In such cases, the act of telling the truth about oneself would take the chimeric form of pure self-documentation, a sort of collection of 'protocol sentences' that apparently testify to the truth of the subject's life in an impersonal way. This involves elimination of the distinction between narrator and character, that is, the delay that defines the former with respect to the latter, and that constitutes a condition of self-narration.[13]

A confession is, therefore, always subsequent to that which is being confessed. And the fault to which the subject confesses resides within that subsequence,[14] as does the obligation of detection placed upon the party reading or listening to the confession as regards what is being confessed. If we take this logic to its radical conclusion, both the specific quality of the subjective fault and the need for investigation become superfluous; because subjective culpability is demonstrated by the very act of confessing, the materials of the confession may be supplied directly by the party receiving it. And so NKVD inspectors could prepare such content directly, leaving only the performance of self-accusation to the subject under the investigation.[15]

The very confessional nature of the autobiographical game set in motion by Soviet society is encapsulated by the duty to engage in 'criticism and self-criticism' (*kritika i samokritika*), imposed on all Bolshevik militants and cadres. The importance of this political duty was alluded to by Stalin himself, who sought to launch an extensive self-criticism campaign within the party and Soviet society more generally, beginning in 1927 with the launch of the first Five-Year Plan.

The slogan of self-criticism must not be regarded as something temporary and transient. Self-criticism is a specific method, a Bolshevik method, of training the forces of the party and of the working class generally in the spirit of revolutionary development. Marx himself spoke of self-criticism as a method of strengthening the proletarian revolution. As to self-criticism in our Party, its beginnings date back to the first appearance of Bolshevism in our country, to its very inception as a specific revolutionary trend in the working-class movement.[16]

Self-criticism was, therefore, a fundamental element not only of Bolshevism, but also of Communism itself, rooted in the works of Marx.[17] According to Stalin, its objective was to 'disclose and eliminate our errors and weaknesses', without which 'there can be no proper education of the Party, the class, and the masses'.[18] The development of a revolutionary society through self-criticism, in turn, contributed to the war against enemies of the working class, including bureaucracy within the party, trade unions, cooperatives etc. Stalin defined the 'bureaucratic elements' as those 'who fear like the plague all criticism by the masses, and who hinder us in developing self-criticism and ridding ourselves of our weaknesses and errors'.[19]

This call to self-criticism translated, in practical terms, into group meetings where lower-ranking members of the organization criticized, or reported errors made by, a superior. The latter would then respond by admitting their faults to the group, and atoning for them in the name of the revolution.[20] In general terms, then, engaging in self-criticism meant confessing one's faults following an act of public accusation and, naturally, anyone could find themselves in the role of accuser or accused from time to time.

Given the importance placed by Stalin on self-criticism, it is reasonable to interrogate the motivation behind such emphasis. The need to overcome one's faults in order to improve, even in a revolutionary sense, seems trivial, and presenting it as a cornerstone of the communist movement does not make it any less so. Such insistence on self-criticism can, however, be traced back to thousands of years' worth of Christian tradition. Viewed through this lens, the value of self-criticism – and ceremonies incorporating such practices – stems from a penitential, confessional model of society, revitalized under Stalinism and moulded to suit its. The political needs belong to Stalinism.[21] Beyond the religious reference, however, the rationale behind the practice of self-criticism and confession of one's faults can be clarified using a more recent point of reference, offered by Émile Durkheim's *The Division of Labour in Society*.

> [Punishment] does not serve, or else only serves quite secondarily, in correcting the culpable, or in intimidating possible followers. From this point of view, its efficacy is justly doubtful and, in any case, mediocre. Its true function is to maintain social cohesion intact, while maintaining all its vitality in the common conscience. [...] We can thus say without paradox that punishment is above all designed to act upon upright people, for, since it serves to heal the wounds made upon collective sentiments, it can fill this role only where these sentiments exist, and commensurately with their vivacity. [...] The result of this chapter is this:

there exists a social solidarity which comes from a certain number of states of conscience which are common to all the members of the same society. This is what repressive law materially represents, at least so far as it is essential.[22]

Durkheim regards punishment as the act by way of which social bonds manifest. Only through punishment do those collective sentiments upon which social unity is founded become visible to the members of that society. It is no coincidence that the penal process does not focus on the criminal, but on the innocent party, who can fully enjoy his condition of innocence thanks to the expiation of the guilty party. As such, the essence of a society, its defining legal and cultural core, can only be perceived through the lens of crime. Or, to be more precise, the symbol of social unity is repressive law and its system of sanctions, and this is true even in a modern context, where repressive law is secondary to co-operative law, and civil law mitigates the weight of criminal law.[23]

Durkheim's decision to present law as the symbol of the unity of a society is born of his desire to establish social bonds outside of the economic space. It involves constructing an image of society that is not primarily based on commercial competition among individuals, as liberal theories would have it, nor on the irreconcilable conflict between the Bourgeois and the working class, as Marxist approaches would suggest.[24] Such theoretical strategies as underpinning Durkheim's sociological construction give rise to paradoxical consequences. If the social substance – the 'states of conscience which are common to all the members of the same society' – is only manifest through crime and punishment, then its essence is negative, not positive. Rather than a state of being, then, it may be regarded as a duty to be. Or rather as a duty not to be, given that the method by way of which it becomes visible is punishment (in accordance with the laws) of the criminal, that is, he who did that which should not have been done. In other words, Durkheim's social bond is characterized by the fact of being deficient, and becomes apparent only when it is broken. Furthermore – to consider all consequences of such a situation – if criminal law is a symbol of the social bond, we face just two options, neither of which is appealing: either ours is a society of law, in which the social being is defined by his or her judgeability, or it is a society of crime, in which man's being social equates to being a criminal.

From this perspective, Stalin's enthusiasm for self-criticism positions him as a sort of more orderly Durkheim. Indeed, he understands that the formal solemnity of courts, law and punishment conceals the social game of charges and counter-charges that fuels the law itself. If, indeed, the social bond exists in negative terms, then its greatest symbol is not criminal law, but the act of reporting that which should not have happened and that nevertheless did happen. The act of reporting sheds light, for the first time, on that which the subject should not have done, conferring upon it a discursive existence. The fact that an event should not have taken place becomes apparent not on the plane of simple facts – which, as facts, are all identical – but purely on the plane of language, which can state that what happened should not have happened.

1. Institutional Communist Autobiographies
17

The highest expression of the social bond, however, is not the act of reporting, but rather the act of self-reporting. Only by confessing one's own inadequacies, whatever their nature, can a subject exist in a truly social sense. Recounting one's life as a story of mistakes and faults makes it possible to understand oneself as a being that has always been inadequate and that only exists as a being that should not have been what it was – just like Durkheim's criminal. Naturally, I do not wish here to imply that Stalin was a better sociologist than Durkheim, nor a deranged follower. Rather I would suggest that, when interpreted through Durkheim's lens and despite its frightening nature, the confessional foundation of Stalin's society begins to seem conceivable within our own political and social rationale.[25]

Autobiographical control and a self-critical posture were not the exclusive domain of the Bolsheviks. They were also a feature of European and non-European communist parties, incorporated into their organizational mechanisms by the coordinating body, Communist International (Comintern). Communist cadres travelling to Moscow from abroad were met with extensive and pervasive autobiographical mechanisms.

> Foreign communists first came across the insistent Soviet demand for autobiographical narrative immediately upon first arrival, a demand renewed upon every change of role and institution. [...] Party members had to fill in questionnaires (*ankety*) and write CVs in the form of 'autobiographies' (*avtobiografii*). They had to offer self-criticism in party and school meetings and evaluate their own work in 'self-reports' (*samootchety*). Such declarations would be recorded by a stenographer, or, at the international cadre schools by the students in turn. Many of these narratives were oral rather than written. An oral autobiography, or more precisely a public autobiographical declaration had to be given before the relevant collective on first joining the party [...]. On the other side of the fence, the apparatus produced 'characterizations' (*kharakteristiki*) or evaluations of cadre, and all sorts of certifications or declarations (*spravki*) to be sent to other institutions. It also collected denunciations.[26]

Foreign cadres' initiation into Bolshevik self-enunciation practices was also facilitated by the Comintern's educational system. The year 1921 saw the opening of the Communist University of the Toilers of the East and the Communist University of the National Minorities of the West. These institutions aimed to establish cadres in areas with no existing workers' party to carry on the legacy of the communist organizations, such as in colonial countries or parts of Europe with significant national minorities. The International Lenin School, founded in 1926,[27] served to train cadres from communist parties emerging from a schism with the old socialist organizations.[28] It engaged, therefore, in a cultural Bolshevization of militants arriving in Russia, which corresponded to the organizational Bolshevization of their parties. Becoming acquainted with Soviet forms of autobiographical assessment and the language of self-criticism was an integral part of this process.

The communist cadres that passed through the Comintern and its associated pedagogical institutions served, then, as vehicles for dissemination of the Bolshevik culture of autobiography. In the interwar period, the French Communist Party (PCF) became the first in Europe to adopt the practice. It was effectively the only communist organization in the West at the time; Italian communists, followed later by their German counterparts, had been reduced to a few thousand members, forced to operate clandestinely as they struggled to survive under Fascism and Nazism, respectively.

The use of autobiography for disciplinary purposes took root in the French organization at the beginning of the 1930s, with the closure of the 'Barbé-Celor group' and management of the party by Eugen Fried, a Comintern delegate to France.[29] Fried reorganized the Central Control Commission and established a dedicated cadres division, headed by Albert Vassart. Maurice Tréand, a graduate of the International Lenin School in Moscow, was appointed executive secretary. The cadres division set to work swiftly and, by 1937, at the peak of Stalin's reign of terror, it had already collected more than 6,000 biographies of communist cadres and militants.[30]

The biographical assessment of PCF militants revolved around a questionnaire featuring open-ended questions, which also functioned as a starting point and template for preparing the accompanying autobiographical accounts.[31] The latter varied in length – ranging between two and forty pages – and touched on a series of issues that centred, on the one hand, on the subject's social history – focusing on school, professional life and private relationships – and, on the other, on their ideological journey and party career, examining its evolution. The party autobiography was also used extensively after the Second World War, up until the De-Stalinization crisis in the second half of the 1950s. From then on, it was gradually relegated to a mere routine activity, and eventually replaced, in 1974, by the simpler *Résumé d'activité du militant*, in which the section on the militant's private life was essentially omitted.[32]

As with the Soviet model, the French autobiography did not limit itself to establishing the 'objective' details of the subject's history: this 'genealogy of social origin' aspect merely represented the first, most elementary level of assessment. Here, too, the 'revelation by deeds' – the specific form of presentation of the details in the autobiography – played the central role. In this way, the cadres division sought to highlight the 'reflexive' dimension of the political history of the cadre subject to biographical assessment, or the discursive construction of the militant self.[33]

In addition to its use for strictly organizational purposes, the PCF also used autobiography in a more traditional way, as an external validation tool. The PCF achieved seventy-two deputies and two senators in the 1936 election. A volume was published at the end of that year containing each of their biographies.[34] *La voix du peuple en Parlement* was later followed by a biography of Stalin, written by Henry Barbusse in 1935 and republished in abridged form in 1936. A celebratory issue of *Les cahiers du bolscevisme* dedicated to Stalin was also published in 1935; this time, his autobiography took the form of an article entitled 'Stalin's Example'.

And, as a final example of the French communists' biographical endeavours, the autobiography of Maurice Thorez, secretary of the PCF, entitled *Fils du Peuple*, was published in 1937. In a certain sense, this work represents a public monument to the autobiographical culture developed by the communist organization. Here, too, the enunciation of the self coincides perfectly with the discursive space made available by the party to its members, to enable them to recount their personal stories.

The Italian way to autobiographical control: Elements of context

The Bolshevik autobiographical assessment mechanism emerged in Italy with Palmiro Togliatti's return to the country and the re-establishment of the communist party, of which he took firm control. Togliatti arrived in Naples on 27 March 1944, having left the Soviet Union.[35] The country had been torn in two: the South was occupied by allies struggling to make their way back up the peninsula, while the centre-North – including Rome – was still under German control. This critical military situation – marked by violent clashes between Germans and Americans along the Gustav line, and at Cassino, in the far South of Lazio, in particular – was mirrored by an equally difficult political climate.

In fact, Togliatti's return coincided with a bitter struggle between the National Liberation Committee (Comitato di Liberazione Nazionale – CLN) – which had met in Bari, on 28 and 29 January 1944, with representatives travelling from the Italian provinces liberated by the allies – and Italy's King Vittorio Emanuele III, who had appointed Marshal Pietro Badoglio as his prime minister. The CLN called for the resignation of Vittorio Emanuele III and Badoglio who, immediately after the announcement of Italy's armistice with the allies on 8 September 1943, had not sought to defend the capital, but rather had fled to Brindisi in search of refuge, leaving the Italian army and administrative system in disarray, while German troops occupied the country. The allies, meanwhile, and Churchill, in particular, would only deal with the Italian monarch.[36]

Faced with such circumstances, Togliatti's decision was clear. Given the absolute urgency of the struggle against German occupation of Italy, he revised the communist's official position, supporting recognition of Badoglio's government by political forces within the CLN. In so doing, the Communist leader prioritized the issue of national liberation over the future constitutional form of the country – as a monarchy or republic – and the anti-fascist nature of the political system over class issues. This repositioning of the PCI gave rise to Togliatti's 'progressive democracy' as a political approach. It also heralded the establishment of the so-called 'new party' as an operating tool, the fundamental feature of which was its accessibility to the masses. Togliatti's position on the matter was utterly clear in his speech to communists in Florence on 3 October 1944:

> We must be a mass party and must therefore not close the party's doors, it should not be a party made up solely of old people who have always stayed in the same

place, we need to attract all elements active in the working and intellectual classes to our party and make it a party with mass character.[37]

The political strategy, therefore, involved leaving behind the organizational model of the old Communist Party of Italy (Partito Comunista d'Italia – PCd'I), as employed between the two wars, and moving towards an identity founded on revolutionary spirit and based on the struggle for national liberation from Fascism. The transformation of the PCI into a mass party was, therefore, subject to a specific limitation, which must be taken into account when reading communist autobiographies.

> We do not accept party members who just carry a card but do nothing for the party. This is not acceptable. [...] If we end up with a situation where just one group of comrades works and everyone else has a card in their pocket but does nothing, basically ours won't be the party we need; it won't be a mass party, but rather a large organisation of sympathisers congregating around a small number of active members, who will grow tired, become exhausted and ultimately won't be able to perform the tasks that the party sets itself.[38]

The PCI is, therefore, a cadre and a mass party, but the two sides of this identity are not placed on the same level. While cadres must aim to achieve quantitative mass, that is, they must seek to increase their numbers, mass groups must aim to transform, qualitatively, into cadres, because belonging to the party does not merely mean being a 'sympathiser', but rather requires mobilization within the organization. Basically, the process of debolshevication of Togliatti's 'new party' – including overcoming the Lenin-style cadre system – was only partially achieved, despite the discontinuity between the PCI and the PCd'I.[39]

Togliatti's strategy proved successful, at least from an organizational perspective.[40] The PCI enjoyed organizational growth that was unprecedented in Europe, with a striking acceleration in membership numbers even in the first two years following the communist leader's return to Italy. At the time of the collapse of the Fascist regime on 25 July 1943, it is estimated that the party had between 5,000 and 6,000 members. At the end of 1944, approximately a year and a half later, there were an estimated 700,000 party members, while in Northern Italy, which was still occupied, there were approximately 90,000. Numbers had doubled by the following year, totalling around 1,800,000 members. The rate of expansion of the party seemed unstoppable. On 31 October 1946, the figure reached 2,166,448, while the updated information presented at the sixth party congress in September 1947 put the figure at 2,252,715. By the end of 1950, communist party members, including those in the Italian Communist Youth Federation (Federazione Italiana dei Giovani Comunisti – FGCI), exceeded two and a half million. This upward trend began to slow in the first half of the 1950s, when party numbers began to consolidate, reaching the peak of their expansion in 1954. The year 1957 saw the beginning of a reversal of the trend. The crisis triggered by de-Stalinization saw the PCI lose 11 per cent of its members, causing it to fall below the symbolic threshold of 2 million.[41]

In the context of hard opposition to communism, triggered by the start of the Cold War, control and regulation of the growing number of militants – to protect against infiltration from the outside and prepare for a protracted trench war in a hostile environment – were, to some extent, indispensable. This was known as 'revolutionary vigilance', and became increasingly pronounced, particularly after 1953. The biographical control of militants, therefore, proved valuable as a tool for governing the population of new members that now flocked to the communist organization. From an operational perspective, new members not only had to be recommended to the organization by existing comrades, but also had to fill out a rather detailed biographical questionnaire, entitled the *Biografia del militante* (*Militant's Biography*) when joining. The latter, or at least the version used by the Bologna Federation, was divided into three sections.[42]

The first section mainly covered basic personal details. The party first required the subject's identification details: their name and surname, date of birth and address. This was followed by questions regarding the militant's level of education, the type of work they performed – employed or self-employed – and any criminal history: 'Have you been arrested for common offences? What was the nature of the offence?' Finally, the focus of the questions shifted to any relatives in the security forces: 'Do you have relatives in the Police Forces?'

The second section of the *Biografia del militante*, meanwhile, was much broader and more detailed, and tellingly entitled *Political Activities*. Of primary interest here was the militant's political past. The section opens with a generic question – 'When did you first become involved in politics?' – before moving on to explore any Fascist background in greater detail, through a series of specific questions: 'Were you a member of the Fascist party?' Respondents were asked to specify the year and reasons for joining, together with any positions held: 'Were you a member of other Fascist associations? Which ones?' 'Which Fascist wars did you participate in?' 'At what level?' 'Were you a volunteer or called to arms?'

The purpose of these rather significant questions was to distinguish between those who had joined the National Fascist Party (Partito Nazionale Fascista – PNF) because they had no other choice, and those who were active members of the Fascist movement and, therefore, could not be admitted into the communist party. The problem represented by Fascist membership is clear from the responses provided by certain communist militants: 'Entered the Fascist Party in '36 and left in '37 because I was arrested. After a year of unemployment, I joined to get work';[43] 'I applied to join the Fascist Party in 1935 when I was doing school leaving certificate exams, because I was asked for a certificate proving Fascist Party membership. But I never picked up the card'.[44] The delicate nature of the question, concerning as it did the country's dark past and the individuals who participated in it, is also highlighted by the response of one militant who, it seems, suffered from a bizarre form of political amnesia: 'I do not remember having been a Fascist.'[45]

Having completed its questioning on Fascism, the *Biografia del militante* moved on to examining the methods and circumstances surrounding the militant joining the PCI. It first asked if the subject had participated in anti-Fascist parties or associations, followed by when and where they had joined the communist party, asking them to provide the names of comrades who would support their application. The questionnaire later examined the possibility of whether those applying to join the 'new party' had, in the past, expressed dissenting opinions with respect to the party's position, perhaps through affinity with the various heresies condemned by the orthodox principles of the communist movement: from Trotskyism, at an international level, to Bordigism in the Italian context.[46] Here, too, the question is carefully worded: 'Was your membership of the Communist Party ever interrupted, or was there any period in which you ceased to be part of it? (In the latter case, indicate the reason for your dissent, and when you returned to the Party)'.

The focus of the interrogation then shifts to any positions previously or currently held by the subject within the party, to their union membership and membership of other 'mass organizations'. From this point, the questionnaire became a sort of self-assessment test, exploring whether the member has any particular aptitudes or specific skills, whether they could be used for 'journalism activities', 'tasks of a political and administrative nature', 'tasks of a technical or administrative nature relating to production' or 'artistic and literary activities'. The *Political Activities* section of the *Biografia del militante* concludes with questions on the subject's partisan past – 'were you a member of the Volunteer Corps for Liberty [Corpo volontari della libertà – CVL]?' – and communist scholarship: 'What communist books have you read that have contributed to your communist militant education?' Almost all militants' bookshelves, at least among those in my sample, included a copy of *History of the Communist Party of the Soviet Union (Bolsheviks): Short Course* and *The Foundation of Leninism* by Stalin. A number of Lenin's works such as *What to Be Done* and *'Left-wing' Communism: An Infantile Disorder* also featured, as well as texts by Marx, including the classic *The Communist Manifesto*. In one instance, the list also included *The Iron Heel* by Jack London. Perhaps it is Comrade Giorgio S., however, who best sums up the bibliographical persuasion of the militants, summarizing his reading activities as follows: 'works by Lenin, *History of the Communist Party of the Soviet Union* and other works by our masters'.[47] And so, while communists certainly read the Marxist classics, and recognized their pedagogical value, Stalin's work emerges as the classic among classics. It is, therefore, no coincidence that Giorgio S. cites the name of one of Stalin's better-known works almost in full, while relegating the others to the category of 'other works by our masters'.

The final section of the questionnaire is entitled *Persecutions Suffered* and once again focuses on the militant's past during the Fascist era. Under investigation here are not the forms of political participation in Fascism, but rather the subject's conduct in the face of the violence and judicial coercion characteristic of Mussolini's twenty-year reign. Militants are, therefore, asked if they were subject to beatings by the Fascist party, if they were arrested – under Fascism or during Nazi occupation of the country – if they were tortured, and how they conducted themselves before judges and Fascist police.[48] Members who had been put on trial were then asked to specify whether any of their co-accused had engaged in 'reprehensible' conduct – in other words, if they had betrayed the trust of their comrades and the party. The interrogation of the subject's behaviour in the face of Fascist coercion involved asking them to specify what jails they were detained in, before asking telling questions about how their period of detention ended. The party wanted to know whether the militant was released at the end of their sentence, having been granted amnesty, or whether they had entered into an agreement of some sort with the security forces. The very wording of this question alludes to the dishonour of such behaviour: 'Did you perform an act of submission to the Fascists or the police?'

The line pursued by the questionnaire, which by this point had evolved into a sort of loyalty test, is maintained in the two final questions: 'Were you ever punished in the Party?' and 'Have you ever adopted a dissenting position towards the Party's political line? Why? On what issues? In what period?' This question – though it essentially reiterates and clarifies the query previously posed in the *Political Activities* section concerning potential interruptions to the member's militant past – leaves no room for negative responses. Rather, it encourages militants to express pride in their party membership. Simone S., for example, responds with a 'never' that precludes further questioning, and touches upon the issue again in his autobiography, when he makes a declaration of absolute loyalty: 'I have never [sic] disagreed with the party line. The party can always [sic] count on me.'[49] Among the questionnaires I examined, there is just one instance of a militant expressing dissent in relation to the PCI, and this is done in a way that entirely invalidates his stance: 'General lack of confidence in the party in 1947–48 due to moral depression, caused by difficult life circumstances, as I was unemployed at the time, and insufficient ideological engagement.'[50]

Overall, the *Biografia del militante* served as a sort of guide to help militants prepare their autobiographies. Indeed, members were invited to elaborate on their answers on 'a separate sheet of paper, to be annexed to the biography'. The biographical questionnaire and accompanying autobiography, while serving an important role in terms of control and screening of militants in the context of significant organizational growth, had other purposes too. In particular, self-narrative production was a crucial formative practice engaged in at PCI party schools, significant from both a critical and self-critical perspective.

> The autobiographies that comrades were required to present in the final months, in the presence of the entire group, were the best indicator of a course's success. The practice involved a critical examination of one's entire life: social background, the influence of parents and friends, life experiences, links to the party and to the working class. Each comrade's critical and self-critical maturity was assessed according to his capacity to analyse himself and his life circumstances. Any points requiring clarification were highlighted by fellow comrades' insistent questioning.[51]

As such, the autobiography also served as a pedagogical tool, enabling the transformation of the militant within the party cadre. A description of the forms of its production – suspended between the collective and the individual, oral production and writing – does not, however, suffice to understand its functioning. Rather, it must be considered in the specific context of the organizational culture of Togliatti's 'new party', and in light of the fundamental political oscillation that characterized it. An understanding of the organizational and political context in which militant autobiographies were produced helps to clarify how the discursive mechanism underpinning the communist self-narrative operated.

Togliatti's quotes referred to above provide a good starting point in that regard. The communist secretary believed that the party should be open to all, but simply registering was not enough. Working for the party and engaging in political activity were also required. As such, militant mobilization was a key issue for the 'new party'. Pietro Secchia, who served as head of organization and propaganda for the communist party between 1946 and 1954, returned to this issue often in his writings, attempting to clearly determine what it meant 'to activate' party members.

> Stating and repeating that all comrades must be active, that each comrade must be assigned a role, is just the first step – it means taking a general view of the issue. To activate all comrades, male and female, young and very young, it is not enough for us to preach. The issue, instead, involves ensuring that all comrades can be active, it means organising the work in such a way that everyone has a role to perform, and it means establishing a basic organisation that makes activation of comrades possible.[52]

According to Secchia, then, it is not sufficient to state that comrades must be active, there is also a responsibility to actually mobilize them; this is more or less what he means by 'it is not enough for us to preach'. How? By assigning each militant an organizational task to perform. From this perspective, then, PCI members' 'activation' should be immediately apparent from their *Biografia del militante*, as militants were required to specify the positions held within the party.

> 1. Front of the Communist Youth [FDG – Fronte della Gioventù]. Organiser 1945–1946. 2. *** Italian National Partisan Association [ANPI – Associazione Nazionale Partigiani d'Italia] Circle. Organiser and Secretary 1947–1948. Div. ***. 3. PCI Collectors Manager – Organiser – Secretary. Div. ***. 1948–49–50. The above refers to work performed outside of working hours. 4. In Div. *** (Ducati factory) Cell Press Prop.[aganda] Manager *** 1946–47, Cell Secretary 1948–49. Secretary of the Italian Workers' Recreational and Welfare Centre [CRAL – Circolo Ricreativo Assistenziale Lavoratori] Ducati from November 1949 to the present.[53]

> 1945 head of press and propaganda in the *** cell 1946 cell secretary, 1947 head of union matters for the *** branch. In February '48, I was elected Secretary of the Chamber of Labour and was then nominated as a member of the Coordination Committee for the [illegible] of ***.[54]

After being discharged on 26 July 1946 Cell Secretary until 17 December 1947, then party Activist and Cell Head of Press until 1 November 1949, from 1 November 1949 I joined the Head of Press and Propaganda Division Committee until 4 September 1951 and then head of Amici Unità [Friends of Unity].[55]

The summaries of roles performed by these three militants suggest, in fact, that being 'active' actually means being 'superactive', holding multiple roles simultaneously. The term 'activation', therefore, does not simply mean to assign a task to each comrade. Also because, strictly speaking, once a militant becomes 'active', they are no longer in a position to stop, given that any break in their 'activity' would result in them being considered 'inactive', something that was unacceptable within the communist organization. On the other hand, the number of tasks that can be assigned to any comrade is finite, as are the time and skills at his disposal. There is, then, a limit to 'activation', which is not, however, easy to identify.

This is probably why Secchia, returning once again to this issue, offers an alternative perspective on the intended meaning of 'activation'.

> We must bring an end to this habit of distinguishing between organizational work and propaganda work and political fervour. Such a distinction deprives organizational work of its political content, reducing it to mere technical activity, basic practical tasks. [...] For us, organizational. work is far removed from simple administration, which is incompatible with the spirit of our Party. [...] The bureaucratic, administrative approach must not be tolerated in party work, because it undermines, drains and erodes the self-generating nature of the organization, preventing communists' sense of initiative from emerging.[56]

The issue of limitations on 'activation' is completely reformulated here, favouring a qualitative, rather than a quantitative, interpretation. 'To activate' comrades does not mean to assign countless tasks to them. Rather, it means enabling them to engage in politics through organizational tasks, transforming administrative processes into political acts. 'Activation', therefore, involves discovering previously elusive meaning in one's activities, which cannot be measured in terms of the amount of time one dedicates to the party.

In other words, 'activation' is an internal condition, a sort of communist state of the soul, to use an outmoded, but essentially accurate, term. Secchia was clearly well aware that such transubstantiation of the organizational into the political is by no means an automatic process, but must instead be achieved through specific techniques. Or rather, the organization itself must transform into a sort of educational machine that simultaneously produces organizational acts and an understanding of their meaning that goes beyond the organizational to become political.

> Democracy means constant activation of party members, raising their consciousness and increasing their engagement not only in discussions of

political issues, but also when managing work. [...] The key method for educating and mobilizing comrades is through general meetings of all the members of a cell, or all the members of a branch. [...] There are, however, still branch and cell executive committees that, though they meet fairly frequently, do not consider it their duty to consult with the militants, that do not view the general party meeting as a school for political education and mobilizing the comrades.[57]

The meaning of 'activation' broadens further. On the one hand, it corresponds to the very idea of democracy, while on the other it denotes a sort of Foucauldian 'direction' of organizational work that, if properly applied, enables the transformation of general cell and branch meetings into a veritable 'school of political education'. In this sense, the call for greater emphasis on study for all party members complements such a pedagogical preoccupation.

Cadres are trained, as I said, through work and study. Very little study happens in the party. Cadres in charge of a branch or a cell, and even the cadres in charge of many federations, don't study, or study little. We ourselves, as comrades in the C.C., study very little, and this is evident in our work. This is evident in meetings, where it is sometimes apparent that the issue under discussion has not been studied in advance, leading to scant contributions and inadequate criticism and self-criticism. We need to read and study more, all comrades need to read and study more, otherwise we'll never turn the party into a body that can work intensively, politically and with continuity in all matters. We must organize more regional, provincial and branch schools. Perhaps we should also try to organize a correspondence school for our cadres. [...] We must also give the comrades the opportunity and the time to study.[58]

'Activation' originally meant assigning a task to each militant, and later came to refer to discovering the political meaning in all organizational tasks. Such political significance is simply party democracy, or rather the experience of the party as a democracy. It is achieved by taking a sort of pedagogical approach to the general meeting, by establishing schools at all levels – regional, provincial and branch – and bringing schooling into comrades' homes – through correspondence courses.

In this way, then, the party tended to present itself as a school and, in turn, the school became the organizational model that the party apparently sought to emulate. Party activities tended to focus on 'activation' of the cadres, which was presented, in turn, as an educational pursuit, rooted in the system of the schools where such education was provided. In short, politics was reduced to pedagogy, and the relationship between party leaders and militants mirrored that of educator and educated or, more accurately, teacher and pupil.[59] The communist organizational bond, therefore, produced a sort of scholastic society in which the obligation to obey became a right to learn, and the right to command became a duty to teach.

The dual inversion that defines the relationship between command and obedience, in turn, conferred upon the pedagogical bond between communist militants a specifically pastoral flavour. Indeed, the defining characteristic of pastoral power is its essentially oblational nature. The shepherd's right to command is, in fact, essentially a duty that he assumes. He sacrifices himself for his sheep, for the sake of their salvation – whatever form that may take.[60] It is no coincidence that cadre 'activation' can also be reframed as a form of watchful attention' paid by party leaders to those under their direction.

> Care for people is the essential element in the art of the organization. A party is made of people, and people must be taken as they are. We must seek to improve them, to educate them, to give them what they lack but, in the meantime, we must work. A political organizer should not simply be a person with powers of observation and analysis […] he should also have that knowledge, that ability to understand the human element that makes up an organisation.[61]

The party, then, educates its members and improves them through ongoing care, starting from the principle that 'people must be taken as they are'. In other words, care is provided by way of a relationship that regards the militant as a fully fledged individual, and not through application of an abstract rule. This intensely individual relationship between those who direct and those receiving direction is, in any case, situated within a rigidly hierarchical structure.

> Even the best comrades and bodies, if left unsupervised, can turn to bureaucracy, even the most well-built gears can rust over time, if not given the proper care. […] Superiors should be in the habit of regularly summoning lower level executives and asking them to take account of their work, of what they have achieved in implementing the party political line. If we often call upon comrades in charge of a particular activity to take account not only of this or that aspect of their work, but of all the work performed, these comrades will be forced to rise above the numerous issues involved in ordinary administration […] in other words, we will get them into the habit of focusing their attention on essential issues.[62]

The relationship between those providing and receiving direction dictates that the right to summon lies with the former and not the latter, who must submit to the other's judgement and demonstrate whether, and in what way, they can implement the party line. This practice of taking account does not, in itself, seem likely to be enough to 'activate' members, unless we consider that the superior is in possession of a broader and more profound truth than their inferior. Bringing various levels of truth into contact with one another in this way reframes the knowledge held by the inferior, thus enabling 'essential issues' to emerge. Basically, the party takes care of its members, regarding them as absolutely singular beings, but when its pastoral care ends, what remains is the exercise of power of hierarchical command and the transformation of 'activation' of the comrades into 'stronger discipline'.[63] What counts, in this context, is the ability of the individual militant to act in unison with the organization of which it is part.

Why should 'activation' of party cadres lead to greater organizational discipline and, therefore, better political performance? There is no real answer to this question. Or rather, Secchia provides various answers, continuously deferring the issue, without succeeding in clearly defining the connection between 'being active' and 'being disciplined'. The term 'activation' at once covers the assignment of an organizational role to each member, the party's pedagogical pursuits, dedication to study, careful direction of those being directed and the discipline demonstrated by the latter group in performing their tasks. All of which culminate in the overall impression of going around in circles. We can draw together the various descriptions of what it means, for a communist, to 'be active', without, however, ever obtaining a succinct answer.

This definitional uncertainty seems to me to stem from the paradoxical nature of the 'activity' required of cadres and militants. Or, rather, from the fact that the direction provided by the party to its members was based on the paradoxical injunction to 'be active!' Strictly speaking, it is nonsensical to order someone to be active: either they are active or they are not. Which once again raises the problem of the limitations of 'activation'; once a person is 'activated' within the organization, there can be no limitations on their 'activity', otherwise it immediately becomes 'inactivity', and they would cease to be such.

The organizational imperative to 'be active!' promoted by the PCI and Pietro Secchia, its head of party cadres, operates in the exact same way as the command to 'be spontaneous'. The subject to whom the command is addressed is placed in a double-bind situation that cannot be resolved. If they comply with the injunction, and are 'active' – or spontaneous – they are, in reality, disobeying it. It is not actually possible to be 'active' – or spontaneous – in response to an order, given that doing so means that one is not 'active' – or spontaneous – but is simply obeying a command and, therefore, in a passive state. If, on the other hand, one is actually 'active' – or spontaneous – one is not fulfilling the command because the 'activity' – or 'spontaneity' – is not performed upon request.

In the first instance, then, the subject to whom the injunction is addressed abides by the form of the command, but violates its substance, as he or she is not truly 'active'. In the second, the subject complies with the substance of the command, because he or she is in fact 'active', but disregards its form, because he or she is not obeying any order. In neither case, then, does the subject obey the instruction. As such, he or she is placed in a lose–lose situation by the person with the power to command. The true significance of such a paradoxical injunction is not, however, the actual failure to obey the order received, but rather the situation of potential non-compliance in which the subject is placed, whatever choice is made.

> The most important distinction between contradictory and paradoxical injunctions is that in the face of a contradictory injunction, one chooses one and loses, or suffers, the other alternative. The result is not a happy one – as already mentioned one cannot eat one's cake and have it too, and the lesser evil is still an evil. But in the face of a contradictory injunction, choice is logically possible. The paradoxical injunction, on the other hand, *bankrupts choice itself*, nothing is possible, and a self-perpetuating oscillating series is set in motion.[64]

'A self-perpetuating oscillating series': this is perhaps the image that best captures the full significance of 'activation' of communist militants. The fact that, faced with a paradoxical injunction, choice becomes impossible does not, in fact, mean that no choice is made – otherwise there would be no 'oscillating series'. Rather, it means that the decision that is made is always potentially wrong. More specifically, militants who are 'activated' by party superiors, through examination of their political performance, are never in a position to verify the meaning of what they are doing, as such meaning is only available to those within the organization with the power to command. The didactic nature assigned by the party to organizational acts transforms the impossibility of knowing the meaning of one's actions – as PCI militants – into the pedagogical promise of a future in which grasping such meaning will finally become possible. In the same way, the pastoral tones adopted in managing the militants and the human care required of those organizing the masses within the party serve as a method to dilute and sweeten the violent substance at the heart of the paradoxical injunction.

Ultimately, it is a feature of pastoral care that the form in which it is provided transcends law and command. In pastoral relationships between those giving and receiving direction, the latter wants to realize the will of the former as though it were their own will. In this way, obeying the other is confused with obeying oneself, and the most profound obedience – that which sees the will of the other becoming my will – can easily be mistaken for the greatest freedom as, even if what I want is the will of the other, it is nevertheless me who wants it.[65] And so the pastoral dimension of the party's direction of the cadres partially obscures the command aspect of that direction and renders the alienation of meaning – produced by the paradoxical injunction to the detriment of the subject to whom it is addressed – barely perceptible. This does not, of course, change the fact that 'activation' is exercised by way of a command from hierarchical superior to their inferior – legitimized by a valid right, guaranteed by the Marxist classics, the USSR, democratic centralism, the partisan struggle, the Republican Constitution etc. – and not in accordance with methods of pastoral direction and the unmediated relationship of will.

The paradoxical 'activation' to which communist militants are subject does not simply represent a method of managing subjects within the party organization. It seems to me that it also has a specifically political value, although the significance of the organizational act – as political action – should not be sought in a mysterious pedagogical sense that would enable a leap from the former to the latter. A brief passage by Carl Schmitt is useful to help us understand what is at play here.

> The sovereign produces and guarantees the situation in its totality. He has the monopoly over this last decision. Therein resides the essence of the state's sovereignty, which must be juristically defined correctly, not as the monopoly to coerce or to rule, but as the monopoly to decide. The exception reveals most clearly the essence of the state's authority. The decision parts here from the legal norm, and (to formulate it paradoxically) authority proves that to produce law it need not be based on law.[66]

The organizational act can become a political action only to the extent that it confers upon the militants the sovereign prerogative of the capacity to decide.[67] This is only exercised, as Schmitt reiterates various times, in concrete situations and, ultimately, consists of an autonomous choice that separates foe from friend. The problem with framing the politicization of militants as acquisition of the power to decide is that the latter goes beyond the mere application of a procedure. Consequently, the idea that a political subject can be produced starting from his positioning within the organization is utterly contradictory, as it is political decision-making that makes organizational norms possible and not the other way round, just as law is not produced starting from the law, but from decisions made by those with sovereign power.

From this perspective, then, the paradoxical organizational injunction underpinning the communist party represents an irresolvable political contradiction, as it seeks to establish an organizational machine capable of producing, regulating and managing the decision-making power that it aims to awaken in its members.[68] A problem expressed, albeit in a distorted way, by the concept of the PCI as a mass party made up of cadres, or by Togliatti's own definition of the communist party as a giraffe, an anatomically impossible animal that nevertheless exists. An issue not grasped – except perhaps in very superficial terms – by Giancarlo Paietta, a communist leader, when he stated that the relationship between communist militants and party leaders should take the form of obedience *perinde ac cadaver*, mirroring the commitment undertaken by Jesuits.[69] Communist militants should obey without obeying and, as politically active subjects, disobey without disobeying. A task impossible to actually fulfil.

All that remains, at this point, then, is to consider how the paradoxical construction of the communist political subject – in organizational and political terms – shaped the militant's self-narrative.

The communist autobiography: Plot and story

The simplest way to approach the issue of the relationship between organizational sphere – and political sphere, which, however, is of less interest to me here – and narrative sphere, is through the direct reading of an autobiographical text written by a communist militant. I have selected the self-narrative account provided here not so must because it represents a sort of average or median of my sample of autobiographies; such concepts are only meaningful in the context of statistical analysis, which I have not performed. Rather, if I had to identify the criteria underpinning my choice, I would say that the self-narrative that I have transcribed possesses, in some sense, the qualities of an ideal type, in the Weberian sense of the term. As such, I regard it as an exemplar. It does not represent the average experience contained in autobiographies of Italian communists who began their political militant careers after the Second World War, offering an adequate description of that type of document and that type of person. Rather, in various ways, including thanks to a series of distortions, it enables us to highlight certain characteristics of the communist self-narrative that might otherwise be elusive. Aside from this, it serves as an example precisely due to its absolute visibility, and not because it adequately represents something else.[70]

> Born on *** 1921, an only child from a family of not uncomfortable financial means, until just a few years ago, as my father is a retired former railway worker. [...] My whole childhood certainly had an influence on my personality, as I was used to living in station houses far, always far, from residential areas, and also the fact that up until now I never experienced serious family circumstances and I was mainly in contact with country people [...]. I was never involved in factory production work in direct contact with the working class in the workplace [...]. Though I had contact with the partisan movement, who even gave me clandestine publications to read, I did not participate in the movement because I was afraid [...]. My father was always an anti-Fascist, having been a member of the Italian Socialist Party [Partito Socialista Italiano – PSI] since his youth, but he never gave me sufficient political education to protect me from the influence of the Bourgeois and Fascist mentality [...]. For me joining [the PCI] was not something conscious or thought out [...]. I came to the school with great enthusiasm [...]. The flaws that were revealed to me are: opportunism in [political] practice, vulgar language, presumption and lack of self-criticism. If I were to say I had [overcome] such flaws, I would be committing a falsehood towards myself and the Party; at the same time, I don't believe it can be said that I have not made improvements. [...] [I can assure] the Party that I have deeply understood my faults and commit to overcoming them through greater and better effort. I am certain that I can do this and undertake to demonstrate it through the work that the Party assigns to me in the future.[71]

As is often the case with the texts I have examined, this self-narrative, written as part of a communist cadre training course, opens with a statement of the writer's personal details. As such, the beginning of the text coincides with the moment of the writer's birth, rooting his communist history in his biological and family origins and, in a certain sense, immediately placing the biological system – that is in itself only an uninterrupted cycle of births and deaths – within the movement historically oriented towards achieving his communist self. The institutional nature of the autobiography, then, makes it possible to circumvent the problem that usually presents itself when one begins to write the story of one's life: why write such a story? Why should anyone read it? This is the discomfort spoken of by Rousseau as regards writing his *Confessions*,[72] and the unease expressed, in particular, by the Italian communists who wrote their autobiographies after the end of twentieth-century communism, as we will see in the third chapter of the book.

If writing one's autobiography at the instruction of the party rendered discussion of the significance of the self-narrative redundant, autobiographical discomfort is shifted from the beginning of the self-narrative to its progression. The story recounted by Simone B. is, in fact, riddled with failures. He lives in railway station houses that are 'always' far from the city, and he was 'mainly in contact with country people'. Consequently, during his childhood, he lacked the key relationship with 'factory production' required for an authentically communist upbringing, and only had 'casual contact' with the workers who lived in his area.

This picture of shortcomings is compounded by the fact that Simone B., though aware of the existence of the partisan movement, whose clandestine publications he read, decided not to get involved, 'because he was afraid'. These personal flaws are combined with family inadequacies: his father, though an anti-Fascist, was a member of the PSI – a sort of weak forerunner to the PCI, which emerged from a split in the PSI – and did not provide his son with a 'sufficient political education'. As such, when Simone B. decides to join the communist party, he does so 'spontaneously' and not in a 'conscious' or 'thought-out' way.

This self-narrative, made up of negative elements of varying degrees of significance, culminates, at the end of the text, in an attitude of negation of the self and his formative story, giving the autobiography that specific critical and self-critical arc expected by the party school. Simone B.'s recent educational journey has taught him that he was vulgar – in his language – as well as presumptuous and lacking in self-criticism. He also confesses to one of the greatest flaws in the communist world, political opportunism, that is, the inability to be flexible in tactical terms, open to alliances while remaining firmly anchored to the global strategy dictated by party leaders.[73] Finally, as though all that was not enough, Simone B. also tells us that he would be committing 'a falsehood' towards himself and the 'Party' if he claimed to have overcome such flaws.

The CV presented by Simone B. to the PCI in his autobiography is dispiriting. It does not require too close an analysis to note that what he is not is firmly foregrounded over what he is, and what he has not done over what he has done. Nevertheless, his political autobiography is perfectly accomplished. On the one hand, the militant complies with the obligation to tell the truth about himself to the party, and there is no better guarantee that one is not lying than the presentation of an unappealing version of the truth about oneself, which would be better kept hidden. On the other hand, the member puts the revelation of this negative truth about himself at the service of the party and allows the latter to guide his conduct, using the knowledge of the self provided by the autobiography. The negative nature of one's life story, made up of shortcomings and faults, takes on a positive slant through the proclamation of such faults to the person who has asked for an account of one's failings. In this sense, the perfection of this autobiography lies in the fact that it takes the form of a confessional act – in the sense of 'speech acts', as discussed by Austin and described here by Peter Brooks.

> The confessional rehearsal or repetition of guilt is its own kind of performance, producing at the same time the excuse or justification of guilt (by the fact of confessing it) and the accumulation of more guilt (by the act of confessing it), in a dynamic that is potentially infinite. The more you confess, the more guilt is produced. The more the guilt is produced, the more the confessional machine functions. The act of confessing necessarily produces guilt in order to be functional. As a speech act, 'I confess' implies and necessitates guilt, and if

guilt is not there in the referent, as an object of cognition, it is in the speech act, which simultaneously exonerates and inculpates.[74]

So not only does a confession always inculpate, because it is retroactive, but the expression of one's guilt also operates according to 'a dynamic that is potentially infinite'. This infinite dynamic between justification of guilt and accumulation of new guilt is similar to the 'self-perpetuating oscillating series' that defines the paradoxical injunction. Autobiography as confession, then, involves the translation of the fundamental organizational act upon which the PCI is based – that is, the injunction requiring militants to 'be active' – into a specific speech act. Indeed, the structure of the communist self-narrative document enables the subject to reach a compromise with the organizational environment in which it is placed.

The militant confesses to a set of more or less serious political faults and shortcomings, thus expressing his inability to meet the organizational standards set by the party. In other words, he acknowledges that he does not grasp the meaning of his actions within the organization, unlike the party leaders, who perceive such meaning and govern according to their various bureaucratic mechanisms. And so Simone B. has accumulated a series of personal inadequacies, which are nothing more than shortcomings in his political decision-making capacity, as he is not capable of having a proper relationship with the organization and the world beyond it. He lacks self-critical ability, on the one hand, and a sense of appropriate behaviour on the political battlefield on the other.

His admission of guilt, however, also serves as a means to atone for his faults and overcome them. Having acknowledged his flaws and demonstrated his sincerity through negative assertions – he does not want to be insincere towards the party – Simone B. immediately states that 'at the same time, I don't believe it can be said that I have not made improvements'. This declaration is promptly mitigated, however, by his subsequent reference to his enduring 'shortcoming', specifically 'not having made enough progress' towards overcoming his 'opportunism'. As such, the conclusion of his autobiography is somewhat tortuous, oscillating ambiguously between inculpation and exoneration.

The main argument presented by Simone B. to exonerate himself, however, is rather generic. He states that he has improved, that he has 'deeply understood' his faults and that he undertakes 'to overcome them through greater and better effort'. And so, though his faults have been laid out clearly, what exactly is involved in overcoming them? Certainly not a set of actions that the subject has undertaken to implement, as the autobiography makes no reference to anything of the kind. Rather, it seems clear that atoning for one's faults simply means confessing them and – by virtue of the mechanism of discursive self-propulsion characterizing the confession – repeating that confession, because the more one confesses, the more one inculpates oneself, and the more one inculpates oneself, the more one needs to confess to exonerate oneself. The organizational paradox thus becomes a paradoxical discursive mechanism: the most important organizational 'activity' – by way of which militants can be directed – becomes using reiterated confession to communicate one's inability to be 'active' as the party desires. And so being 'active' means confessing to not being so, and confessing to not being 'active' provides the opportunity to be 'active' within the party and gives it meaning. This paradoxical act ties the militant to the party, as he awaits the day when being 'active' simply means being 'active'; as Simone B. says, 'I am certain that I can do this and undertake to demonstrate it through the work that the Party assigns to me in the future.'

The link between the communist organization's imperative to 'be active!' and the confessional form of the militants' self-narrative enables us to understand the latter as an autobiographical speech act, but it does not tell us much about the 'literary' quality of the autobiographies themselves, for want of a better term. This requires us to step down another level, beyond the organizational and discursive tiers, to focus on the strictly narrative elements and consider how the relationship between author, narrator and character is arranged within the text, beyond their formal identity within the autobiography. This issue is best approached by examining what I consider to be the 'degree zero' of the party autobiography.[75]

> C. Carlo from *** and *** born in *** on *** 1914, now living in *** at Via ***. My mum and dad were born labourers, and were part of the PSI when Fascism began to take on Italian workers. Dad was caned by the Fascists, and then joined the Fascist trade union at the end of 1925. From that point I learned to hate Fascism, and never endorsed it [...]. In 1940 I was conscripted and sent to Yugoslavia as a soldier. On 8 September 1943 I was made a prisoner of war by the Germans, and was in Germany until *** May 1945, when the Soviet army freed us. I returned to Italy on *** August 1945, and immediately signed up to the *** branch of the PCI. For a very short period I was secretary of the cell, and then secretary of the branch itself. In May 1946 I became an executive member of the Camera del Lavoro [the local centre for labour unions] and manager of the Lega Trasporti [Transport League], and in early 1947 I became a district organizer for the Lega Braccianti [Farmworkers' League] and a member of the managing committee of the branch of the PCI. During this period I never had disagreements with the party.[76]

Like Simone B's, Carlo C's self-narrative opens with an immediate account of his autobiographical details. Unlike the latter's autobiography, however, the former barely constitutes an appendix to the *Biografia del militante*. In fact, Carlo C. presents a brief CV of his activities before and after the Second World War, and ends his account with reference to the final question on the membership questionnaire, repeating that he had never disagreed with the party's political line. A similar approach to the party autobiography can be found in the following text.

> During the period of the Italian Social Republic, I taught in three professional development schools: ***, ***, and *** as headteacher. I had to flee from *** because I publicly approved of the actions of the deputy head *** (D.C.) who, in my absence, fired the then secretary of the *** Fascist party, and both of us refused to resurrect the Opera Nazionale Balilla [the Fascist youth organization] for our students. Between 1934 and 1943 I attended the weekly meetings that my

companion *** (the first secretary of the *** branch) held with a group of friends, almost all of whom were in the PCI (***, *** etc.). After 1943 I often met my companion ***, especially to recover weapons. I joined the PCI officially in April 1945. I joined the Cooperation in the same year, where I was responsible for the structure of the Cooperative Federation. In 1946 I moved to the Consumer Cooperative of the People of ***, where I remain at present.[77]

There are no significant differences between the two texts. Both are 'nonchaotic enumerations',[78] presenting a sort of administrative epic of the self, consisting of a detailed description of one's life. Comrade Enrico C., for instance, notes that he met with a group of communist militants on a weekly basis for nine years, from 1934 until 1943. These somewhat two-dimensional representations seem to suppress the temporal dimension in favour of the spatial, replacing the spiritual transitions in the subject's life with a detailed list of their institutional actions. This approach is modelled on the Catalogue of Ships contained in Book Two of the *Iliad*, revealing the same geospatial passion evident in Homer's enumeration.[79] The following autobiography fully embraces this penchant for topography.

I was born on *** 1931 in Via *** in ***. When I was about five years old, we moved to Via ***. I went to school in *** until the second year of primary school, then did my third and some of my fourth year in Marconi School in ***. I finished primary school in Via ***. In November 1941 we went to live in Piazza ***, as custodians of the German Academy. [...] In 1943 I ran away to my aunt and uncle's house in *** with my brother. We returned in October of the same year, not to Piazza ***, but rather a villa on Via *** that the Academy had occupied to keep the school going. I too attended the German school. In Autumn 1944, after school finished and the German teachers left, the villa was occupied by soldiers. We returned to our residence in Piazza *** one week prior to the Liberation. Between the years *** and *** I attended the *** Business School in Via ***. In 1948, I took a shorthand course with the Società Stenografica Bolognese [Bologna Shorthand Association] in Piazza ***. From November 1948 until February 1949, I worked with Prof. *** from the Clinica Medica dell'Ospedale S. Orsola as a shorthand typist. Since then, I've not been able to find proper employment. In August [illegible] I joined the Communist Party and the FGCI [Federation of Young Communists], at the *** branch in Via ***. My father has been the car park manager for the restaurant *** in Piazza *** since 1945 (and still holds this position).[80]

The self-narrative of Giovanna C., a young shorthand typist, takes the form of a detailed map of her movements in Bologna. Her story is reduced to a chronological series of events that, in turn, are closely linked to the toponymy of the city. The autobiography becomes a series of cartographic references, which even includes the restaurant car park managed by her father.

Why do these three texts represent the 'degree zero' of the party autobiography? To answer this question, I must refer back to an observation made in the

Introduction. Lejeune notes that the autobiography is based on the shared identity of the author, narrator and character, but can assume profoundly different forms, depending on how the power relations between these three figures are arranged. The autobiographical 'degree zero' occurs when the author function represents the pole of attraction for the narrator and the character. As mentioned previously, identity documents represent the extreme example of such a configuration, expressing the elementary statement that I am equal to me. The three autobiographies that I have transcribed here – the first and third almost in full – are little more than an evolution of the identity document in the form of a CV.

The precision with which the details of one's life are presented is the result of an approach, whereby the sense of plot is subordinate to the verifiability of the information provided in the autobiography. And naturally, of the various functions involved in the autobiographical text, it is the author who is responsible for the accuracy of the information presented in the self-narrative. The latter is the guarantor of the proper relationship between text and world or, if you prefer, of the *adequatio rei et intellectus*. The privileging of space over time is merely an effect of this bias in power relations in favour of the author: description prevails over narration and the text comes to resemble a mere commentary on the identity document photo, lending itself to a two-dimensional interpretation, like a map, as is the case with Giovanna C.'s autobiography.

What does it mean, though, when we say that description prevails over narration? It certainly does not mean that the autobiographies in question are boring – as curriculum vitae usually are – or that the texts are of poor literary quality. Giovanna C.'s text, for example, is, in its own way, extraordinary, representing an extreme version of one dimension of the party autobiography, by responding to the institutional request to write about oneself with a sort of *Nouveau Roman*.[81] The problem, rather, is that these texts do not have an ending. This phenomenon is particularly evident in Giovanna C.'s case, but the same could be said for Enrico C.'s and Carlo C.'s autobiographies. The young shorthand typist's autobiography could, in fact, be disproportionately expanded in terms of volume, with an even more detailed description of her movements, of the places she went with family and for work, or by specifying the address of her relatives' house in the countryside or the location of the clinic where she worked. We could easily imagine Giovanna C. intent on describing where she was during the Italian parliamentary elections or when Togliatti was wounded in an attack in 1948. Naturally, the more detail provided, the more the text loses its geometrical order, evolving from a 'nonchaotic' into a 'chaotic enumeration'.

The subordination of narration to description, however, is not limited to the potential for the former to be crushed by the weight of the latter, resulting in an abundant series of disconnected – or only superficially connected – events. The central issue is, in fact, another.

> Temporality is a problem, and an irreducible factor of any narrative statement, in a way that location is not [...] It is my simple conviction, then, that narrative

has something to do with time-boundedness, and that plot is the internal logic of the discourse of mortality. Walter Benjamin has made this point in the simplest and most extreme way, in claiming that what we seek in narrative fictions is that knowledge of death which is denied to us in our own lives: the death that write *finis* to the life and therefore confers on it its meaning. [...] Benjamin thus advances the ultimate argument for the necessary retrospectivity of narrative: that only the end can finally determine meaning close the sentence as a signifying totality.[82]

Peter Brooks' observations relate to fiction, but they can be equally applied to autobiography. Not only is there no narrative without time, but the time that characterizes narrative is that which is defined in relation to the experience of death: the time that has the final word in our lives and confers meaning upon it. In other words, the end of life is what enables us to find purpose in life and give it form. Autobiographies made up purely of CV-like elements and descriptions, such as those presented previously, have no ending and are completely lacking in form; they could continue to unfold endlessly before the reader. It is not so much excessive description, then, that makes narration impossible, but rather the fact that the series of descriptions lacks direction of any kind, resulting in a text that is devoid of form though not, obviously, devoid of interest. Such direction can only be provided by the narrator itself, as an independent figure separate to the author, who has the power to decide upon a story's ending and who, based solely on that final decision, can impose order and retrospectively select the events to end up in the account from the confused tangle of the infinite.

The absence of a narrator in communist autobiographies is not simply a literary problem. As the bearer of Lejeune's 'accuracy', the author function is naturally indispensable for the purposes of performing the most basic controls on an individual's identity and the potential that they are lying about significant aspects of their story. The party's control over this area of the autobiographical account corresponds, in a certain sense, to the genealogical investigation discussed by Kharkhordin, which considered the communist militant's past. It is the narrator, however, engaged in bringing the autobiographical story together, who enables the party, as a reader, to grasp the otherwise elusive dimension of the militant's own subjectivity, which manifests in the way one tells one's story.

This broadly corresponds to Kharkhordin's 'revelation by deeds', with the caveat, as stated previously, that the fundamental revelation is not what is revealed, but rather how that revelation is made; that is, how the narrator recounts the story they are narrating. Kharkhordin's categories of 'genealogy' and 'revelation' can be translated, in narratological terms, as story and plot, *fabula* and *syuzhet*. The autobiographical degree zero, then, depends entirely upon the author, resulting in a story without a plot or, more accurately, in a story to which the plot cannot give shape and to which it does not provide any specific narrative identity. A 'good' communist autobiography, then, cannot rely solely upon the story; it must also present a clearly visible plot with a narrator who is engaged with what he is recounting and who – given that it is his story being told – also appears as a character in the events being recounted. The issue, then, shifts to understanding the type of relationship that exists between the narrator and the main character.

It is worth noting at the outset that the emergence of the character and their sphere of action is rare in communist autobiographical texts and, when it does occur, it is often in a somewhat unexpected form.

> Between 14 and 18 years of age, my life was work, entertainment, play, sport. At 14 years of age I started work, errand boy, barber, mechanic and finally woodworker. I ac[c]epted all company, students, workers, farmers, I made no distinction, I was always opposed to the corrupt life, to the bad life (thanks to my upbringing by my parents). I heard bad things said about Fascism, from my brother and from others, and even though I was in the Fascist organisations, even though I didn't understand the reality of the situation, I never talked. I was always generous, nervous, and very reserved, due to a somewhat reserved life given my mother's death, I was always with my father until the age of 17 I often spent my evenings at home or with my dad. In 1943 with the first bombings in ***, I gave up work and went back to my town. 25 July the fall of mussolini [sic], confusion: people yelling down with mussolini [sic], others – the Fascists were taking off their badges and uniforms, I wasn't able to understand what was happening, drawn by the enthusiasm of the people I too began to yell down with mussolini [sic] (in this period I saw badoglio [sic] as the man who had saved Italy). 8 September, more confusion, soldiers everywhere walking to get to their homes, badoglio [sic] had turned traitor they said, my ideas became more confused, first mussolini [sic] had fallen thanks to badoglio [sic], now badoglio had turned traitor, the soldiers were running away what was happening? I understood later what was happening.[83]

In Luca C.'s autobiography, it is as though the main character suddenly invades the text, almost forcing the narrator into silence for a moment, to enable the action to flow freely. Four years of life are summarized in the first sentence, followed by an equally quick summary of the jobs held from when he was fourteen years of age: 'errand boy, barber, mechanic and finally woodworker'. This description of the militant's whole life is followed by a moral portrait: broad minded – 'I ac[c]epted all company'; morally upstanding – 'I always opposed the corrupt life'; and indisputably loyal – his brother, and probably his friends, are critical of Fascism, but Luca C. never mentions this: 'I never talked.' This moral portrait is followed by a sentimental characterization of himself as 'generous, nervous, very reserved', probably due to his mother's death.

This series of steps that leads from chronology to character description of the subject is orchestrated by the narrator. Suddenly, however, it is 1943, the year Mussolini fell from power, and it is as though the narrator himself, who is administering the plot, is participant in it. Everything is triggered by the 'first

1. Institutional Communist Autobiographies 39

bombing' to which Luca C., the character – not the narrator – reacts almost instantly, giving up work and taking refuge in his hometown. On 25 July 1943, the day Mussolini's reign ended, everything is amplified: the character is surrounded by confusion, people are yelling 'down with mussolini'. The dictator's name is written with a lowercase first letter throughout the text, a linguistic concession by the narrator to the character, leaving us in no doubt as to the latter's attitude towards the former leader. The Fascists tear off their badges and, amidst the general chaos, Luca C. finds himself yelling the same words as everyone else.

'I wasn't able to understand what was happening, drawn by the enthusiasm of the people I too began to yell.' The narrative change of focus is contained in this passage: the narrator, with the temporal distance granted by the retrospective nature of the account, is well aware of what happened, and of what 25 July meant for Italy. The character, on the other hand, knows nothing of any of it. And that is not all: that lack of awareness is not measured in terms of the superior position of knowledge occupied by the narrator as compared to the character. The account does not, for instance, say 'I was not able to understand what was happening, but I would come to realise it later'. Instead, the failure to understand is presented as a symptom of the enthusiasm that grips the character as he hears people shout and sees Fascists of all ranks shedding the symbols of their power.

This whirlwind moment is followed by the brief re-emergence of the narrator, in a parenthetical role, to finally provide the clarification he was previously unable to: 'in this period I thought of badoglio [sic] as the man who had saved Italy.' The undertone of this observation is subtly negative, as the narrator is using his knowledge here to highlight the character's naivety in regarding Badoglio as a great patriot, unaware of his dishonourable flight to Brindisi, sacrificing the country's interests for the sake of his own safety.

The somewhat arrogant figure of the narrator is quickly relegated to the background again, however, due to the events of 8 September 1943, the day of the Italian armistice with the allies. Confusion once again takes centre stage. The confusion of the Italian soldiers setting out for home in disarray, with no military guide, is coupled with the dismay of the character who cannot understand the course of events: 'first mussolini had fallen thanks to badoglio, now badoglio had turned traitor, the soldiers were running away.' The passage ends with a 'what was happening?', marking his presence within the text.

There are few instances in which the character so forcefully invades the account, but at least one more deserves a mention, due to the particular way in which the character's overpowering of the narrator manifests.

> Though I can't linger on this matter for long, I can't forget to mention here my joy the day (November 1944) I was assigned the card (it was pink at the time). The comrade that handed it to me said: 'Remember that you're the youngest registered comrade in Bologna'. I felt like I was someone or something. Everything I said that day, even the most foolish, seemed great to me, because I had said it, and I was a member of the communist party.[84]

In this case, too, the narrator is secondary to the character, who is given the right to express herself directly without mediation by the narrator's voice. The right to speak independently is not, however, granted to the main character recounting her experiences, but rather to one of her interlocutors, a comrade in the communist party. The text does not report any direct statements made by Franca A., the autobiography's author, on such an important moment for her. We only know – and it is the narrator who provides a condensed report of the event – that the main character spoke that day, and that even the most foolish things she said were ennobled by the fact that her discourse was backed by the party. And so the narrator withdraws, and the right to speak directly is granted not to the main character, but to the party and its representative.

This struggle by the main character to gain independence in relation to the narrator and be released from the latter's tutelage is not coincidental. In part, it is a product of the space available to the writer: the communist autobiography does not have the same scope of a novel and, given that it is underpinned by preoccupations with referential correctness and accuracy, characters whose stories are being told – including the main character – cannot be granted much freedom to move. Issues of textual brevity and conciseness are, however, secondary to what is, in fact, a distinctive feature of the communist autobiography, specifically the subordination of the – main – character to the narrator. A comparison of two drafts of a single autobiography sheds light on the operation of such a mechanism.

> [My father] tried to work after a year with a coalman after being at a contractor's firm[.] I remember one evening he came home being nasty to my mother [who] gave out to him because he had come to Bologna [and] she said he should join the Fascist Party and he didn't want anything to do with politics not because he was anti-Fascist, all he wanted was to go to church and stay home, I remember when I was six they made me go to church and learn the doctrine. And so in 1940 the war broke out and I saw everyone talking about war like it was a game; that's how wartime life began. At school people talked about war all the time and they taught us who was the enemy and who was the ally. I never suffered from hunger during the war because I had my farmer grandparents who brought me wheat; but I remember at school when I gave my classmate my half snack, he asked me how I was eating white bread and he told me he only ate two hundred grams of brown bread I think it was the first time I felt pity for a classmate and I had never heard such a thing said before.[85]

> But then my family struggled financially when we came to Bologna they didn't give my father anything and so life had become hard and what's more my mother got sick and my father [was] unemployed. To work you needed the Fascist party card and my father didn't want to join not because he was against Fascism but because he wasn't interested in politics, as long as he went to church he was happy. From 1938/39/40/41 he worked tough jobs and didn't earn much he was

a coalman and what happened to him, they offered him good positions but he refused because you always needed the Fascist party card, at school I learnt a bit of history I really admired Garibaldi and Fascism not so much, in fourth class I never suffered hunger like many of my classmates and inside I felt a sense of shame at the situation but I couldn't understand it.[86]

The two passages are from two separate rewritings of Patrizio G.'s autobiography. The first is undated, but it is plausible that it precedes the second, written in 1951. The second text is much longer than the first – four pages compared to two – and describes a series of events that occurred after the time when the account provided in the undated document ends. What changes between one draft and another? The same period in the life of the autobiography's author is presented in a significantly more concise form in the 1951 version – approximately one quarter of the text is missing. This reduction is essentially achieved by means of two rather significant cuts. First, the episode involving the argument between father and mother is missing – the former 'came home being nasty to my mother' and the two probably fought over the issue of Fascist party membership. It also does not include the somewhat pathetic anecdote involving sharing his snack with the child who only had brown bread to eat.

While the account of these life episodes is undoubtedly already mediated by the narrator in the first draft, a margin for action and reaction by the character nevertheless remains. While it is the character who sees his father being 'nasty' to his mother, it is the narrator who elegantly omits the child character's reactions, limiting himself to summarizing what had happened by stressing that his life had become hard also because of his mother's sickness and his father's unemployment. Similarly, the immediacy of the episode with the brown bread disappears, to be replaced with a laconic 'I never suffered hunger like many of my classmates'. The different weight assigned to plot and story and to character and narrator is most evident, however, in the concluding passage. The first version states that it was 'the first time I felt pity for a classmate and I had never heard such a thing said before.' Here, the subject of the pity is the character, who for the first time encounters the misery of the world. In the second version, however, the passage ends with 'I felt a sense of shame at this situation but I couldn't understand it.'

Not only do we move from pity to shame, that is, from an immediate to a mediate sentiment, but the impression left by the conversation with the classmate is also replaced by a claim not to understand. The passage is particularly ambiguous: what is, in fact, the unit for measuring such a lack of understanding? Is it the child, discovering that another child only eats two hundred grams of brown bread, that does not understand, or is it the child character that cannot interpret what he encounters because he does not have the knowledge of the adult narrator? In other words, is the character's lack of comprehension temporally situated in the present tense of the episode or in the future tense inhabited by the narrator? The text itself does not offer a definitive answer to these questions, but a comparison of the two versions of the story at least makes it possible to conclude that the state of not knowing is suggested to the character by the narrator. In the brief moment in which he was not entirely under the tutelage of the narrative voice, the former experienced pity and wonder at what was before him.

The subordination of character to narrator is evident not so much in the closure of spaces, within the account, that the character can use to assert itself through action or direct discourse, but rather, specifically, through the motif of lack of knowledge. This dimension, which permeates the first of the autobiographies I presented – written by Simone B. – in its entirety, and also emerges in the second version of Patrizio G.'s account, defines the specific condition of the character within the autobiographical plot. The epistemological issue, as a distinctive trait of the character, emerges in full force in Paolo A.'s text, written while he was attending a course at one of the party schools.

> In July of '45 I was repatriated. My Father was a partisan and I was welcomed warmly by all the Partisans. I joined the C.P. [Communist Party] I believed that everything was already over. I went to meetings and always talked about killing. The leaders corrected me and looked for books to read. But I still didn't understand what reading meant I was an enemy of books and study. […] In fact at this school I have learned that I am an instinctive comrade. While before I thought I knew a lot about it, whereas even now I realise that I have a lot to learn. I have already learned something, whereas before I couldn't stand books, now I read whenever I can and using the study techniques they taught us I have also learned to understand what I read. And so the end of this school is the start of study for me.[87]

When Paolo A. joins the PCI on his return from Germany where he was imprisoned, his desire is to 'kill', that is, to take part in a revolution, as is stated in certain passages of the text that I have omitted here for reasons of brevity. This need for action is coupled with a 'hatred' of books. At the end of his time at the school, the description of which is placed at the end of the autobiography, he understands that his desire for revolution has made him an 'instinctive comrade', and that study is essential. Of significance, in this text, is not just the presentation of the character in negative terms, from a cognitive perspective, but also the fact that the beginning of his communist educational journey coincides with an act of depoliticization – at least in the sense attributed by Schmitt to politics, to which I refer in this work. Becoming a communist means transferring to the party one's right to determine who is a friend and who is an enemy, a decision that takes the form of a revolutionary act and that is crystallized, in Paolo A.'s discourse, in the action of 'killing' one's adversary.[88] The character appears as an 'instinctive comrade', engaged in unregulated action in the eyes of the narrator who, having reached the end of his educational journey, and thanks to the knowledge he has acquired, can perceive the character's recklessness.

The communist autobiography, therefore, takes the form of a *Bildungsroman*, characterized by a clear separation between chronological order and logical order. The significance of the personal story, in other words, is concentrated at the end of the account and not at the beginning, so that the point of origin of the story does not coincide with the point of origin of the meaning of that story. Instead, the events that constitute the story acquire their meaning only in retrospect, starting with the definitive delineation of the plot.

> They become meaningful: this is the point. The novelistic episode is almost never meaningful in itself. It becomes so because someone – in the *Bildungsroman* usually the protagonist – gives it meaning. He prolongs the encounter, he probes into the conversation, he recalls it, he puts hopes in it. The novelistic plot is marked by this curvature towards the interiority, which dispenses meaning and thereby creates events. 'Remember to live': remember that all you run into can be used for the building of your life; it can all be made meaningful. It is the uneven glimmer of 'experience'.[89]

For the protagonist of the *Bildungsroman*, the meaning of an event always comes afterwards: 'he prolongs the encounter, he probes into the conversation, he recalls it.' Likewise, one's life story, in itself void of significance, becomes an experience, and its telling tends towards interiority as a space in which what happens becomes significant. A shift occurs, then, from chronological to logical order, and time becomes meaning.

In the case of the communist autobiographies I have presented, however, the 'curvature towards interiority', takes on a more specific meaning. The folding of events back on themselves, achieved through memory, which reflects their interior value, translates into the long journey taken by the autobiography's main character to become the narrator of their own story. Ultimately, the final accomplishment of the communist self-narrative is represented by the moment when the character, as bearer of the action, becomes one with the narrator, as the centre of knowledge.[90] The communist's life story thus becomes a run-up by the character in relation to the narrator, something that is only realized at the end of the account, when the character, having finally become a self-narrator, makes his story subordinate to the meaning conferred upon it by the plot that imposes order on that story. The subordination of character to narrator could not be clearer: the story of the self only has value if it is understood, and understanding occurs by way of the narrator presenting it in the form of a plot.

It is not enough, however, to become the narrator. As mentioned previously, in terms of the organizational conditions of its production, the communist autobiography is ensnared in the paradoxical command to 'be active'. This dictates the fundamental quality of the narration and of the evolution of character into narrator.

> I should begin by saying that my way of performing the activity has always been instinctive, as I also have a very low level of political maturity, I limited myself to simple practical messages to lead the workers in my factory and in my area to fight for economic and political causes. It's only now that I realise how certain issues and matters could have been resolved more easily with better

results. Thanks to the teachings of this course at the working class school that introduced me to the theory of the labour movement and the importance of political parties as a guiding force in the labour movement struggle.[91]

When the character becomes the narrator, he understands the meaning of his past. The past, however, appears to him as a set of faults and shortcomings: 'it is only now that I realise how certain issues and matters could have been resolved more easily with better results.' The perception of one's own story as a journey of faults is even clearer in the following text. This extract is taken from a document that often accompanies the communist militants' autobiographies in their personal files. The *Cosa mi aspetto dalla scuola* [What I expect from the school] composition was written at the beginning of cadre and militant courses, while a corresponding document entitled *Cosa mi ha dato la scuola* [What the school has given me] was prepared at the end.

> While it may be true that I was a political leader, it's also true that I lack many of the qualities of a leader, for example I am semi-illiterate to this day and this prevents me from better understanding while reading, and learning what I read. And so starting from such a low point I expect many things. First, because I'm behind, I will have to make more sacrifices in reading than another comrade who is better than me [...] To do this I expect that in school there is discipline in study and in all interactions in the school, a foundation required of a true student, a member of the working class.[92]

A character who has finally become the narrator of his own story cannot help but tell it from a critical and self-critical, and, therefore, negative, perspective. This is how, on a narrative level, the pragmatic paradox – 'be active' – used to organize the communist militants within the party, is resolved. Autobiographical 'activation' translates into absorption of the character by the narrator, and action by the awareness of the meaning of that action. The narrator's awareness, however, is purely negative, and so reflects the organizational alienation of the meaning of the actions performed by the militants.

The narrator knows significantly more than the character, but his knowledge is disappointing, limited to a Socratic awareness of what he does not know. The narrator, however, knows that he does not know, while the character, considered from the narrator's perspective, does not know that he knows. This awareness, of which the character himself is ignorant, does not ennoble his presence within the autobiographical text, but rather definitively relegates him. The absorption of the character by the narrator does not, in fact, result in the disappearance of the former in favour of the latter. Rather, it entails the transformation of the character into something less than the character, in a foreshadowing of meaning to be revealed by the narrator at the end. As such, the character becomes a *figura*.

> Beside the opposition between *figura* and fulfilment or truth, there appears another, between *figura* and *historia*; *historia* or *littera* is the literal sense or

the event related; *figura* is the same literal meaning or event in reference to the fulfilment cloaked in it, and this fulfilment itself is *veritas*, so that *figura* becomes a middle term between *littera-historia* and *veritas*.⁹³

The character as *figura* does not exist for its own sake. Rather, it exists as a vehicle by way of which the *veritas* – the truth borne by the narrator – emerges in the *historia* – in our case, in the *story* upon which the autobiography is based. The assertion of the rights of the narrator against those of the character, then, translates into imposition by the former onto the latter of a sort of figural interpretation,⁹⁴ according to which the events of the character's past become allegories that can only be deciphered from the present inhabited by the narrator or, to be more precise, by the character who has finally become the narrator. Naturally, what separates the past to which the character is confined from the present inhabited by the narrator is the encounter with the party, and preparation of the autobiography seals that event.

The most fascinating example of figural transformation of the past is found in Benedetta R.'s autobiography, which is among the best that I have read.

> Around that time I began to hear talk of Socialist Russia, and from what I heard I understood that there were no bosses in that country, that everyone worked and earned, that everyone could study, in my mind I imagined a large country full of kind, intelligent and good people, where everyone greeted each other and used informal forms of address, and so I developed a great respect and affection for the communists and the partisans, as soon as I was told that person is one of them, I instantly found them kinder, more intelligent, I imagined them to be better and I even considered them better looking, I had a great dislike for anyone who spoke badly of them.⁹⁵

Benedetta R. is not even fourteen years old when she fantasizes about 'Socialist Russia', but she is already involved in distributing partisan movement leaflets and publications. Did she really dream of the Soviet Union as a country where all residents are friends? The question is irrelevant. What matters is that Benedetta R.'s membership of the PCI was in some way influenced and foreshadowed by the adolescent fantasy of socialism's native land as a country where everyone is 'intelligent and good'. Or rather, Benedetta R., as narrator of her own story, chooses – from among all the events that she could recount to represent herself as a character – to describe the fantasy that prepared her for the decision to become a communist.

Of significance here, however, is not that the child's fantasy of Russia, inhabited by 'kind, intelligent and good people', foreshadows the adult's experience of communism, characterized by 'great affection for comrades', 'blind trust in them' and 'great love for the Division', according to Benedetta R.'s description in her autobiography. Of relevance, rather, is the fact that the action is reduced to mere prevision. What defines Benedetta R. as a character is that – through her fantasy – she provides advance notice, without fully realizing it, of knowledge that Benedetta

R. will only truly possess at the end of her self-narrative: an awareness, guaranteed by the party, of Russia as a land of human emancipation, the Italian equivalent of which is represented by the party division. From this perspective, Benedetta R. as an adolescent character is a *figura*, whose truth is only perfectly realized by way of Benedetta R. the adult self-narrator.

The communist autobiography is, therefore, built on repetition. Not, however, in the sense that the narrator repeats what happened to the character. Rather, it is the character who, as a *figura*, repeats the meaning possessed by the narrator. Indeed, foreshadowing the future means repeating in the past that which has not already happened in the future. The character's action, however, as it is mere foreshadowing, makes the future appear as through a veil – an open-eyed dream – that is only removed when the character becomes a narrator and, finally, as self-narrator rather than character, grasps the meaning of her own story.[96]

The ultimate significance of this story, however, is disappointing. The communist self-narrative simply reveals that the meaning of one's actions is a flawed meaning, destined never to stand the test of the narrator's final judgement, due to the insurmountable gap between action and knowledge, between the former's stubborn randomness and the latter's need for order.

Chapter 2

FEMINIST SELF-ENUNCIATION: BETWEEN SILENCE AND INFINITE SPEECH

The paradox of emancipation and its autobiographical strategies

Italian neo-feminism, which emerged at the end of the 1960s,[1] introduced profound changes to the political forms of use of the self-narrative. Indeed, completely different mechanisms are at play in the feminist 'autobiographical pact' as in its communist equivalent. First, the autobiographical act is emancipated from the organizational strictures previously placed on it. The self-narrative is, therefore, no longer one of a range of tools – together with coercive devices such as reprimand or expulsion – used by the party to discipline its militants. Instead, the organizational forms availed of by the neo-feminist movement – and, in particular, the small group consisting solely of women – become instrumental to making it possible to speak about oneself. Whereas in the communist context, the organization and its requirements provided the conditions for production of the party autobiography, in the feminist sphere it is the self-narrative and its needs that give form to the organizational structure – that is, the small group – within which it can finally develop.

The feminist self-narrative's freedom from the organizational shackles placed on the party autobiography, in turn, gives rise to a variety of textual forms not found in the communist domain. Whereas PCI militants filled out a political questionnaire and enclosed an autobiographical account that – though it took different forms – remained faithful to the CV-style model, neo-feminists drew on a much broader range of autobiographical styles to recount their self-narratives, from diary form to lyrical fragment. Though the latter form technically falls outside of the scope of autobiographical enunciation, as we shall see, the decision to employ this literary genre results from feminist exploration of the political opportunities offered by autobiographical discourse. Among the idiosyncrasies that characterize feminist self-enunciation, the lack of simple, straightforward autobiographies, in the form of a memoir of one's life, is notable. The latter did not begin to emerge until the 1980s, and is discussed in the next chapter. Given the 'experimental' nature of the feminist self-narrative, however, this absence is not particularly surprising: established methods of narrating the self were inevitably going to be regarded as expressions of the male power of words, to be rejected or simply abandoned to the oblivion of history.

Consciousness-raising groups – a phenomenon widespread in Italy from the second half of the 1960s until the beginning of the 1970s – provide the starting point for a discussion of the variegated setting in which feminist autobiographical discourse emerged. Made up of a small number of women and focused on practising consciousness-raising, they may be regarded as the 'basic structure of the [feminist] movement', the 'spontaneous organisation that women adopted for acquiring consciousness' and the 'place where personal behaviours are changed in order to change society at large'.[2] What exactly does the consciousness-raising practice consist of? While Carol Hanisch and the North American consciousness-raising groups represent the political and fundamental theoretical point of reference,[3] it is the operational translation of this practice performed by Italian feminists that is of relevance here.[4] Carla Lonzi, a leading Italian feminist, described it as such in her *Significato dell'autoscienza nei gruppi femministi* (*Meaning of Consciousness-raising in Feminist Groups*):[5]

> It is here that the feminist consciousness-raising groups acquire their true physiognomy as nuclei that transform the spirituality of the patriarchal era: they operate, by way of a sudden leap, on women who come to know each other again as complete human beings, who do not need approval from men. Feminist consciousness-raising differs from all other forms of consciousness-raising, in particular that proposed by psychoanalysis, because it raises the issue of personal dependence within the female species, as a species that is itself dependent. [...] And this transition give rise to the opportunity for creative feminist action: it is in asserting oneself, without the guarantee of male understanding, that women reach that state of liberty that undermines the myth of the couple.[6]

It would seem that the value of consciousness-raising, as a practice, is primarily cathartic and, therefore, eminently negative. Its objective is to break the chain of subjugation that links women to men, allowing the former to overcome their need for the approval of the latter. As such, the feminist group serves as a mechanism that enables women to reject the 'myth of the couple' and the relationship of dependence that this imposes. Finally, Lonzi clarifies that feminist consciousness-raising is opposed to its psychoanalytical counterpart. Why so? Beyond the explanation provided in the text itself – 'because it raises the issue of the personal dependence within the female species, as a species that is itself dependent' – the rejection of psychoanalysis does not seem to be rooted in the therapeutic nature of the latter, but rather in the fact that it is practised by men.

The significance of consciousness-raising, therefore, seems to reside in the act of separation, from the male sex, which gives rise to the emergence of groups of women who dedicate themselves to practising feminist self-awareness. At the end of her article, however, Carla Lonzi presents a dialectical argument that puts a positive spin on the separation of women from men. Feminists do not, in fact, exclude men. Rather, they exclude the exclusion that men have historically reserved for the female sex. And so consciousness-raising is the (feminist) negation of a (male) negation that culminates in the affirmation of women.

Though this argument is appealing, the text in question does not reveal much to us about feminist consciousness-raising, except to imply that it does not involve women achieving immediate consciousness of themselves; rather, it is a consciousness obtained by rejecting male consciousness, and, therefore, in a mediated way, with the small women's groups serving as a tool. Nothing is said of how consciousness is materially acquired. The following text is useful in this regard:

> There are many misunderstandings and misinterpretations of the significance of the small consciousness-raising groups, which may be regarded as the base unit for almost all feminist movements. It's nothing new, some say. [...] Other, more sophisticated, commenters regard it as a psychotherapy group. This interpretation is also inaccurate. The very term 'therapy' suggests that someone is ill. [...] But what is the small consciousness-raising group, then? It is a limited number of women (between 6 and 10) that meet periodically (at least once a week) to talk about themselves, their lives, their experiences. There is no abstract discourse, no ideological discussions. These would presuppose that we already know what we are and what we want, or that we accept the definitions that male culture has always attributed to us. The principle is that of 'politics of experience'. And so not a mode of politics that takes a readymade ideology as its starting point, but one that starts with fundamental needs. An ideological moment may have a place, but as a point of arrival, and one that should always be assessed and revisited through discussion.[7]

This text, too, and with greater insistence than Lonzi's, underlines the idea that feminist consciousness-raising is not equivalent to psychoanalytical therapy. The latter presupposes that 'someone is ill' and must be cured in order to heal. From a feminist perspective, however, to the extent that it is appropriate to talk of illness, it is clearly (male) society that is afflicted by a disorder and in need of treatment. This position, on the one hand, seems to echo the Frankfurt school of criticism of psychoanalysis[8] and, on the other, reveals a certain degree of preoccupation with the fact that consciousness-raising may become a consolatory practice, devoid of emancipatory value and disengaged from the political objectives of the women's movement. It should be noted that the quoted text dates from 1974, the year in which Italian feminists were resolutely and triumphantly engaged in mobilization on the referendum, instigated by the Christian Democrats, to repeal the divorce law introduced in 1970.

More relevant to my work than the rejection of the notion of therapy is the description of what happened at the consciousness-raising group. We are told that the women talk about themselves and their experiences when they meet, avoiding 'ideological discussions' and 'abstract discourse'. This is clearly an important point, as it is reiterated at the end of the passage, emphasizing the rejection of 'readymade ideology'. If ideology must play a part in consciousness-raising groups, it must do so at the end, serving as a provisional 'point of arrival', to be regularly revisited through discussion. Feminists, then, do not simply reject male – and sexist – ideology, replacing it with feminist ideology. Rather, they dismiss the very concept of ideology as a political tool that could serve women. Why so? Because ideology is simply a synonym for abstraction. What is, in fact, being rejected is the movement towards the universal – which leaves a set of individual experiences, or 'fundamental needs', in its wake – that forms the basis for abstract (and, though not explicitly stated, male) universality.[9]

And so if, in political terms, feminist consciousness-raising is the rejection of a rejection, as Carla Lonzi asserts, in epistemological terms it is the rejection of an abstraction and, therefore, of the (male) *logos* that produces 'abstract [and ideological] discourses'. What occupies the discursive space left vacant by the rejection of the (male) *logos*? Though not explicitly identified, the only candidate eligible to fill the resulting epistemological void is the female (and feminist) *mythos*. If male power operates by way of mechanisms of logic and abstraction, female counter-power choses to tackle it using narration as its strategy, anchoring the account in personal experience.[10] These women combat abstract ideology with autobiographical concreteness, the immobile objectivity of male knowledge with the living subjectivity of the act of telling the truth about oneself.

This tendency towards the immediate recounting and expression of the self, rooted in the consciousness-raising experience, essentially defines the autobiographical textual field of feminism. The political experience of *Sottosopra* [*Upside Down*] offers a good starting point for exploring the latter. This publication was produced between 1973 and 1976 – by a group based in Via Cherubini in Milan – as a tool to gather the *Experiences of Italian Feminist Groups*, as the subtitle of the first two editions from 1973 and 1974 clearly states. The publication not only devoted space to feminist experiences across Italy but also included a particularly wide range of forms of expression in its women's writing. It contained poetry, political documents, transcripts of feminist group meetings, theoretical articles, open letters, songs, translations and writings from women describing their condition. Leaving aside the ideological and theoretical documents, the autobiographical inclination of the materials is apparent. In particular, the 1974 edition of *Sottosopra* contains a collection of office stories, whose protagonists are female office workers, oppressed by their male colleagues and bosses. One, which tells the story of a young woman moving from one job to the next, without any satisfaction, is particularly sad:

> Another office (you can't find anything else!), worse than the first but at least the pay is decent. All the people you have to deal with (the three owners: a husband and wife and their son) are over 60, and there's the usual filth, the usual bare desk and the usual ancient typewriter. And you spend all day correcting the three old people's mistakes![11]

This sense of unhappiness is also evident in other tales, such as Liliana's 'story from ten years ago, which still pains me inside'. In her description, the offices, this time in a large company, are a place of sexual alienation with nowhere to escape to:

Pussies, tits, arses, blondes, gingers, brunettes, fat women, skinny women, whores, actresses, young women and old women, hard women and decrepit women: these were the conversation topics of the male graphic designers and copywriters, some with degrees, some without, in the canteen, in the toilet and during after-work drinks and coffee breaks. We women who were on hand were lusted after and at the same time scorned because we were not attractive enough.[12]

Another woman, also a secretary, described the same meaningless atmosphere:

My job is very simple: I number the pages of documents, I sort paperwork sent from my office to other branches, I remove the various pieces of carbon paper joining the counterfoils for the data processing department and the various Italian agencies, I write down information from documents in a notebook, I type letters and turn the pages of the calendar in my office and in my boss' office … 'because otherwise I'm not taking care of him … ' This has been my working day for roughly three years … Every day is more and more similar and more and more alienating.[13]

The atmosphere of office alienation that these stories exude is far removed from the sense of – sometimes excruciating – pain that characterizes many communist militant autobiographies, strewn with war, unemployment, poverty and hunger. The differences between the communist and feminist autobiographical horizons cannot, however, simply be reduced to the underlying emotional tone linked, naturally, to events in global and Italian history, specifically the transition from the post-war years and reconstruction[14] to the period immediately following the great Italian economic and industrial boom of the 1960s. What is different, rather, is the fundamental orientation of the feminist self-narrative. Whereas communist militants followed a CV-style template to write about themselves, feminists adopted a testimonial-style writing strategy.

In the first instance, despite the undeniable creativity and variety in the subject's modes of recounting their stories to the party, the primacy of reader over writer and narrator over character gives rise to a sort of general autobiographical rulebook. The militant could only recount his or her story on the condition that it provided an accurate description of his or her life, including personal details, and presented the political meaning of his or her existence in accordance with the system of expectations established by the party. Failure to comply with such obligations was met with reproach, or even expulsion, from the party organization. The adoption of a testimonial strategy by the previously examined texts overturns this power relationship. In what way? The following explanation is offered by Paul Ricouer.

What is a true witness, a faithful witness? Everyone knows that it is something other an accurate or even conscientious narrator. He does not limit himself to testifying that … but rather testifies for … and bears testimony to … By way of these expressions, language intends that the witness seals his attachment to the cause he defends by publicly confessing his conviction, with the zeal of a propagandist and devotion that can lead to him sacrificing his life. A witness is capable of suffering and dying for what he believes in. When life is the price to be paid for proving one's conviction, the witness is known by a different name: he's called a martyr. [...] A man becomes a martyr above all because he is a witness. But to become a martyr, a man must be a witness to the very end and this cannot arise from a purely legal reflection: in a trial, it is not the witness who risks his life, but the accused.[15]

As mentioned in Chapter 2, communist autobiographies also feature a testimonial dimension, but in the traditional 'legal' form to which Ricouer refers. The communist militant is called upon to testify to his political innocence before the party court. The risk she faces is not, therefore, rooted in her being a witness, but rather a person accused, at least potentially, of having betrayed the communist cause. When a feminist subject testifies to her alienation as a woman, on the other hand, she does so in an extra-legal or, more accurately, anti-legal dimension. Her testimony does not corroborate the account of an accused before any court. Rather, precisely because in this instance testifying means putting one's life on the line to assert one's conviction, it countermands the authority of the court and the law that upholds it.

To testify, then, means to accuse law itself. And, because the act of accusation is no longer founded in the law, it can only be legitimized by the power of the subject performing that act. Testimony that accuses must, therefore, necessarily take the form of first-person testimony, where what is being testified to acquires its antinomian power only by virtue of the fact that it is also a self-narrative. As such, the three feminist texts above can be regarded as going beyond mere 'accurate or even conscientious' reporting of everyday sexism in the workplace, or alienation produced by the monotony and insignificance of one's role. Rather, their affirmative character is the product of their desire to tell a truth that only exists in the enunciation of the subject's personal story, by way of which she puts herself and the world at risk.

The rejection of the male *logos*, then, translates into a transition from third to first person in the act of enunciating the truth – from the impersonal nature of abstract discourse to a first-person account that bears witness to the truth. This first shift is accompanied by a second that affects the recipient – listener or reader – of the autobiographical words. Removed from the legal context, the primacy of the recipient, as a judge of the adequacy of the self-enunciation, is diminished. The figure of the narrator – as the interface between the rights of the reader/listener and the duties of the character – also loses power, as a result. In this new 'autobiographical pact', sealed by feminists, the account that testifies to one's own truth is no longer addressed to a figure that judges it, but rather to the community of women, defined by the equality of its members. Once again, however, equality should not be interpreted in legal or mathematical terms: the feminist community built around the autobiographical word is characterized by an I–you bond. The I recounts her narrative to a you that recounts her narrative, in turn, and responds to the narrative of the other.[16]

The feminist account, then, resembles that presented by Scheherazade in the *Arabian Nights*,[17] but diverges from the latter in one important way. The daughter of the grand vizier of the King of Persia – at the request of another woman, her sister, Dunyazade – tells the last story of her life and, by repeating it night after night, succeeds in saving herself and overcoming the king's homicidal fury towards womankind. Both Scheherazade and the feminists recount their stories in dangerous circumstances, in the face of male power. The feminists, however, tell the one story that Scheherazade never recounted: the story of the self, which is delivered in the *Arabian Nights* by an anonymous narrator.[18]

Might we, therefore, regard Italian feminists of the 1970s as more radical Scheherazades? To some extent we might, provided that we refrain from lavishing generic praise based on that radicalism alone, and instead examine the effects that it produces, including those that are problematic.

> The only 'historical' method that we have at our disposal for engaging with one another, consciousness-raising, as it has been practised thus far, that is, as an often merely episodic account of our experiences, no longer satisfies us [...]. Actually, for me, gradually becoming aware of the inadequacy of this tool that had seemed to me to be one of the key elements of our time together, has contributed greatly to my current uncertainty, which has me feeling that I need to find new meaning, a new dimension to the act of being among women.[19]

Margherita's words reveal a sense of tiredness with the self-narration practised by the consciousness-raising groups, expressing not so much personal fatigue, it would seem, as the general condition of the feminist movement in 1974.[20] Margherita observes that accounts are 'often merely episodic', alluding to a sort of inability to adequately say what should be said, or a struggle to articulate, in narrative terms, what one wishes to express. Such aphasia does not seem to me to be a simple issue of narrative tiredness. Rather, the discursive difficulty touched upon by Margherita is linked to what I regard as the focal point of the self-enunciation mechanism employed by Italian neo-feminism.

> *Lea*: the great strength of the 1970s was that it shed light on material that had been simultaneously denied, deleted and mythologised by male culture, never recounted from a female perspective. In this way, women opened up a crevice in the crust of culture. What made this bearable? [...] It marked a break in centuries-old, historical complicity.[21]

This quote is from a work by Lea Melandri – a leading Italian feminist, though not as well known as Carla Lonzi or figures such as Adriana Cavarero or Luisa Muraro who gravitated to the Milan Women's Bookstore Collective – the title of which, tellingly, is *Una visceralità indicibile* (*Unspeakable Viscerality*). In a nutshell, Italian neo-feminists' central concern was to recount a story that had 'never [been] recounted from a female perspective', thus alluding to a profound dimension – visceral, according to the title of the work – that resists speakability and that is, in fact, 'unspeakable'. Not a simple task and one that, not by chance, the text describes as 'a break in centuries-old, historical complicity'.

In this way, Lea Melandri outlines the narrative agenda of 1970s Italian feminism, which innovatively rewrote the paradoxical autobiographical command integral to the communist organizational space. If the communist militants' self-narrative was a response to the paradoxical injunction to 'be active!', its feminist counterpart was marked by the command to 'be yourself!', in opposition to millennial male and patriarchal power that prevented previous generations of women from truly being women. The *ontological imperative*, for want of a better term, that commands one to be what one is, is already innately self-contradictory: if I must be myself, it is because I am not actually such, that is, I am not myself, but rather something other than myself. As such, the injunction to 'be yourself!' is not aimed at the – female – subject to whom it is addressed, but at another, who is not that same subject. In this sense, it is an instruction that is impossible to obey, because the subject at whom it is aimed is always absent. On the other hand, if one is simply oneself, the command is superfluous: I am me without the need for anyone to command me to be such. Or, from another perspective, if I do obey it, I do so by breaching it: *I can* be myself, in other words, *if I do not have* to be myself.

If we shift our focus from the ontological to the discursive plane, the substance of the question does not change; the problem becomes more evident, but also more complicated. As we saw previously, the condition for being oneself, from a feminist perspective, is to recount what has never been recounted or, in more general terms, to say what has never been said. In this case, the self-contradictory nature of the injunction to be oneself is compounded by the problem of understanding precisely what that 'never' – which also appears in Lea Melandri's quote – actually means. The three stories of office alienation examined previously suggest that the 'never' in question is essentially historical in nature: the women telling their stories consent to the emergence, on a discursive level, of a state of oppression that language had previously been prohibited from expressing. Viewed in this way, the feminist self-narrative is simply the autobiographical manifestation of a more general – and not particularly original – politics of testimony and denunciation, wherein the purpose of expressing one's personal pain is to inspire moral indignation.[22]

Italian neo-feminists were not content with such an interpretation of that 'never', and this discontent is at the root of their originality, as well as their torment. In my view, the sense of fatigue and inadequacy as regards the self-narrative that emerges during the consciousness-raising experience derives from the impossible task entrusted to feminist self-enunciation. As with the title chosen by Lea Melandri for her account of the feminist 1970s – *Una visceralità indicibile* – the 'never' does not indicate a condition of chronological anteriority, but rather a linguistic and ontological void. Women are not required to strive to recount something that has not yet been recounted. Rather, they must speak something that cannot be spoken, because that which must be spoken – male violence and oppression – continuously eludes the language. *And so, women are not required to speak the unspoken, but the unspeakable.* The experiences of the Italian feminist movement of the 1970s, involving the liberal reworking of the psychoanalytical tradition, were simply an attempt to rise to the challenge that neo-feminism had set itself as regards the unspeakable, which, in feminist discourse, often manifests in the more reassuring guise of the unconscious.

From a psychological perspective, the idea of unspeakability can certainly be linked to that of trauma. Indeed, trauma, by its very nature, though produces discursive effects, rejects discourse itself: manifesting while hiding and hiding while manifesting in language, always to be found in an unexpected place. In order to be spoken, then, it requires the limits usually placed on self-narration to be broken.[23] In sociological terms, however, the following observations by Georg Simmel regarding the secret and the secret society – which at first glance seem unrelated to our topic – are much more useful:

> The secret puts a barrier between men, but at the same time, it creates the tempting challenge to break through it, by gossip and revelation – and this challenge accompanies its psychology like a constant overtone. [...] In this respect, therefore, the further development of every relation is determined by the ratio of persevering and yielding energies which are contained in the relation. The former rest on the practical interest in secrecy and its formal attraction. The latter are based on the impossibility of bearing the tension entailed by keeping a secret any longer, and on a feeling of superiority. Although this superiority lies in a latent form, so to speak, in secrecy itself, for our feelings it is fully actualized only at the moment of revelation or often, also, in the lust of confession, which may contain this feeling of power in the negative and perverted form of self-humiliation and contrition.[24]

Feminist consciousness-raising groups are, at their core, secret societies that work in reverse. They form around a secret, but one that is not theirs; rather, it is the very secret on which the society around them is based – millennial patriarchal power that oppresses women, clear yet unconfessable, to which women themselves have adapted over the course of history.

The feminists' task is to reveal this secret – which, as women, they could also choose to keep, to derive some secondary benefit from it – and, through its confession, establish themselves as feminists. As such, their strength is derived from this very secret, by way of its confession. It is the superiority referred to by Simmel, which 'is fully actualized only at the moment of revelation', and that can, however, be accompanied by a 'feeling of power in the negative and perverted form of self-humiliation and contrition'. It is ultimately this very oscillation between power and impotence that is at the root of the emotive tone found in the testimonies of workplace alienation examined previously: the power of denunciation serves as a counterpoint to the sense of humiliation at a life of subordination – to master and male power.

The relationship between feminism and secrets, however, is more complicated still. The feminist movement did not limit itself to revealing another's secret – that of male power. If it had, it would not have moved beyond the politics of testimony examined earlier, that is, indignant denunciation of what was and must no longer be. Rather, the intellectual and political interests of feminism focused on the secret behind the secret revealed by the women's words, that is, the secrecy of the secret on which male power is founded. To put it in platonic terms, the women's movement did not focus on white things, but on the whiteness that makes them white.

On the one hand, this means tackling the sexist secret with a sort of feminist counter-secret that serves as the foundation for a society of free women. On the other, this counter-secret is, in fact, nothing more than the ever-elusive secret of the oppression suffered by women: that obscure backdrop against which human history had so far played out. This, in turn, gives the feminist movement its separate identity – making it publicly recognizable – but, as a secret, albeit one that is inverted in relation to male society, it will also produce oppositions that mark feminism internally. To paraphrase Simmel, we might say that 'the secret puts a barrier between women', a barrier caused by the different meanings that the women attribute to that secret. Finally, given the link between secret and confession, feminist groups found themselves engaged in attempting to claim the secret of the secret for themselves. A much more onerous task than simply confessing to *a secret*, as scary and horrible as it may be, because it involves enunciating *the secrecy of the secret*: the slippery surface of the latter, which enables it to operate as an oppressive social order that does not reveal its oppression.

This desire – to tell not the secret, but the secrecy of the secret – translated into a paradoxical injunction that allowed neo-feminists to talk about themselves, which might be expressed as the imperative to 'speak the unspeakable (about yourself and about yourself and the world)!' Once again we are faced with a command that is impossible to abide by, because it can only be complied with by breaching it. If, indeed, one speaks the unspeakable – which is not simply the unspoken, but specifically that which cannot be spoken – then one is not speaking the unspeakable, because once the unspeakable is spoken, it ceases to be such. The only solution that remains, then, is to not speak the unspeakable, in order to preserve its defining quality, that is, its unspeakability. In this way, the unspeakability of the unspeakable is expressed, but at the cost of saying nothing. In the first case, then, the subject abides by the form of the command – in that she complies with the order to speak the unspeakable – but fails to achieve its material objective – whatever she says, she is certainly not speaking the unspeakable. In the second example, the situation is reversed. The subject is entirely oriented towards the substance of the injunction – unspeakability as a condition of silence of the dominant language – but infringes the form of the command. The subject is placed in an aphasic state as regards speaking the unspeakable: she does not speak, although she has been ordered to speak.[25]

Feminist self-enunciation is, therefore, set in motion by way of a paradoxical injunction that is isomorphic to its communist counterpart. The fact the command does not originate within an easily identifiable organizational structure, as in the case of the PCI, is immaterial. First, the small consciousness-raising feminist groups took on the task of enforcing the injunction just as the communist bureaucratic structures had administered it in relation to the cadres. Second, the idea that the communist injunction is heteronomous – that is, that the party, from its dominant position, forces its militants to be 'active' – whereas its feminist equivalent is autonomous – that is, the feminists freely chose to speak the unspeakable – is incorrect. As noted previously, paradoxical injunctions arise and operate only in double-bind situations, in which subjects are linked to one another by way of 'an intense relationship'.[26] In this context, distinguishing between an injunction imposed heteronomously and one assumed autonomously is simply impossible. The only real distinction between the contexts of communist and feminist autobiographical enunciation is the different degrees of formalization – the party, in one case, and the women's movement with its groups, in the other – but this difference is quantitative, rather than qualitative.

If the communist paradoxical injunction made it possible to control the cadres, what effects did the neo-feminist paradoxical prescription have on the activists within the women's movement? Or rather, what does enunciating oneself mean in the context of the impossible obligation to speak the unspeakable? First, it is important to note that the task of expressing the unexpressable did not have a paralysing effect on feminist women's desire to speak about themselves. Rather, it gave rise to certain strategies of self-enunciation that sought to address that paradox, in an attempt to overcome the challenge of unspeakability in an innovative way. The best starting point for describing the direction taken by feminist autobiographies, in my view, is a brief essay by Tzvetan Todorov – *Le discours psychotique*.[27] Todorov defines psychotic discourse as follows:

> If psychosis is a disturbance of the relationship between the 'I' and external reality, then it follows that psychotic discourse is discourse that fails in the act of evoking this reality, and so in its task of referring.[28]

This definition helps to clarify that feminist self-enunciation works only on condition that psychosis is not interpreted in pathological terms. Indeed, the feminist account avails of a discursive strategy similar to that of a psychotic nature, characterized by a break with reality. Unlike the psychosis referred to by Todorov, however, this break is not the product of a 'failure'; rather, it is consciously sought out. The 'disturbance of the relationship between "I" and external reality' is not experienced as an illness; instead, it is an effect of the political rejection of that reality, defined by a condition of female submission to men. Ultimately, the very idea that to enunciate oneself one has to speak the unspeakable – about reality – is based on the conviction that referring to everyday reality is simply useless. At most, it may be discussed in negative terms, as in the feminist testimonies to workplace alienation cited above.

Psychotic discourse takes three distinct routes: paranoid, schizophrenic and catatonic. *Paranoid discourse* is characterized by the fact that 'the referents evoked do not have a real existence as far as we are concerned'; the 'we', here, refers collectively to non-paranoid subjects. This distinctive trait is, in fact, of less interest to me and, in a certain sense, Todorov himself gradually fades it out over the course of his description, stating that paranoid discourse 'is quite similar, as discourse, to normal discourse'. The problem lies in the fact that the paranoid speaker, unlike the subject to whom he is speaking, does not realize that what he is speaking about is not real. From this perspective, then, the paranoia of discourse is not a feature of the discourse itself, but is instead the result of a disconnect between the persons producing and receiving it. Basically, the psychotic element arises from a power relationship that dictates what is real and what is not.

The second feature of paranoid discourse referred to by Todorov is much more interesting: it dictates that 'nothing happens without reason and nothing is devoid of meaning'. To consider this slightly differently, we might say that all elements within it are subject to a process of over-interpretation and, consequently, they become bearers of additional significance that must be carefully deciphered. In that sense, a person affected by interpretative paranoia is no different to the 'philosopher', the 'scientist' and the 'critic': 'The latter figures, like the paranoid subject, perceive everything that regular individuals perceive, as well as many things that the latter do not even suspect.'

Schizophrenic discourse also eliminates reference to the real world, but in a completely different way to its paranoid counterpart. Whereas the latter, as we have seen, appears as 'normal' discourse – with the elements fused together, for want of a better word, in a single block of meaning – the former, on the contrary, is disengaged from reality by way of a process of internal flaking. What the subject enunciates is devoid of coherence, and the meaning of the discourse becomes obscure and difficult to understand. Reference to reality is, therefore, no longer possible because, in order to refer to something, discourse must first have meaning, and to having meaning, it must be at least minimally coherent.

The hierarchical structure of discourse is, therefore, lacking: what comes after does not depend on what came before, clauses are often incomplete, transitivity disappears – in the sense that transitive verbs are used in an absolute sense, without being followed by an object complement. Overall, schizophrenic discourse appears as a mass of 'clauses juxtaposed one on top of another, without any relationship in terms of content, nor conjunctions that indicate their hierarchy'. The conclusion that Todorov draws from this description is rather significant as regards my interpretation of the feminist self-narrative. Schizophrenic enunciation is 'discourse that does not derive justification from outside itself, discourse that is simply discourse'. In this sense, it is very similar to literary writing that 'wants representation [of the world] to make way for non-representation'.[29]

Catatonic discourse, finally, radicalizes the aggression of language towards reality that characterizes paranoia and schizophrenia. It does so, however, in a paradoxical way: not by abolishing discourse's reference to reality but, more directly, by silencing discourse that refers to the world. The term 'catatonic discourse' is in fact a misnomer: catatonic discourse is non-discourse; it is, essentially, a 'rejection of language'. These psychotic enunciation tendencies correspond, I believe, to the three strategies of enunciation employed by Italian neo-feminists in their attempt to resolve the unspeakability paradox at the heart of their self-narratives. If speaking the unspeakable is simply a means of actively rejecting reality – understood, in this case, as the surrounding social world – and producing innovative discourse that is not limited to simple passive mimesis of what it is, this break may be achieved by way of rather different general strategies.

The *paranoid strategy* of self-narration is characterized by the narrator's assertiveness with regard to the character. The narrator is the function that imposes direction and, therefore, meaning on the self-narrative, and it is the issue of meaning and the spasmodic pursuit of it that characterizes paranoid discourse. The primacy of the narrator in feminist self-narratives in no way resembles the sovereignty exercised by this figure in communist autobiographies. As previously noted, the feminist narrator responds to the imperative to speak the unspeakable or, rather, unspeakable meaning; it is not being called upon to reveal its 'active' nature, as was the case for the party militant. In other words, though it directs the narrative, the feminist narrator does not impose order in the same way as its communist counterpart, or serve as a pole of attraction on which the character and its action ultimately converge. In this way, the paranoid self-narrative gives rise to a specific autobiographical form that I would call *infinite discourse*. The latter expands itself indefinitely in the pursuit of a meaning that constantly flits along the surface of the language without being possible to grasp it.

The *schizophrenic strategy* moves in the opposite direction. The pursuit of the unspeakable is not entrusted, in this case, to the narrator and their attempts to find meaning in what is being recounted. Rather, the power of that which cannot be spoken emerges through a series of fractures in the text, which diminish the figure of the narrator almost to the point of making it disappear. All of this only partially translates into emancipation of the character from the guardianship of the narrator. What occurs, instead, is a profound remodelling of the autobiographical text that ultimately diverges in a series of directions: the simple account of day-to-day life, the dream-like report and, finally, lyrical illumination.

As regards the *catatonic strategy*, there is not very much to be said in a strict sense. The rejection of everything that is ordinarily speakable, in pursuit of the unspeakable, translates into silence, that is, an absence of self-narrative. To pursue this route would, therefore, lead into impossible territory involving autobiographical texts that were never written. The paradox of feminist self-enunciation would, therefore, necessarily be accompanied by a Borges-style paradoxical textual investigation. While it may not be possible to trace the *catatonia of discourse* – because this equates to an absence of discourse – we can, however, highlight a specific form of *discourse of catatonia*. This manifests as a sort of hesitation to recount, common across the board of feminist self-enunciation, which reflects profound doubts regarding the actual ability of the discourse to speak what should be spoken.

There remains one last point to be made. These three narrative strategies do not necessarily correspond to three different types of texts. Rather, such strategies often co-exist within a text, like field lines that deform the space in an irregular way, depending on which of them prevails in any given moment. This is particularly the case in Carla Lonzi's *Taci, anzi parla*, which offers examples of all of the enunciation strategies I have discussed here, though the paranoid strategy prevails. It is for this reason – rather than on any theoretical grounds relating to her philosophy of feminism[30] – that I have chosen her work as my preferred gateway to the world of feminist self-enunciation. The next section will look at paranoid self-discourse, while the third one will consider both schizophrenic and catatonic discourse. The latter, emerging as it does at the margins of the text, is the strategy to which I dedicate the briefest, and inevitably least satisfying, textual analysis.

Paranoia: The infinite discourse

Taci, anzi parla was published in Italy in 1978, in the twilight of the season of protest that began in 1968. The movement of 1977, the heir of a decade of struggles, celebrated its end with a convention held in Bologna in September of that same year, which closed with a demonstration that was relatively well attended but lacked in any actual political following. In March 1978, Aldo Moro, the leader of the Christian Democrats – that remained Italy's leading political party despite the excellent results achieved by the PCI in the elections of 1975 – was kidnapped and killed by the Brigate Rosse. Two years later, in September 1980, workers at the Fiat Mirafiori plant in Turin began a long strike against the wave of dismissals by company management, which ended in clamorous failure. This culminated in the so-called 'march of the 40,000', on 14 October 1980, when employees and management took to the streets in protest against the strikers and in support of resuming work at Turin's car manufacturing plants.[31] In some ways, *Taci, anzi parla* marks the end of a decade of feminist political effort. Likewise, her establishment of the Rivolta Femminile group – which published its *Manifesto di Rivolta Femminile* (*Manifesto of Women's Revolt*) and *Sputiamo su Hegel* (*Let's Spit on Hegel*) in 1970, followed by *La donna vaginale e la donna clitoridea* (*The Clitoridian Woman and the Vaginal Woman*) the following year – marked the beginning of the season of feminist theoretical awareness.[32]

As clearly evinced by its subtitle, *Diario di una femminista* (*Diary of a Feminist*), *Taci, anzi parla* is not structured as a memoir, as was the case with the communist militants' autobiographies. As such, the account is not provided from the vantage of an end point, with the narrator describing the events of his or her life as the character. Rather, it takes the form of a casual collection of notes and impressions, accumulating day by day. The temporal arc of the work spans the period from August 1972 to January 1977. In geographical terms, the diary opens in Macari, between Trapani and San Vito Lo Capo, in Sicily, but it is difficult to pinpoint exactly where it ends: the last reference to a place puts the author on a train moving towards Montevarchi, in the province of Arezzo (Tuscany), on 20 December 1976 – one month before the diary concludes.

Providing an analytical summary of what happens in the four and a half years of the diary would be practically impossible, given its – at least apparently – episodic nature. In general terms, the account begins with the protagonist's separation from her husband Raffaele, and deals with the series of meetings and relationships that tie her to her friends and fellow members of the Rivolta Femminile group – Piera,

Monica, Gemma, Isa, Anita, Felicita, Agata etc.[33] This tangled web is held together, and narratively driven, by Lonzi's series of failed relationships: her broken friendship with Ester (a pseudonym for artist Carla Accardi), the end of her relationship with Sara (actually Tuuli Tarina, the Finnish member of Rivolta Femminile)[34] and the gradual unravelling of her relationship with Simone, representing none other than sculptor Pietro Consagra. To summarize the narrative progression of *Diario di una femminista* in its broadest terms, then, we could say that it is an itinerary of constantly renewed disappointments. All contained in a 1,300-page pocket book.

The volume of the text, its tightly typeset pages and the diary form are reminiscent, in a certain sense, of the brief autobiography by Giovanna C. examined in the previous chapter. In the case of the young communist typist, her obsession with accuracy in detailing the schools she had attended, houses she had seen and places she had worked culminated in an informal text, incapable of closing in on itself from a narrative perspective. Carla Lonzi achieves a very similar effect using the diary form. Dates follow each other in quick succession right up to the very last one presented in the book – 29 January 1977 – but there is no specific narrative reason behind the timing of the conclusion. The diary could just as easily have finished on 28 or 30 January, or any other date, without changing the meaning of the narrative itself. Basically, the story recounted in the diary is interrupted at a certain point, but this conclusion has no bearing on the plot. This is also true of the starting point of the diary. It could have opened at any other moment than 1 August 1972 without in any way disturbing the narrative: in fact, the indifference to plot in the story does not so much mean that the story is devoid of an ending, but rather that it lacks a purpose.

It is not, therefore, possible to identify a narrative teleology that, by way of the plot structure, holds the various elements of the account together – or at least it seems that way, as we will see at the end of this chapter. In Giovanna C.'s case, this feature is a flaw of the autobiographical text, preventing it from assuming the form of a first-person *Bildungsroman* in which the character chases the narrator for the duration of the story, before finally merging with the latter at the end. For Carla Lonzi, however, the disarticulation between *fabula* and plot is a strength of her autobiographical strategy.

The Florentine feminist is tasked with resolving the issue of speaking the unspeakable, and the mechanism used to cut the Gordian knot of this paradoxical injunction is ingenious. She resolves the problem via a sort of frontal assault: by deciding to say everything. Indeed, if everything is said, there is nothing left to say. In a certain sense, the narrative strategy adopted in *Taci, anzi parla* consists of draining the great ocean of words spoken by men and women. Saying everything leaves no space for the unsaid: the power of feminist self-enunciation breathes words into spaces that have been obstinately silenced by male power. The significance of this operation can also be formulated in a different, more specific way: if I say everything, there will be no space left for others' words, because I have appropriated everything that can be said – there is no unspeakable left – and in doing so I can be certain that I have discursively re-appropriated myself, and can assert that 'I am myself'.[35] It is this decision that dictates the size of

Lonzi's diary, its informal nature and the lack of ending to its story. If, indeed, the Florentine feminist has performed the inaugural act of enunciating everything, the historical work of saying everything must be performed by women as a discursive community engaged in this mission of total expression. And, indeed, the female characters in Carla Lonzi's diary are engaged in a continuous process of writing about themselves and exchanging autobiographical documents – but we will return to this point further on in the analysis.

It is worth noting that while the strategy of self-enunciation set in motion by *Taci, anzi parla* may validly be described as *infinite discourse*, it would nevertheless be entirely inappropriate to speak of paranoia here. Saying everything does not, however, simply mean speaking all possible statements. This is already a rather complicated task given, at least in theory, that it not only involves speaking all statements relating to the past without omitting any,[36] but also includes future statements that have not yet been spoken. The lack of closure in terms of story in *Diario di una femminista* alludes precisely to this future that is yet to be enunciated but that, in principle, is perfectly enunciable by way of the feminist self-narrative.

This first problem, of a quantitative nature, so to speak, is accompanied by a second, that I would define as qualitative. To say it all does not, in fact, simply mean exhausting all statements that language makes available to the enunciator. Indeed, many linguistic combinations, though formally possible, are entirely devoid of meaning and, therefore, there is no point in wasting energy enunciating them. From this perspective, then, it is not so much a case of enunciating all possible statements, but rather of enunciating all statements that have meaning – from a feminist perspective, naturally. And so the objective is not to pronounce and write all possible statements but rather, on a deeper level, to exhaust all possible meaning through self-enunciation.

In this way, the primacy of the narrator is once again established, albeit in a paranoid form. Or, to reframe it, while the narrator is no longer capable of guiding the story – which has neither a beginning nor an end – or of giving it direction, it is, nevertheless, responsible for finding meaning within it. As such, the narrator finds himself or herself constantly engaged, throughout the account, in deciphering narrative material, the meaning of which is problematic. It must, therefore, contend with a set of signs without well-defined meanings, which condemn it to the gruelling task of over-interpretation.

> **13 April [1974].** Is it right to assert that women have never expressed an experience of liberation as has happened, instead, in the male world? Is this not perhaps an ideological assertion? A corollary of my previous feminist mindset? Teresa d'Avila, Teresa Martin what did they express? A religious, mystical experience. And therefore liberating. Or not? And female writers? But then, do I intend to suggest that it is me who expresses and will express an experience of liberation? From a certain perspective it seems so yes, me, Sara, and some friends from Rivolta.[37]

The narrator opens the entry dated 13 April with a question presenting a sort of hyperbolic doubt: is it true that 'women have never expressed an experience of liberation'? This first reflection is followed by six others, which culminate in a response that, though hyperbolic, like the initial question, nevertheless reveals a certain uncertainty: yes, Carla Lonzi courageously asserts, women have never liberated themselves but, 'from a certain perspective' me, Sara 'and some friends from Rivolta' are achieving that emancipation, long sought after by women. She is, therefore, only capable of defining the significance of the Rivolta Femminile experience with interpretative effort, by placing her feminist group in the context of centuries of history.

The exercise of hyperbolic doubt, which translates into a textual accumulation of questions, not only concerns such broad issues as female emancipation – addressed by way of enormous uncertainty and an equally grandiose response – but also extends to private aspects of her life.

> Why do I promise, promise, promise? These highs and lows are scary, but it is what I am. I am different people, opposing people, this is why I am more complex than others, but less stable, and I end up not being able to expand upon the contradictory complexity. I have a real, cursed crisis. Now I am more aggressive and Simone likewise. When I feel desperate he is always and only ever protective, kind. Do I hurt him? Limit him? [...] Is there no other way to be oneself other than doing like Mansfield? Relationships lead to compromise: is freedom solitude?³⁸

At the centre of the entry dated 27 October 1975 is a question, the dramatic nature of which is heightened through the triple repetition of the verbal form 'I promise', which loads it with meaning.³⁹ The text then proceeds with the same degree of emotional intensity – 'I have a real, cursed crisis' – and finally, as in the previous case, dilates to encompass a horizon that extends beyond that of the mere couple relationship, through reference, presumably, to Katherine Mansfield and her many pseudonyms – corresponding to the 'different people' that make up Carla Lonzi – and, finally, through a universal question on freedom: 'is freedom solitude?'

The erratic process of self-interrogation does not cease that day and, a few lines later, moves in the direction of other enigmatic territories.

> Why does Gemma not speak more loudly and, when she recounts something, why does she not take the time to clearly state what it's about? Why does Nicola not ask if she doesn't understand? Why do they leave it up to me to intervene? Why can I not help but intervene?⁴⁰

The constant and anxious questioning is not merely reserved, then, for the great questions of history, and the smaller, but no less important issues pertaining to a sentimental relationship; it also extends to everyday matters associated with the women's meetings.

Naturally, other feminist texts also present a similar flurry of questions, but with completely different meanings.

> But is all this truly of benefit to women? Personal success? A source of pride, glory? We have many doubts in this regard. [...] But then, if the protagonists of the human reproduction process are no longer men or women, who is left? What is left, unfortunately, is science, which has become women's real partner in this anomalous relationship, aimed more at producing abortions that children. [...] The objective? The glory of science, affirmation of (male) human intellect, the myth of man as demiurge and creator.[41]

This quote is not from an autobiographical text, but rather from an article, published in an Italian feminist magazine discussing two births made possible by scientific advances. In this case, the persistent repetition of questions is of purely rhetorical value – albeit critical rhetoric. To some extent, the reader already knows the answers that will be provided by the author of the article, as it appears in a feminist periodical, which is expected to criticize the status quo.

Carla Lonzi's questions do not serve as rhetorical amplification of a critical thesis. Instead, their dispersal throughout the text is an expression of the disarticulation between story and plot to which I referred earlier. In a certain sense, the presence of the narrator within the narrative fabric becomes purely negative. No longer able to direct the story, it manifests as a constant disturbance: faced with the impossibility of determining the meaning of events, it resorts to repeating questions without answers,[42] slowing down the narrative, almost to the point of immobilizing it, and consuming it in its incessant interrogation.[43]

If, however, as Todorov claims, paranoid discourse is characterized by the fact that 'nothing is devoid of meaning', in *Taci, anzi parla* it would seem, on the contrary, that 'nothing has meaning'. The narrator's inability to give the story any significance is, in fact, at the heart of the anguished questions that it poses to the world and to itself. In reality, the inquisitive attitude underpinning Carla Lonzi's diary is perfectly compatible with Todorov's definition. The impossibility for the narrator figure to direct the story is, in fact, not merely a manifestation of impotence, but also an opportunity for emancipation from the story and its demands. In other words, the inability to guide the account in teleological terms translates into freedom from the obligation to establish an internal hierarchical structure and assign different weight to characters and events. It also offers the opportunity to seek the meaning of the narrative material in all of its nooks and crannies, without limitations imposed by a significance threshold. The narrator searches for the significance of any given event because meaning has a vertical, rather than horizontal relationship with the story. It is not produced by way of the linear progression of the story itself, but is instead vertically imposed on each event that is recounted. As such, the persistent repetition of a question by the narrator does not indicate a lack of meaning. On the contrary, it alludes to an excess thereof,[44] precisely as described by Todorov in relation to paranoid discourse. The issue of paranoia also emerges directly – albeit marginally – in the pages of the diary.

This morning again Simone alluded to my paranoia in social interactions. But what does that mean? Is it possible that it's a stupid complex, a stupid oversight and that a situation that makes me so uncomfortable that I lose a sense of myself is in fact acceptable? Because that's the problem: I don't accept it, as in I don't accept myself in those circumstances, I start with the assumption that 'going there' is wrong. In fact if it were up to me I certainly wouldn't go, and nor would I be invited. And so I go for reasons of social propriety, to please Simone. I surrender the initiative of my preferences and immediately forfeit my eyes, I lose self-respect and, with that, everything. […] My shame would be greater if, from this state of disorientation, I was able to simulate and reconstruct my normal sense of confidence. And so I project the contempt I would feel for myself onto other women, because I see them engaged in some sort of performance when I know that, like me, they are there as courtesans and they don't notice, it doesn't unsettle them.[45]

This text perfectly demonstrates the operation of paranoid discourse. Addressing the protagonist of the diary, Simone raises the issue of paranoia – albeit in relation to the specific context of social interactions. Carla's response is negative, but is expressed in the form of a question that distils the essence of paranoid discourse: 'but what does that mean?' This first question is followed by a second that, this time, is mainly rhetorical: 'is it possible that it's a stupid complex?' The response once again is negative. Carla does not love social engagements and only attends 'to please Simone'. This makes her lose confidence in herself and feel contempt for those women who, like her, are there as mere courtesans, engaged 'in some sort of performance' of themselves, without even noticing what is actually going on.

The paranoid interpretation process, therefore, moves from a specific situation – in our case, just prior to the quoted passage we are told that it is a 'mundane evening' – towards universal meaning that is articulated according to opposing poles. Women are courtesans due to the presence of the men, and it is for this reason that they deserve contempt. Elements that do not corroborate such an interpretation are omitted. Indeed, there is no reason for us not to believe the narrator when she says that the women in attendance that evening were servile and deferential. But the men? Bizarrely, in a world where everything is appearance that must be deciphered, men are the only elements that manifest as they are, specifically as beings that exist solely to be adulated by women.

The possibility that the dinner or vernissage – the text does not specify – is a performance from start to finish and that the milieu – consisting of individuals regarded socially as artists and intellectuals, the constant backdrop for *Taci, anzi parla* – is founded on adulation and lies, distributed unevenly between men and women as dominators and dominated, is not even considered. Each interpretative act is, of course, unilateral, and is interesting precisely because of this. We must, however, seek to understand the effects of the interpretative operations proposed by Carla Lonzi on the autobiographical universe that she builds.

To consider this issue, let us briefly set aside our examination of *Taci, anzi parla* and turn to the transcript of a feminist debate held in Milan on the 1st and 2nd of February 1975, included in the third edition of the feminist journal

Sottosopra. This edition is dedicated to the issue of abortion, which was gaining increasing ground as a key topic in Italian feminist debate.[46] The transcription of the discussion in question – *Il corpo politico* (*The Political Body*) – takes up just over half of the publication. The remainder consists of heteroclitic material – letters, posters, reviews, a poem, further transcripts of women's meetings.

The text merely specifies the time that the debate began – 'Saturday 1 February 1975, 3pm, all together' – and then presents the participants' contributions, one after another. In a certain sense, this represents a sort of degree zero of narration: the narrative figure does not recount an event, but rather simply reports it in chronologically linear terms, delineated by the succession of speeches by the various contributors to the debate. Naturally, this is a pretence, given that transcription always constitutes rewriting,[47] that is, putting the contents of a story, however incidental they may be, into narrative form – in our case, the story of a feminist meeting that took place over two days in Milan in 1975.

This situation in which the narrator is present, but silent, serves as a counterpoint to the content of the text itself. Here, the meeting's participants present one after another, reciprocally defining themselves by an action that connects them all, that is, the narration of the self, focusing on the experience of female sexuality and abortion. And so the silence of the first-level narrator corresponds to the extraordinary loquaciousness of the second-level narrators, so that – to use categories introduced by Genette[48] – the diegesis is transformed into a series of metadiegetic acts. What characterizes the acts of self-expression engaged in by the meeting's participants?

> [**Si.**] I was interested in a discussion on sexuality for a personal reason. [...] The reasons are also worth investigating ... I said it the other evening, too, and I can't express myself in any other way, and I'd also like to discuss it with other women, this feeling of having been blocked before, in terms of sexuality. *I always experienced sexuality as something that brought me into direct interaction with the man, this inevitably brought with it the image of procreation and not just this, because there's a less-defined thought, closer to violence, I'd like to express it with an example* [italics my own]. When I was ten or twelve years old and I'd see a couple, and they'd say: they got married, I'd think 'Oh God, she survived! So it is possible'. In my imagination marriage was obviously the sexual relationship, and this was linked with something so violent that it seemed strange that a woman could survive it. This perception of the extreme violence of sexuality, I think that it's what makes me keep my distance somewhat from such matters, but not actually in reality, because at a certain point I did have sexual relations [...]. But I'd have liked to investigate this link that perhaps not all women make, but surely many do, between sexuality and violence.[49]

Si. refers to a previous meeting at which she would have liked to speak about what she is discussing now, and her childhood experiences. When faced with married couples at twelve years of age, she was startled to consider that a woman was capable of surviving the sex act with a man. Subsequently, Si. actually had sexual relations with a man and, in fact, she did not die.

The action contained in this narrative is barely perceptible. The centre of the text is, instead, occupied by the narrator herself decoding the meaning of the story. Her primacy emerges very clearly from the wording of the section in italics. The narrator feels that there has 'always' been a relationship between sex, man and violence. It is a feeling – which is like confused knowledge – defined by its atemporal nature: indeed, the 'always' to which she refers means 'from the beginning', but this beginning does not coincide with the birth of the character. Rather, it refers to the absolute intensity of the feeling – and knowledge – in question. Taking this timeless state as a starting point, the childhood startlement at the married couple becomes a mere 'example'. It is transformed into the illustration of a sense that goes beyond the story, possessed by a figure – the narrator – that, while close to the character, is external and cognitively superior to the latter; indeed, the narrator has always known that of which the child character is unaware.

Once the hierarchy among the character, her story and the narrator has been established, the account becomes an account of the difficulties faced by that narrator in correctly expressing her narrative – because it involves a 'feeling' that requires clarification. In that regard, it is worth noting the various hesitations expressed in the transcription: Si. would like to investigate why 'for a personal reason' she is interested in discussing sexuality, she would like to express herself, but she feels she was 'blocked before, in terms of sexuality'. And, in any case, she always kept her 'distance somewhat in such matters', but not 'actually'. The text doubles back on itself, it is no longer the narrative of a story but instead the story of a narrative and its obstacles. Or, to put it differently, the narrator becomes the character in the story, and the only action she performs, with great effort, is the narrative itself.

A similar situation is also found in *Taci, anzi parla*. In this case, it certainly cannot be said that the narrator is silent and gives over space to the characters. However, just as the characters that appear one after another in *Il corpo politico* are engaged in a series of meta-diegetic acts – the activity they perform in recounting is to recount themselves – likewise, the characters in Carla Lonzi's diary are distinguished by their 'meta-diaristic' activities, that is, by being constantly engaged in writing or reading diaries.[50]

> Isa gave me her diary to read casually, hiding a touch of nervousness. [...] I immediately understood why I became so close to Sara so quickly. The knowledge that a diary creates a link that cannot be dissolved: compared to this, other relationships are almost like those between strangers.[51]

The feminist social world that Carla Lonzi depicts is, therefore, held together by the circulation of diaries, that is, the exchange of autobiographical products. In other words, the idea that there exists – initially – a social feminist bond that is – then – presented in a diary and reflected in the pages of *Taci, anzi parla*, is but a referential illusion. On the contrary, it is the diary that creates the world, exhausting every possibility of a social bond. And so all that Carla Lonzi recounts is the account of her serving as her own narrator by way of her diary.

The characters that surround her are, in turn, essentially consumed by the process of becoming their own narrators. And so, what we are presented with is not a diary, but a meta-diary. Within it, the negative presence of the story's narrator – represented by the questions – can only superficially be regarded as a form of weakening of the narrator figure. The indifference as regards the story, the refusal to give it form by choosing to write a diary rather than memoirs, alludes to the absolute primacy of the narrative act over its contents. The former, in a certain sense, distorts the latter, folding the contents in on themselves, with the result that the narrative act can only recount itself and its performance, referring to itself – the narrator writing the diary – or a series of characters whose only actions involve narrating themselves – by way of writing and reading their diaries, letters and poems. In this way, the second condition for paranoid discourse referred to by Todorov is met, that is, elimination of the referent. In our case this translates into the loss of a story that, indeed, I was able to summarize in a few short sentences.

Is this an excessive interpretation that is, in turn, paranoid? To answer this question, it is sufficient to check whether or not the aforementioned elimination of reality occurs in the text – with the caveat that, obviously, such elimination cannot be total because there is no transcendental narrative act, that is, a pure narrator who is fully free from narrative materials.

> [17 October 1973] Simone tells me I seem melancholy, as though I no longer intend to deal with the very stress of life; that he believes in distraction, it's good to distract oneself with art, he does not place any hope in human interactions as a sort of solution, he wants to have an intense relationship with me, otherwise 'grazing' is enough for him. He says of himself 'I am an easily contented little soul'. Initially, I feel convinced and restored by his sense of reality, of magnitude, of fantasy. Initially, he is more at ease in his existence than me, and therefore has a greater right to it than me. Today however he was stressed 'You are more stressed than me now'. Because I am a balloon that crushes everything and makes everything fly. What I can't do is comport myself with à plomb, like a rock. [...] Are we moving apart while seeking each other? I note how we become reactionary. Through pessimism, which may even be justified, like Malraux, for example, who went from being a revolutionary to rekindling all of the bourgeoisie myths. [...] As a girl I was nihilistic, and I still am. I don't fall for progressive traps.[52]

I have already spoken of the dilation of meaning of minutiae and day-to-day situations, so that they take on universal value, and I have nothing further to add in this regard. Rather, I wonder where Simone and Carla were when they had the conversation reported in the diary. From the entries that precede and follow that dated 17 October, it seems probable that they are together in the house in Rome. Beyond this, it is not possible to say much more. There is no clue as to whether this exchange of opinions occurred in the living room, kitchen, bedroom or another part of the house, or in a public place. Likewise, it is impossible to identify the time of day that their conversation took place. Finally, if we had to answer the question 'what did Carla and Simone do on 17 October 1973?', all we could say is 'they talked'. The activities of that day are, in fact, reduced to a conversation in an unknown space at an unknown time. The chronotope of the account has literally evaporated, leaving behind just the two characters and their words. The tone of their dialogue, which almost mechanically reflects the absence of time and space, is, therefore, not surprising. Indeed, Simone is no longer a body, but an 'easily contented little soul'. And Carla's condition is equally evanescent: she is simply 'a balloon that crushes everything and makes everything fly' and cannot behave 'like a rock'.

To better understand this process of metaphysical erosion and the direction it takes, I will use the writings of Raymond Carver as a contrast agent. First, I will present the description of a dinner found in *Cathedral*, a collection of short stories, involving Jack, the protagonist and first-person narrator, his partner Fran, his colleague Bud and his wife Olla. This is followed by the description of a Roman dinner as narrated by Carla Lonzi.

> Bud passed me the platter of ham and helped himself to some mashed potatoes. We got down to them. We didn't say much except now and then Bud or I would say, 'This is real good ham.' Or, 'this sweet corn is the best sweet corn I ever ate.' 'This bread is what's special,' Olla said. 'I'll have some more salad, please, Olla,' Fran said, softening up maybe a little. 'Have more of this,' Bud would say and he passed me the platter of ham, or else the bowl of red gravy. From time to time, we heard the baby make its noise. Olla would turn her head to listen, then, satisfied it was just fussing, she would give her attention back to her food.[53]

> [**18 October 1973**] These Roman dinners are terrible, both in terms of how much one eats and for what they signify. Luckily, I went ten years without dealing with them. But this morning Simone was puzzled because of my bad mood, I can't deal with such grotesque situations. [...] Simone returned to the idea that I hate people. He's interested in everyone because he can get information from them. I understand that it's important to keep each other up to date on exhibitions, stories, movements, moods, prices, prestige ... Super-important. He declared 'I don't think I'll meet God.' Then he came close to me – I was still in bed – and began kissing me sweetly and we made love.[54]

While I have transcribed Carla Lonzi's diary entry almost in full, to complete Carver's account it should be noted that Jack and Fran also have sex after their dinner with Bud and Olla. In this case, however, the deed is introduced in a rather more prosaic way by Fran, who says to her partner 'Honey, fill me up with your seed!' – and, of course, the latter couple are members of the proletariat, rather than a sculptor and an art critic with feminist leanings. The works from which these passages are taken are relatively contemporary to each other – *Taci, anzi parla* is from 1978, while *Cathedral* is from 1983 – and, crucially, they have something in common: elimination of the referential horizon.[55]

The two texts differ radically, however, in how they achieve this erosion of reality. Carver pursues it by way of a faithful and detailed description that adheres fully to the situation that he is recounting. The events, presented in the terse language used to describe them, become entirely intransitive, as though frozen in the moment of their occurrence. What do the characters in *Feathers* do at dinner? They talk about the food and how good it is, as though nothing exists beyond that meal. What do Jack and Fran talk about before going to Bud and Olla's? Naturally about what they should bring Bud and Olla as a polite response to their invitation – wine or dessert. It is not difficult to imagine the four of them talking about smoking if they smoked, or discussing work if they were at work.

This gives the impression of a surreal reality unfolding before the eyes of the reader, where things – the people and events described by Carver – crumble under the weight of their banality, at once losing substance and reality and becoming devoid of all meaning. Indeed, the end of the story, which confirms its meaning, arrives without the slightest foreshadowing by any signs that the characters, or the reader, could have interpreted in advance. After that evening and the meeting with Olla's 'ugly baby' – and the peacock wandering around the couple's garden – Fran gets pregnant, gets fat and cuts her beautiful hair and the two have a son who, however, 'has a conniving streak in him'. A fatal evening, then? Maybe, but not even the narrator is truly convinced of this: 'The change came later – and when it came, it was like something that happened to other people.' In a certain sense, the realistic representation of the characters' lives, pursued through the description of their dreary day-to-day existence, is missing because centre stage is occupied by the nonsensical randomness of events. These accumulate without forming a coherent whole, the meaning of which might be identified by the narrator.

This could not be further from Carla Lonzi's account of a Roman dinner. Here, too, the referential horizon dissolves but, in this case, this results in the disappearance of the meal itself, in all its trivial materiality. What did Simone and Carla eat? How many people were invited and who were they? Where did the diners meet? What we do know is that they probably talked more about artists than art, about their respective statuses and the monetary value of what they do. Of the dinner itself, we only know that it was 'terrible'. Why? Both because of what was eaten and for what it signified. It seems fair to say that the significance of that social occasion literally devours its culinary substance. Instead of 'ham' and 'salad', we have Carla and Simone's reactions. The former tells us that she waited 'ten years' to attend such an event, while the latter observes that he didn't meet God among his fellow diners. And so, instead of a meal, we are presented with the two characters' interpretation of the meal.

Another case of a fatal dinner? It is hard to provide an unambiguous response. No, given that the sexual encounter that concludes the evening does not result in a birth, and that the two characters continue with their lives more or less as before. Yes, given that a dinner that one has waited more than a decade for is necessarily an event in which the stakes – in terms of significance – are very high. This might also explain the reference to God who, however, remains stubbornly *absconditus* on this occasion. Elimination of the referent, in this case, does not involve the transformation of reality in a mirror that reflects perfect images devoid of any substance, and, therefore, empty of any meaning that might make them three-dimensional. Rather, its erosion occurs by way of a sort of epistemic violence, which crushes things and people, overloading them with meaning until they become signs available to the subject that interprets them – our first-person narrator.[56]

> The universe must always show itself as inhabited by cosmic ethical forces ready to say their name and reveal their operation at the correct gesture or word. To figure such a world, rhetoric must maintain a state of exaltation, a state where hyperbole is a 'natural' form of expression because anything less would convey only the apparent (naturalistic, banal) drama, not the true (moral, cosmic) drama. [...] Such bombastic sublimity forcibly removes us – and no doubt is intended to remove us – from the plane of actuality, to place us in a more rarified atmosphere where each statement is a total and coherent gesture toward the representation of the cosmic moral drama.[57]

Carla Lonzi's autobiographical account is, finally, a melodrama of the self. Reality becomes mere appearance (though not in the style of Raymond Carver), or even disappears, to be replaced with a series of hyperbolic transfigurations: a dinner that one has waited ten years for, a missed encounter with God, a nihilistic childhood, the suspected presence of 'progressive traps', the figures of Katherine Mansfield and Teresa D'Avila.[58] Lonzi's paranoid self-enunciation strategy is, therefore, steeped in 'melodramatic imagination', described by Peter Brooks, much more profoundly than can be captured in a single quotation.[59] It shares its binary structure with the world of the melodrama, characterized by the opposition between evil and good, where the driving force behind the action is mainly represented by the malign principal, in this case, man, and more specifically Simone, the traitor in the situation, who breaches Carla's trust. The enclosed garden, meanwhile, is a 'space of innocence',[60] corresponding to Turicchi's country house and representing the literary backdrop for the sociological foundation of the small feminist groups, that is, the place where the Simmellian secret is guarded. Finally, we are also presented with what Peter Brooks calls 'the text of muteness'.[61]

> **[10 November 1972]** I almost burst out crying on the telephone to Germana, I was speaking through a wave of tears and the other. [...] I doubt myself, I doubt I understand, I doubt, I doubt, I doubt. I cry rivers, and what good it does me. [...] Ignazia cried lots on the telephone once. She cried pointlessly with me. I remember that I used to cry as a girl, I used to find myself writing in my diary in tears, like now. I'm going back to being a girl, if I can cry, my inner spring is plentiful, it has not dried up. I have to leave here. Other things will come out later. But now I must continue to cry, there I am truly me.[62]

Carla Lonzi is true to her word and cries a lot throughout the work, as do others, to tell the truth.[63] Why? Naturally, the tears are rooted in the complex relationship circumstances in which the protagonist finds herself. There is, however, a broader explanation for her recourse to tears, which is ingrained in the paranoid self-enunciation strategy. Faced with the profound nature of meaning and its omnipresence, words do not suffice. The series of questions running through the text, causing it to dilate and hindering its progression, does not simply indicate the constant pursuit of meaning; it also expresses the inability to adequately express such meaning. As mentioned previously, the narrator's endless interrogation of the events that she recounts remains, for the most part, unresolved. This makes it necessary to transcend verbal language and move towards elementary gesture, where words are reduced to silence and meaning flows directly from the body.

In a certain sense, we have reached the limits of the autobiographical strategy of speaking the unspeakable about oneself and the world. Overcoming the paradoxical injunction by choosing to say everything, however, raises an issue that, in turn, needs to be resolved: what if the unspeakable cannot be fully articulated in language? This problem is resolved precisely through tears, an act by way of which meaning that cannot be spoken or conveyed through language can, nevertheless, be expressed. The 'muteness' resorted to does not involve simply renouncing discourse, but rather increasing its modes of expression so that it also includes non-verbal dimensions.[64]

The final element that positions Carla Lonzi's self-narrative strategy within the context of melodrama, demonstrating the close connection between this and paranoid discourse, is the preoccupation with the issue of innocence.

> [**8 April 1975**] I had thought every possible bad thing about me and her: having navigated the sense of guilt and the mirage of her innocence, I had discovered her to be blind, unfair, selfish, hateful, absurd. I had accepted that she felt like my victim because I was hers too. [...] Then I cried bitterly, disconsolately, desperately at my illusion that I might have been an opportunity for her to free herself, an enlightening opportunity.[65]

To avoid repetition, I will not examine the hyperbolic language – which manifests here in excessive adjectivization, both in terms of quality and quantity – or the recourse to tears. Instead, I will focus on the issue of innocence that permeates the entire diary. Carla has been tricked by the 'mirage of her innocence' – she refers here to Sara, expressing her disillusionment with a rather significant relationship. It seems that this mirage might more correctly be considered blindness on Carla's part – 'my illusion' – than wilful deception by Sara. And, indeed, a few pages later, the narrator states that she had loved the Finnish girl 'with a sense of awe at her innocence'.[66]

Further proof that there was no malevolence on Sara's part, and that the relationship between the two women was characterized by reciprocal innocence, is alluded to directly by the manner in which their bond is described: Sara had the right to feel like Carla's victim because Carla was Sara's victim. This wording is rather curious, because generally, if someone is – or feels that they are – the victim of someone else, the latter is a persecutor and not a victim. In our case, however, this dualism is absent. Instead of victim and persecutor or two victims and two persecutors – in the case of a symmetrical relationship of aggression – we have just two victims. Why? Because though both Sara and Carla suffer, they both suffer unjustly; they are victims – and not persecutors – because they are completely innocent. Malice and cruelty – traits that tear down the innocent, turning them into faultless victims – are to be found elsewhere.

This leads us to the issue of the unspeakable faced by the narrator of *Taci, anzi parla*. The innocence referred to here is, in fact, much more than a moral or even legal condition. The innocence that Lonzi claims for herself is, on the one hand, a driving force that enables the plot of the diary to progress: something lost, that may yet be saved. On the other hand, it is essentially an epistemic condition: only an innocent person can say everything, understand everything and, therefore, know everything. And so, if for Carla Lonzi speaking the unspeakable means saying everything, both in the sense of saying as much as possible and of speaking all of the meaning that she herself is capable of grasping, this can only be achieved as innocent speech, that is, as discourse by an innocent person. An innocent person is one who can say everything, breaking the rules of ordinary enunciation, precisely because that person is in a state that simultaneously precedes and follows the corrupt, disfigured language spoken by men. Innocence is the condition that makes feminist discourse possible: it is the place from which it is possible to speak of oneself in a manner that transcends male discourse. Likewise, feminist discourse is the condition that makes innocence possible: the latter only exists at the end of the self-narrative, as a product of it.

This concludes my analysis of paranoid self-discourse. Obeying the paradoxical command to speak the unspeakable by deciding, like Carla Lonzi, to say everything is a brave decision; to some extent, nevertheless, its effects are as paradoxical as the injunction to which they respond. If speaking the unspeakable means speaking meaning that resists expression through ordinary discourse, the result is that which we have just examined. A voluble narrator, who is, however perennially insecure (and anyway, who can be truly certain that they are speaking the unspeakable?), a narrative paralysed by the pursuit of its meaning and, as a consequence, a main character with no narrative world in which to act. Its primary action consists of recounting itself to itself and to others, while the narration is reduced to the account of an account – or of many accounts, but the essential situation does not change. And while the character's world is progressively erased, crushed by the elusive presence of meaning that cannot be grasped, this anguish of loss is, to some extent, contained by way of the melodramatic structuring of that universe of mysterious signs and messages to be deciphered.

Is the paranoid self-narrative strategy, therefore, inherently destined to fail? I would suggest, instead, that it is not wholly satisfactory, which is one reason why the feminist self-narrative also pursued other routes.

Schizophrenia and catatonia: Poetry, dreams and discursive hesitations

Carla Lonzi's infinite discourse seeks to say everything in order to achieve the objective of being herself through self-narrative, thus obeying the paradoxical command to 'be yourself!' I speak of myself to be able to be myself. But, if to be myself I have to speak of myself, it is because in reality I am not truly myself, that is, I am something other than me. My task, therefore, is to overcome that otherness hiding within me and to do this I must say everything. From a discursive perspective, then, I must speak the unspeakable and tell the untellable. This titanic effort culminated in the paranoid monument that is *Taci, anzi parla,* and the primacy of its narrator to the detriment of its character. A superiority, as mentioned, that manifests in a very different way compared to the communist narrator. In fact, the account is not oriented towards the ultimate coincidence of the character's action with the narrator's wisdom. Instead, it involves the character and its action being crushed by the narrator and its need for meaning, giving rise to the anxious interrogation that permeates the entire book.

The pursuit of the unspeakable and rejection of the male discursive system can, however, take routes other than the frontal assault contained in *Taci, anzi parla*. One possible solution is offered by the schizophrenic strategy of self-enunciation. To describe its operation, let us briefly return to Todorov's observations on schizophrenic discourse. The most striking characteristic of the latter is its lack of coherence: it is at once incomplete, disjointed and contradictory. From a discursive perspective, then, schizophrenia presents as a jumble of linguistic materials that accumulate with no apparent order and that, as such, have no meaning and, therefore, no referents, because discourse must have meaning to be able to refer to something. It may be useful, at this point, to examine a schizophrenic account to gain a better understanding of its features.

> A donkey was carrying salt and he went through a river and he decided to go for a swim and his salt started dissolving off of him into the water and it did it left him hanging there so he crawled out on the other side and became a mastodon it gets unfrozen it's up in the Artic right now it's a block of ice and a block of ice gets planted in it's forced in a square right? Ever studied that sort of formation, block of ice in the ground? Well, it fights the perma frost it pushes it away and let things go up around it you can see they're like, they're almost like a pattern with a flower they start from the middle and it's like a submerged ice cube that got frozen into the soil afterwards.[67]

A schizophrenic subject was asked by researchers to recount the fable of *The Monkey and the Load of Salt*. The text above is the astonishing product of that request. Should the schizophrenic self-enunciation strategy engaged in by Italian neo-feminists produce a similar result?

I believe that the response to this is generally affirmative, although it is more difficult to reconstruct schizophrenic enunciation than paranoid self-discourse. There is no single key reference work like *Taci, anzi parla* for this strategy, and we must go beyond the bounds of the autobiographical account, at least in part, to define its main features. This is, however, no real surprise: if schizophrenic discourse is disorganized and incoherent, it can only be reconstructed by way of that disorganization and incoherence.

The starting point for describing this discursive object is alluded to in the previous paragraph and consists of a discussion among feminists, the transcription of which is contained in the third edition of *Sottosopra* in 1975. This is not an autobiographical text in the strict sense of the word; instead, it takes the form of documentation of a group experience, the value of which seems to lie in its ability to offer a faithful summary of what happened at the feminists' meeting. The narrative structure of such a text, however, also lends itself to immediately autobiographical use. And indeed, Carla Lonzi takes the literary form in question in that direction.

> C[arla]: But do you not believe that I achieve consciousness on all fronts? It's not as though consciousness becomes consciousness in one field and not in another. [...] P[ietro]. Of course. C. In all areas. Once you have it, it works like a ball, it's not a diaphragm that works here but not over there. P. We'll have to see whether the consciousness works to keep us together or to separate us. C. The consciousness works to maintain contact with another consciousness. P. There are also atavistic, general desires. For example, I have a desire to be with you [...] C. You want to be with me? P. Why? If I wanted to be with you it would be resolved, giving and having, giving and having, we settle it and don't speak of it again. But in fact there is another matter upstream. There's a fundamental basis, right? C. Yes. Sorry, does it not seem to you that if I am with you it's a sign that I want to be with you?[68]

To better understand this dialogue, we must first understand the nature of *Vai pure* (*Please, Go*) the text in which it is included. Carla Lonzi and Pietro Consagra – Simone from *Taci anzi parla* – met in Lonzi's house in Rome, between the end of April and the beginning of May 1980, and recorded their conversation for four days. At the end of this process, the former left the latter. Although the book does not take the traditional form of a self-narrative – structured as a diary or as memoirs – it can, undoubtedly, be considered a form of autobiographical report. In fact, it is doubly so, given that it is not only Carla Lonzi but also Pietro Consagra who reveals their life. Although we have moved away from *Taci, anzi parla* in terms of form, the substance of the autobiographical diary by the Florentine feminist is more or less the same.

The metaphysical erosion of reality is comparable, as is the reduction of the world to consciousness of the world. In fact, to be more specific, the intentional object of the consciousness is not even the world, but another consciousness: the consciousness to which Carla Lonzi refers is, in fact, consciousness of a consciousness. The idealistic reduction of the world is so strong that even Consagra's absurd objection contains a grain of truth. It is not just consciousness that exists, he says, but also 'atavistic, general desires' and, included among these unsubstantiated original desires, is the 'desire to be with you'. The statement is meaningless, but it should be regarded as a form of *captatio benevolentiae* addressed to the woman who is about to leave him. In any case, the end of the passage reiterates the idealistic tone of the conversation. The sculptor does not understand what is happening because he is not capable of seeing that things are signs of themselves. The fact that Carla is with Pietro means Carla wants to be with Pietro. In truth, the equivalence between the fact and the significance of the fact is not in any way guaranteed. As such, the response to the question, 'does it not seem to you that if I am with you it's a sign that I want to be with you?', is not at all contained in the question, unless we wish to reduce reality to a set of self-evident meanings.

Thus far, then, there is nothing new, either in relation to *Taci, anzi parla* or to the feminists discussing the issue of abortion in the transcript included in *Sottosopra*. As in the latter case, the characters seem to break free from the guardianship of the narrator – and its insistence on meaning – only because the narrator is in fact embodied by them. Of interest, instead, is the brief 'methodological' foreword in which Carla Lonzi introduces her conversation with Consagra.

> This dialogue has not been altered by the presence of a possible future reader because it was not recorded to be published, but proved to be worthy of publication. An act of intervention that breaks the code of silence pertaining to the relationship between two.[69]

It is difficult to agree with the book's author, both in light of a century of social research and, simply, for reasons of good sense. The presence of a recording device already renders the conversation between the two public, introducing a silent third party into what ought to have been a dialogue uniting the I with the you.[70] It does not matter, then, that the recording was not made with a view to publication. What is relevant is the mere potential for publication, which transforms the conversation into a fact – capable of being inspected even by someone not involved in it – and, therefore, destroys the orality of the dialogue, turning it into a written text.

This, in turn, produces a sort of 'Hawthorne effect', in the sense that the actors in the conversation inevitably end up seeking to participate as best they can in the experiment that they themselves have set in motion[71] – foreshadowing reality shows where couples break up and get back together on TV.[72] In this way, then, more so than an 'authentic' dialogue – to use Lonzi's own words – we are faced with what I would define as a monument to 'authentic' dialogue, which has little to do with the latter. On the other hand, the solemn register that characterizes the exchanges between Lonzi and Consagra tempers, in literary terms, the reality of the pain, hatred or delayed sweetness that generally accompanies the end of a relationship in real life.

Criticizing this premise for methodological reasons, however, fails to address the basic question that it raises. The importance lies in the intention underpinning such a statement, the paradoxical nature of which alludes to a different method of resolving the feminist paradox of speaking the unspeakable. The text, though not produced for publication, 'proved to be worthy of publication'. What exactly does this mean? In this case, it alludes to the pure event-based nature that defines *Vai pure*. It is as though Carla Lonzi is telling us that the work in question emerged from a situation of double contingency: the conversation between the two, by virtue of its unrepeatability, and the – unexpected – decision to transform it into a book. In a certain sense, the author is hinting at the existence of *another being outside the self-discourse* who silently conditions it, destabilizes its production and manifests as *another being within the self-discourse*, who cannot be controlled. In this case, that being imposes the publication of something that, perhaps, initially seemed unpublishable and manifests for a moment in the brief introduction to the book, conditioning its structure, at least in part, through the elimination of the voluble narrator present in *Taci, anzi parla*.

And so the transition from *Taci, anzi parla* to *Vai pure* involves moving from experimenting with the speakability of the unspeakable to assuming an awareness of the existence of unspeakability at the heart of the speakable. Naturally, this movement is partial and barely perceptible: beyond the introduction to the text, the discursive landscape is not actually that different to that found in *Diario di una femminista*. Basically, instead of the narrator's restless questions and infinite quest for meaning, we have two characters, placed within a narrative framework that is reduced to the bare essentials, engaged in doing what the first narrator had previously done alone. The initial promise, then, is not kept, but the work alludes to a discursive possibility that is fully availed of and consciously used in other Italian neo-feminist texts.

> Dostoevsky's hero is not an objectified image but an autonomous discourse, *pure voice*; we do not see him, we hear him; everything that we see and know apart from his discourse is nonessential and is swallowed up by discourse as its own raw material, or else remains outside it as something that stimulates and provokes.[73]

The Dostoevsky heroes become 'pure voice'. Their material existence is completely consumed by their incessant discussions about themselves and the world – and, in fact, as Bakthin rightly states, we hear them, but we do not see them. This very much resembles Carla and Pietro's situation: pure voices that echo in an empty space – Lonzi's house in Rome, we are told, though this information is not particularly relevant – where everything is absorbed by the conversation between the two characters. The 'pure voice', as an element, reveals itself as an extremely interesting discursive tool for capturing the unspeakability of the speakable that emerges, for a moment, in *Vai pure*. This necessarily requires leaving behind the autobiographical enunciation space, however, and presenting oneself, instead, as a poetic 'pure voice'.

Inside outside
Inside outside
Inside outside

Inside outside
the obsessive rhythm of hope
life and death intertwined
Inside
Inside
Inside
Inside
the acute heat of ice
Outside
Outside
Outside
Outside
the frozen rhythm of nothingness.
When passion inhabits the world
the skyscrapers will fall singing
the din of the world by now conquered.
Free spaces and fly.[74]

Someone would have considered
romantic
the idea of Paestum
we went there
presented
with thousands of ideas
for stories
before us when we arrive
a stormy see
a very low sky,
inclined impregnated on the wintry
earth,
dark wet and only light
from the yellow summer memory
from the tourist shrieks.[75]

Having the courage to love you
from the silence of the denied body
looking at your breasts
following with a gaze
following …
in the pool of purple water
lilies, they fly
Oh, please, please stop
stop, but really stop.
Shreds of kite outside the

damp cave:
existence freed of its
essence. The tangible evidence of thousands of
fissures that rip through the veil of
survival.
And I ask myself if ...
I am learning to fly or not. Or if I believe
I am learning and actually I flail like
a hen?
No, I no longer want boredom
I finally want to want.[76]

The first two quotes are from much longer pieces of poetry, while the third is the full text of a poem written collaboratively by a group of women from Collettivo pratica dell'inconscio in via Pace, Rome[77]: each verse was written by a different woman. The most visible elements of these poetic products are their experimental character and the use of avant-garde stylistic forms – the image of the skyscrapers that fall singing has a distinctively Rimbaudesque quality. This does not negate the fact, however, that what we are reading is lyrical poetry. Here, the feminist voice frees itself from the self-narrative form to become poetry, which is essentially lyrical.[78]

Why so? Because, by breaking the customary order of the sentence with its logical links guaranteed by syntax and grammar, lyrical poetry projects the lyrical flow beyond time and space, in search of the expression of the ineffable moment. The lyrical attitude, then, is oriented towards the accidental and not towards what is permanent and essential – as stated in the last of the three poems cited here, it is 'existence freed of its/essence'. In other words, such a poetic choice is defined by its capacity to abolish the world of the referent in which we are usually immersed in search of something that it itself, by its habitual nature, conceals – essentially confirming the literary vocation of the schizophrenic discourse discussed by Todorov.

And indeed, the second poem moves immediately from the romantic idea of Paestum to its lyrical representation, in which the earth is made 'light' by the 'yellow' memory of summer, without encountering the real Paestum. The lyrical act, then, produces a word form that resides outside of language, that has meaning, but no longer a referent – thus assuming the form of a lyrical sigh.[79] And it is precisely thanks to these characteristics that it can construct a 'lyrical' community, defined by the destruction of all distance between the author and the subjects to whom the lyrical communication is addressed, who, it seems, are directly summoned to the context of the poetic enunciation.[80]

The dismantling of the logical links that hold the discourse together and the elimination of the referential horizon naturally form part of a lyrical strategy – not an autobiographical one, in this instance – of self-enunciation. The establishment of a community through the lyrical act is, in turn, the political effect that Italian neo-feminist strove to achieve by making use of this specific form of poetic expression. This description, however, is lacking the fundamental element, the intentional object – to use phenomenological language – of feminist lyric poetry, upon which the political community of women can be established. And the intentional object is nothing more than the pure epiphany of meaning that is no longer rooted in the – syntactic, logical or narrative – relationship among the words, but in their lack of relationship, in the crumbling of discourse itself into linguistic islands that can no longer be held together. It is 'the tangible evidence of thousands of/fissures that rip through the veil of/survival', as expressed by the women of the Collettivo pratica dell'inconscio. For these women, the 'veil of survival' is simply the world constructed by men, the discursive cage within which they are prisoners and that must be torn open to discover what is beyond its weighty linguistic bars.

The transition from the autobiographical I to the lyrical I, then, formalizes the impossibility of conquering meaning by way of the linear narration of the self. The relationship with the feminist interpretation of the world is not produced by way of the horizontal progression of the account, but through the vertical lyrical statements that shatter the metonymic chains that form the narrative, experimenting with the splintered route where meaning materializes like a flash of lightning.

Speaking the unspeakable, using this path, no longer means an infinite dilation of discourse to capture the unspeakable through laborious meditation, as performed by Lonzi. Speaking the unspeakable means putting discourse to the test posed by schizophrenia. It means dismantling the plot and tearing down the sovereign power that governs, that is, the narrator. It means abandoning the story, with its characters and their action. And, in a certain sense, it also means allowing the figure of the author to drift away: the poetry of the Collettivo pratica dell'inconscio is written by an anonymous subject, it is a lyrical act without an I to support it. At the end of all of this is the unspeakable and the unexpressable, which manifest in the form of discourse that harms itself in order to go beyond itself. Its existence consists of falling apart and opening up spaces to reveal what cannot be conquered through the patient weaving of linguistic signs.

At this point, it may seem justifiable to conclude that the schizophrenic form of self-enunciation is lyrical by nature – confirming the specific link between schizophrenia and contemporary literature to which Todorov alluded in his essay – and to note that these observations contradict my statement at the beginning of the chapter regarding an autobiographical self-enunciation strategy. The foregoing discussion would, in fact, seem to suggest that autobiographical expression and schizophrenic discourse are incompatible. This is not, however, the case. Rather, the concept of a schizophrenic autobiography is complicated because the discursive collapse that would define it would not allow for the shared identity between author, narrator and character required for autobiographical enunciation. And schizophrenic autobiography should not be confused with the autobiography of a schizophrenic, as the latter should more correctly be defined as a form of biography. Indeed, either it is written when the schizophrenic subject is no longer such – whether during temporary or definitive remission is of little consequence – and is, therefore, the account by a non-schizophrenic subject of a schizophrenic subject, or it is written by a schizophrenic subject with some form of institutional support, and it is, therefore, the institution – usually of a medical nature – that tells its story through the lens of a mental disorder.

If, however, a schizophrenic self-narrative is impossible, schizophrenic textual manifestations are indeed possible, and represent an alternative method of feminist self-enunciation within the confines of autobiographical discourse. I refer here to the transcription of dream-like activity to which many Italian neo-feminists dedicated themselves with commitment and passion. In this case, too, Carla Lonzi's *Diario di una femminista* represents my preferred starting point. In part, this is for purely quantitative reasons – the section of the text dedicated to 1973 contains 117 dreams, while the 1974 section contains 140. As such, dream-like reports represent a non-negligible part of *Taci, anzi parla*. The real motivation, however, is qualitative. The dream-like writing that punctuates the diary gives rise to a sort of schizophrenic counter-writing that works in a constant relationship of attrition with the paranoid self-discourse that gives the text its main structure. This is best illustrated by presenting one of Lonzi's dreams directly.

> I am on the bed with Tito and a homosexual friend of mine. I fall asleep and I wake up in the middle of the night: my friend is reading my booklet on sex and is entirely respectful. … I go to the balcony: there's no railing, but I'm there now and I discard my cigarette butt. A guard dressed in white looks up, but I don't let him see me. It's dark on the promenade: it seems like a man is doing somersaults because he put my lit cigarette butt in his mouth backwards. But perhaps I'm mistaken. Suddenly, I have no means and I give myself over to fate: in an alleyway covered by ancient vaults, I ask a woman if she wants me as a housekeeper. She agrees, I go with her. We climb an external staircase and on the outside landing she lies down gently and pulls up her clothes: a male sex organ appears, plump like that of a boy who is not yet developed. I try to reach the clitoris however, which may be hidden underneath, but I don't find anything and in any case it doesn't work for me, I get tired.[81]

This dream, dated 25 April 1973, quite clearly presents the itinerary of Lonzi's own pursuit of the clitoridian woman – the latter lifts up her skirt, revealing a male member, which, however, may hide a clitoris.[82] At the same time, vaginal characteristics are attributed to the male subject – it is the man who does somersaults because he put the burning end of Lonzi's cigarette butt in his mouth. Here, however, I am not interested in the symbolic content of the dream. My focus is instead on the action and the vertiginous articulation thereof. A number of completely separate locations – bedrooms, balconies, a promenade, an alleyway covered by 'ancient vaults' – and a series of conspicuous characters – Tito, the homosexual friend, the guard, the man doing somersaults, the woman with the child's penis – are covered in the space of a short few lines. This is an example of external focalization,[83] in which the narrator is incapable of adding anything to the character's actions, unfold before our eyes in all of their strangeness.

Basically, Carla Lonzi's dream-like activities share practically nothing with the laborious pages of her diary that we read previously. The paranoid narrator insistent on meditating on every detail is dominated by the schizophrenic action of the character, uncoupled from any form of coherence or logical consequentiality. The narrator's desire to direct the story in her – perennially frustrated – pursuit of meaning is replaced by the simple transcription of a dream-like story devoid of all direction, which opens suddenly and closes just as suddenly, with no justification except 'I get tired'. The poetics of the fragment that characterizes feminist lyrical poetry translates, then, into a dream-like account, the *fabula* of which freefalls towards its conclusion through a series of disjointed narrative parts that, instead of making action by the main character impossible, paradoxically serves to reinforce its strength.

Not all of Carla Lonzi's dreams are structured in this way, however. There is one that is particularly worthy of examination due to the role it plays in the diary and for reasons of interpretative interest.

> A blonde nun lifts herself from her pillows and tells the others that she is about to die. When I return she is dead. Among her personal items I discover a photograph: a kind of baroque headstone with my name engraved on it. And then I see a marble sculpture of me with others, very young, beautiful and intact, looking secular, with a plunging neckline in my sumptuous dress.[84]

Lonzi's book ends with this dream from 29 January 1977. The dream-like material is reported matter-of-factly, without any interpretation to clarify its meaning. From the previous pages, it is clear that the diary's author has managed to overcome her ambiguous relationship with Piera and Simone. The content of the dream, however, raises some further considerations. The dream, on the one hand, appears as a final tribute to the evanescent sovereignty of the narrator of *Taci, anzi parla*. Ultimately, the effort to say everything is achieved in the concluding transcript of that which resists being said and which nevertheless is included in the self-narrative: a sort of trophy to the omnivorous will of the narrator figure, who does not stop at anything in its pursuit to say everything and the meaning of everything. In this case, however, the narrator does not raise any ruminative question or offer the reader any comment on the dream. In a certain sense, it is as though the narrator's strength has run out at the very moment of its final affirmation.

The concluding dream, in fact, is the final realization of the paranoid self-enunciation strategy, which, however, assumes the form of schizophrenic expression of the self, where the narrator stays silent in favour of the character and its action, which the narrator figure is unable to control. At least up to a certain point. The first compromise between paranoid discourse and schizophrenic discourse that concludes the book – the narrating subject who wants to say everything about herself ends her account with a text that she includes in the diary despite being unable to interpret it – is accompanied by a second that is the very epitome of a dream-like account. The freedom of the character, though apparently preserved in the confusion of the dream-like action, is nevertheless subtly limited and subordinate to the overall structure of diary narration.

Carla Lonzi encounters a nun, who dies immediately. The photo she finds among her personal effects tells her that the nun was actually herself: the image before her shows her as a marble sculpture, beautiful and finally happy. In this way, the end of the diary is saved from the casual game of time, the succession of days and years that accumulate page after page. Basically, at the end of the diary we find the end of the diary: the recomposition of the self, the concluding appropriation of the meaning of her life, which had been elusive in the previous 1,300 pages. Finally, Carla Lonzi rediscovers herself beautiful and innocent, without any further need for the exasperated forms of melodramatic rhetoric.

To say everything about oneself, to speak the unspeakable about oneself and recompose oneself beyond male discursive power, however, means to pay a very high price. Carla Lonzi only achieves herself in the guise of a funeral statue. The final word in paranoid self-enunciation, capable of draining the limitless sea of the unspeakable and beyond which there remains nothing else to say, coincides with the declaration of her death. The self-narrative, at this point, sheds the living form of the diary, with its – at least theoretical – claim to be interminable, and shows itself, instead, to be a lengthy obituary. The rights of the autobiographical narrator are re-established, and the story takes shape thanks to the plot that governs it, but the latter reveals itself for what it is, that is, movement towards the end and, therefore, a drive towards death.[85]

And so if *Taci, anzi parla* dabbles in schizophrenic methods of speaking about the self, by way of the dreams that punctuate the diary, the primacy of the narrator is nevertheless re-affirmed at the end of the work – that is, at its most important point. In a certain sense, there is no interpretation of the dream that concludes the diary because, in that dream, it is not the discourse of the other that speaks within the self-discourse; it is not the language of the subconscious that manifests as a dream-like character and harms the voice of consciousness embodied by the narrator. In this case, it is the narrator figure that is dreaming – dreaming of itself – and it is evident that the power of death dominates the narrative. Carla Lonzi's final dream is, in a certain sense, free indirect discourse in a dream-like form.

Naturally, Carla Lonzi is not the only Italian neo-feminist who dreams. The transcription of dream-like experiences is also practiced by other women, beyond the complex narrative strategy that characterizes the *Diario di una femminista*.

> Dream: I am in the via Cernaia residence, with two men one of whom is a cardinal or a bishop with all of his vestments and he is kneeling on the ground and, to my great disgust, these two want me to kiss the bishop's rear end … I escape with another girl, leaving a third one inside (they weren't there before, I feel very guilty that I have to leave her inside but I don't think I'll manage to escape in time if I wait for her to get out too). Precipitous stairs at the pace of a galloping horse. Out onto the street, afraid that they are watching where I'm going from the window. Hunger – pastry stolen from a café. I know I'm

in Milan. ... Then on the steep road that runs alongside the stream, laborious climb, I see them behind me now if I turn, there are more than two of them, but they are not bothering to follow me.[86]

In Alice Martinelli's dream, the action is perhaps even more relentless than in Lonzi's first dream, marked by the protagonist's escape and the multiplication of the women being followed – suddenly there are two, plus a third who does not keep pace – and the men following them – first two, then an unspecified number. And so more action, more characters, more schizophrenic freedom for the action.

Beyond the context of the Rivolta Femminile political group – in which Alice Martinelli also participated – Lea Melandri also transcribed her dreams, probably before anyone else in the Italian feminist movement, in fact, given that the relevant notebooks begin in 1966. Here is an example.

> I am travelling in a car with ***. Destination Faenza. Suitcases and lots of books. Enthusiastic departure. Another scene. I see myself on a nurse's bed, my parents are there and perhaps other relatives; my uncle *** tries to give me an injection of [illegible] in my foot [illegible]. Violent reaction from me, I manage to free myself and the needle breaks and hits my uncle on the head. I arrive in Faenza: an [illegible], sense of desolation. *** speaks to a friend at the window; there are three students there smiling at me, not sure how (it seems to me [illegible] that they were in the car with us before). New departure (perhaps return): lots of mud in the square, suitcases wide open, books scattered in the mud. Desperate and vain attempt to collect them and rearrange them in my suitcase. Two dogs arrive and pounce on me. One attacks me, trying to bite me. Those present don't help me, they advise me to stroke it to calm it down. Sense of my weakness. But now the dog seems to transform into a human being, a cross between a man and a child who, moved to pity, helps me to gather the books and with great effort I manage to fill up the suitcase, which is full of books but also lots of mud. Vague sense of departure, laborious and not very clear conclusion.[87]

In this dream, too, action is tumultuous, moving from one situation to another without interruption and without any apparent logic. In this case, the narrator in the dream-like report also makes a concluding comment – 'laborious and not very clear conclusion' – that is more an admission of impotence than a statement regarding her ability to organize the story. The dream-like arrangement of time – and space – contrasts with the characteristics of the paranoid strategy of self-narration: the single temporal sequence produced by the narrator's meditation on the meaning of the narrated story falls to pieces and is replaced by the scattered and fragmented everyday world, devoid of substantial links. It is a time of metamorphosis – clearly presented in Lea Melandri's dream – in which the protagonist and her world become something other than what they are.[88]

This brings me back once again to Todorov's categorization and his definition of schizophrenic discourse. As I said earlier, the latter is characterized by a form of extreme incoherence obtained by profoundly altering the ways in which the various segments of discourse are joined together, making it impossible to establish an internal causal hierarchy. Lea Melandri reacts violently to her uncle's injection, but it is impossible to understand why. She is attacked by a dog, but none among those present try to help her. Bizarrely, they advise her to stroke it. Alice Martinelli runs away from a pair of perverted men, but suddenly finds herself being followed by three of them, without it being clear where the third man came from.

In this way, abolition of the referent is achieved. Not, however, as in the previous case, through the doubling back of the text on itself in a narrative situation with no story. In a certain sense, the schizophrenic discourse strategy is more radical. Narration as a function of order and meaning is omitted; the linearity of the story and the coherence of the protagonist and the other characters are lost. The narrator no longer serves as guardian of the meaning of the story, committed to directing the activity engaged in by the protagonist. The latter, in turn, reacts to the most bizarre situations with the strangest behaviours. The protagonist and the secondary characters lose all psychological identity. The former exists only in the rush of the action, passively experienced or actively performed: being followed, or throwing a lit cigarette butt into a man's mouth.

The schizophrenic strategy of addressing the paradoxical injunction underpinning feminist self-discourse is, therefore, profoundly different from its paranoid counterpart. The latter achieves the sense of the self through an attempt not to leave anything unsaid. Here, instead, it is as though the paradoxical injunction has been taken literally and turned upside down. If I must express myself, it is because I am not really what I think I am – otherwise I would not need to express myself. And so expressing myself must mean saying that I am not myself. *In other words, a paradoxical command is obeyed in a way that is, in turn, paradoxical. By expressing myself, I am saying that in reality I am another. Basically, I acknowledge the contradictory character of the command by stating that I myself am a contradiction.* And so, through the dream-like report, it is the character that occupies the proscenium in the account of the self, engaged in an interminable alteration of the self, dictated by the unpredictable and meaningless situations in which it finds itself.

The most coherent interpreter of this radical strategy of resolving the feminist paradox of self-enunciation through destruction of the primacy of the narrator is, in fact, Lea Melandri. If Carla Lonzi does not allow the dreams presented in her diary to consolidate into a schizophrenic discourse as an alternative to the paranoid self-narrative, Lea Melandri employs a discursive strategy that overturns that engaged in by the Florentine feminist at every turn.

Let me elaborate. Lea Melandri's dream journals, stored in the archives of the Fondazione Badaracco di Milano – which relate to 1966, 1969 and 1970 – present a structure in direct opposition to Carla Lonzi's diary. For the most part, the daily entries pertain to dreams from the night before, while hermeneutic attempts relating to dream-like materials also appear here and there. In other words, we are faced with a sort of dream-like account of the self, in which the presence of the interpreting figure – corresponding to the narrative voice in the *Diario di una femminista* – is clearly subordinate to the plot of the dreams that form the structure of the text. And so, if in the paranoid self-narrative, dreams, too, are subordinate to the narrator's need for order and pursuit of meaning, in Lea Melandri's schizophrenic narration, the former are given the freedom to manifest in all their scatteredness and incoherence, while the latter is reduced to playing a mere supporting role.

This, however, is not all. Undoubtedly, the schizophrenic self-enunciation strategy destroys the referent, producing a nonsensical discourse. In the case of dream journals, however, the operation is more subtle. The lack of continuity of the dream, as discussed previously, is combined with the complete non-transitivity of the dream-like text. In fact, though the latter manifests as the transcription of a dream-like situation that precedes it and that it tries to document as best it can, in reality it produces the situation to which it seeks to refer. In other words, the dream is but the text of the dream written in Lea Melandri's notebooks. Or, we could also say that the after – transcribing the dream – precedes the before – the dream itself – and, even more radically, that we are faced with an after without a before.[89] The folding of the text back on itself that abolishes the referent is not achieved by arranging an account that recounts an account – or rather, a diary that narrates the writing of the diary of the person who writes it – but rather by producing a non-Euclidean object of reference that only exists within the text itself.

Elimination of the primacy of the narrator in favour of the character, and abolishment of the referent by way of paradoxical texts consisting of transcripts of dreams, are combined, finally, with an equally radical change to the figure of the author and the effects of the authorial act: works that take the form of books. Lea Melandri's journals can only be consulted as archive documents. And, for privacy protection reasons, Melandri's permission is required to access them (she is still alive), together with authorization from the regional administrative authority that manages the archive. On the one hand, this is a practical difficulty that commonly affects research involving documents of this kind. On the other, this barrier to reading the texts may be regarded as the effect of a precise writing strategy: dismantling the ordinary paratextual forms that transform a text into a book and producing a work that is not a work, attributed to an author who is not an author.[90] If *Taci, anzi parla* is the monument to paranoid self-enunciation erected by Carla Lonzi, Lea Melandri's dream journals are the non-monument to schizophrenic self-enunciation: the closest thing that exists, as far as I am aware, to a schizophrenic autobiography.[91]

I will conclude, finally, with some very quick notes about catatonic self-enunciation. Not much can be said about this final feminist strategy of self-enunciation. I include it here for the sake of exhaustiveness, but, in fact, it is a strategy of silence. It involves stepping outside of the paradox of self-expression by not expressing oneself. In this case, the referent is eliminated because, as there is no discourse, there is also no act of reference. In a strictly logical sense, this would mean not having access to any documents that demonstrate the operation of the catatonic strategy. However, while there may not be a *discourse of silence* – which is the absence of words – there is, nevertheless, a *discourse on silence*. In this latter case, the problem of expressing oneself, and female expression, is presented more as a difficulty, than an impossibility, to use words.

> The man is the subject who speaks: the woman can only mime a language that she has not produced. And yet from this silence, this space of non-existence, while listening to the man speak, women discovered that they exist, albeit mutely. ... And so women, formerly objects of consumption and exchange, and therefore silent, began to express their needs, using a different language. In this regard, we wonder whether and to what extent the workers' movements opened up a space for women to begin to express themselves, to state themselves, to speak of themselves ... There are, however, also spaces that are more ours ('women's houses', magazines, bookshops, galleries, editions and holidays) and there is also a mode of communication that is more 'ours', in the sense that it is invented, practised, spoken, sung, shouted and written by women among women. That alludes to the body, to sexuality, to the Beyond, to the removed, to the unconscious.[92]

Women are placed in a state of mutism by male power. The feminist revolution restores self-expression to women but, despite an increase in the forms of orality, writing, singing and shouting, it remains elusive. In other words, it says something that cannot be grasped.

This type of discursive difficulty emerges at various points through feminist discourse.

> These [are] some of the oppositions that caused us to spend the entire period of preparing the magazine in a state of stress and uncertainty as to whether we would ever succeed. Even now as we write, it seems almost as though we don't know whether we will ever read our words in print.[93]

> In fact, we never 'seriously' discussed, all together, how to create the upcoming journal, what the journal is and what it should not be. We have pondered this 'inability' of ours various times, also because the story of the contribution to *Sottosopra* is associated with the story of a 'document' that we have always deeply wanted to produce and that was never born. And so the discourse of 'writers' block' was born (and not just that: a block with regard to many activities), which is a trait of women.[94]

These two quotations are taken, respectively, from the introduction to the second edition of the Roman magazine *Differenze* (*Differences*) and the second edition of the Milanese *Sottosopra*. Both texts serve the traditional function of prologues: the adoption of a modest attitude by the writer – referring to the difficulties with writing – and, more specifically, reconciling a collection of writings that are quite different from one another.[95]

Unlike the traditional approach, however, the feminist prologue emphasizes the problem of adequately expressing the female. If, indeed, women have been victims of a thousand-year-old silence imposed by male power, it is natural that the task of expressing oneself, following such a story of oppression cannot but be rife with obstacles. The issue of self-expression, sometimes, has more strictly technical connotations.

> The greatest problems were associated with the content and mode of expression, in the sense of finding a form of mediation between the moment of disseminating the information and the moment of production, creativity, enjoyment and use of the 'starting from oneself' ... The type of communications produced constantly oscillated between two extremes: on the one hand Radia's consciousness-raising, which inevitably privileged oral expression, separated from bodily communication and, therefore, devoid of actual-emotive engagement with the women listeners; on the other, proper technical-journalistic (!) information on current affairs that relate to women.[96]

Radia is the feminist name given to a radio station managed by women. What is problematic here is language itself as a means of communication. In this case, the difficulty of expressing oneself is a communicative difficulty, an uncertainty regarding the best discursive choices to enable one to be understood and to understand oneself. Drawing on Jakobson's categories,[97] it could be said that discourse is interrogated on the channel that it uses, that is, the possibility or impossibility of coming into contact with the other who receives the message, and the code used, that is, the effectiveness of saying what one wishes to say.

Catatonia is a much more radical discursive operation than those found in the paranoid strategy – even more radical than the schizophrenic. It is no longer a matter of abolishing the story in favour of meaning – paranoid – or dissolving the narrative within dream-like action – schizophrenic. Here, instead, it is discourse itself that is lacking, because language is not sufficient for what it must convey and, therefore, it cannot say anything to anyone. Both the narrator and the character disappear because the author is no longer there to produce any utterance.

The paradox contained in the injunction on self-expression, then, is addressed in a radical way. The self is not expressed by absorbing the discourse of the other in self-enunciation, and nor is the self enunciated by saying that the 'self is another'. More simply, nothing is said because there is no language. The command is not fulfilled because there is no way of doing so within the field of discourse. The paradox of self-expression is met with a paradoxical silence, heavy with meaning.

Naturally, the catatonic strategy of self-enunciation, in a pure state, does not exist. As mentioned at the beginning, it would take the form of pure negativity, absence of work, lack of discourse. Rather, it manifests as an example of Althusser's metonymic causality,[98] a discursive strategy present only as an absence or, as in the texts examined here, a hesitation, a moment of linguistic trepidation that immediately closes over on itself and fades as quickly as possible.

Chapter 3

THE REMAINS OF TWO TRADITIONS:
INSTITUTIONAL MONUMENTS AND
IMPOSSIBLE MOURNING

After the end: The collapse of communism and the self-narrative

War, Fascist violence, unemployment and poverty were very common themes in the communist militant autobiographies presented in Chapter 1. Nevertheless, such accounts invariably convey a 'joy of being',[1] which accompanies the communist militants' decision to join the party and take part in the political struggle. The end of the historical experience of communism – represented most strikingly by the Berlin Wall being torn down in 1989 and the siege on Russian parliament in 1991, resulting in Boris Yeltsin's victory over Mikhail Gorbachev and the dissolution of the Soviet Union at the end of the same year – together with the disbandment of the PCI on 3 February 1991, deeply coloured the tone of subsequent Italian communist autobiographies.

Such accounts lack the energy that characterized the self-narratives written in the decade following the end of the Second World War, that sense of awe and enthusiasm at having discovered profound meaning – in the form of communism – that would forever change their individual lives and the general course of history. The transformative power embodied by the earlier autobiographies – that simultaneously documented a complete existential turn and served as vehicles of personal metamorphosis – is, therefore, extinguished. The documentary dimension remains, but the emotional timbre varies greatly from one account to the next: writing styles range from Pietro Ingrao's emphatic tone to Emanuele Macaluso's significantly more detached presentation.[2]

The clearest distinction separating the later texts from the original communist autobiographies is the absence of a pragmatic objective, at least in its most obvious form: these writers are not writing to become communists and, as such, the act of autobiographical enunciation loses its significance with respect to the autobiographical document. Moreover, communism ceased to be of topical interest and – as the Soviet Bloc crumbled and the Italian party dissolved – it quickly faded into the past, like a great error of history or a lost opportunity for humanity, depending on one's perspective. Writers no longer wrote to become communists, because one cannot become something that no longer exists. In a certain sense, the autobiographies published after the collapse of historical communism are not stories of development; instead, they resemble ledgers, recording the debits and credits of one's political existence, in search of a more or less definitive balance.

This overall description, however, is inadequate. To me, the most interesting aspects of the communist autobiographies written *après le déluge* are the sets of similarities and differences as compared to the earlier institutional self-narratives, coupled with the narrative treatment of one's former communist self at a time when communism no longer exists. I will begin my analysis by making an observation that, on the surface, may seem rather trite: the autobiographies written in the wake of the communist era do not differ greatly, in terms of form, from those penned in the decade of the movement's inception. The primacy of narrator over character and the guidance of the latter by the former appear to have been unscathed by the political catastrophe that befell communism. The character acts, while the narrator is responsible for ascribing meaning to that action. Unfortunately, the meaning of one's life as a communist no longer seems as clear-cut as it was before.

> This is not a history book. It deals with things that surface from my memory when I catch people's quizzical looks and their expressions interrogate me: Why were you a communist? Why do you say that you are a communist? What do you mean, when you have no party, no position, when you have lost the newspaper you helped found? Is it an illusion that you cling to, because you are stubborn or stuck in the past? Every so often someone will stop me and say with great kindness: 'You were a legend!' But who wants to be a legend? Legends are the projections of other people and have nothing to do with me. The idea embarrasses me. I am not a name on a memorial plaque to be honoured, who has departed from the world and exists outside of time. I am still struggling with the world and with time. But the question of what it means to be or to have been a communist nags away at me.[3]

Rossana Rossanda's introduction to the account of her life is emphatically negative. Rossanda is not writing a 'history book'. She is not performing an official function that authorizes her to say what she wants to say, nor is she part of an organization that confers legitimacy on her enunciation. She is no longer involved with *il Manifesto*, the newspaper she helped found – originally conceived of as a magazine and the reason for Rossanda's expulsion from the PCI. Likewise, she rejects the label of 'legend', because she is entirely indifferent to such a mode of recognition. The opening passage of the former communist leader's work bears echoes of Eugenio Montale's words: 'This, today, is all that we can tell you:/what we are *not*, what we do *not* want.'[4]

If the first generation of party autobiographies read like communist *Bildungsromans*, characterized by the more or less laborious pursuit of the narrator by the character until the action of the latter coincides with the meaning possessed by the former, here the situation is entirely different. The narrator of the later texts administers the character's story, but the meaning pursued by the latter is defined in negative, rather than positive, terms. Instead of an affirmation, it manifests as an interrogation – 'why were you a communist?' The status of such meaning is difficult to define. It does not belong to the realm of historical science, as the author is not, herself, a historian. Nor can it be categorized in epical terms, as her refusal to be regarded as a 'legend' equates to rejecting the epithet of 'hero', confined to the 'absolute past', no longer able to communicate in the present.[5]

The narrator, therefore, embarks on presenting her autobiographical account without being able to determine exactly what the set of events that she is about to recount might mean. This issue is common to all later communist autobiographies, which struggle to pinpoint the meaning to be ascribed to the self-narrative.

> I have spoken with Paolo Franchi about the PCI many times, about its history, its leaders, the women and men who attended its events and its elections. More than once, we concluded that perhaps it would be a good idea to write something. Not the history of this party, which is a subject best left to the historians. And not 'my memoirs', either, given that I am not a 'personality' and, in any case, I never kept a diary or saved a document.[6]

Emanuele Macaluso faces the same dilemma as Rossana Rossanda: why write what he is about to write? Like his former party comrade, his work is neither a history of the PCI, because he is not a historian, nor a collection of memoirs, given that, with a certain sense of modesty, he does not consider himself important enough for his autobiography to be of public interest: he is not a 'personality'. The struggle to give the text a solid epistemological grounding is resolved, here, by rooting it in social interaction and presenting it as the product of a sort of 'face engagement'[7] with journalist Paolo Franchi. And so, whereas Rossanda's work is framed as the response to a request by a generic you, Macaluso's approach is more direct. He presents his communist life story as the result of a dialogue with a real person, even concluding the text with a series of letters exchanged with Franchi, whom he credits with encouraging him to put pen to paper.

Pietro Ingrao's solution, meanwhile, is a sort of bizarre hybrid, combining certain features from the opening passages of Rossanda and Macaluso's respective works.

> These memoirs are a sort of reconstruction of a personal and social affair that unfolded against the backdrop of the bloody affairs of my times. [...] But even a memorialist cannot be truly certain that things went this way, according to this underlying 'order'. [...] Did that event happen like that, as it clings to my sweet, painful memory? Or is the key worn, assuming that there is a key, even if only for a collection of fragments? Given the uncertainty of language, how is memory expressed and legitimized? And why are we so afraid of losing our memory? Is it the vanity of remaining always and forever part of the scene, or an attempt at salvation? Or perhaps it is the memory of subjugation to others, that cannot stand silence.[8]

Ingrao follows this passage by thanking some friends – referring to them by name and surname – for their help with 'reconstructing those intense events and bringing order to those troubled memories'.

The preface to his account, then, mirrors the discursive strategies previously examined, pushing them further still. The questions multiply, but their focus is different to Rossanda's, more introspective. They do not seek to determine what it means to be a communist; rather, they attempt to verify the reliability of the writer's memory. Like a Descartes of Italian communism, Ingrao repeatedly questions whether he is capable of remembering what he remembers. Fortunately for him, he is supported in this process not by a Cartesian demon, dragging him into a vortex of doubt, but by his daughter and a group of friends – whereas Macaluso was assisted only by a journalist – who rescue him from the uncertainties posed by forgetfulness and the tricks of memory.

Though Ingrao is not driven by the evil genius to ponder the existence of the world at large, his incipit is, nevertheless, informed by a Cartesian stance, which pushes the narrator to ask a radical question: is writing about the self not, perhaps, an act of narcissism, wherein the rightful place of the object – the history of Italian communism – is occupied by the subject who narrates that history? As Ingrao himself asks, 'Is it the vanity of remaining always and forever part of the scene, or an attempt at salvation?' The solution arrived at by Macaluso is rather staid: I write my memoirs not because I am important (a 'personality'), but because I agree with my interlocutor that something should be written. The uncertainty expressed by Ingrao, however, is somewhat deceptive; it makes no difference, in fact, whether the purpose of the autobiography is to achieve one last hurrah as a celebrity or to save oneself. The writer is at the centre of the account in either case, and will, most likely, achieve both outcomes.

The issue, of course, is not so much that, in a first-person account, the world is filtered by the autobiographical narrator. This is inevitable. Of note, instead, is that first-person narrators have differing degrees of interest in themselves as characters and, as such, dedicate more or less space to matters pertaining to that character in the story. In this regard, if *Moby Dick*'s Ishmael sits firmly at one end of the continuum of self-interest – having saved himself not to tell his own story, but that of the white whale and the captain who hunted him – we might place Pietro Ingrao at the opposite end.

Evidence of the intensely subjective nature of the account is provided by the author's ruminations on memory and its meaning, which cast aside reflections on history and its significance. It also emerges from the tangle of adjectives that make up the text as a whole, and that is by no means limited to the brief passage cited above. Suffice to read back over the first question raised by the Italian communist: 'Did that event happen like that, as it clings to my sweet, painful memory?' If we rewrite the question without adjectives – and without the emphasis added by the metaphor that sees past events 'clinging' to his memory – we can focus on the relevant issue: 'Did that event happen as my memory presents it to me?' This version captures the issue addressed by the question, but what it does not convey is that Ingrao experiences memory as 'sweet' and 'painful'.

The same can be said for the 'intense events' and 'troubled memories' that his friends and daughter work with him to reconstruct. Ingrao does not leave it to the reader to decide how much intensity or troubledness to attribute to his story. He informs them in advance, because his priority is the quality that he – not others – ascribes to his story.⁹ This is not merely a stylistic quirk but rather, as I will illustrate shortly, a means of attempting to address the question of 'why write the autobiography of a communist when communism no longer exists?'

A different approach to this issue can be found in the self-narrative published by Armando Cossutta.

> Effectively, my life coincides with an important period in the history of our country, on which I have a privileged perspective. And yet, in truth, these pages are not intended as anything more than a chronicle. As such, nobody should expect reflections on the evolution of our country over the last fifty years, or analyses of the crucial turning points we encountered. I have limited myself to recounting my personal experience as a communist, seeking, in so doing, to shed light on the reasons behind the passion that drove that experience, a passion shared by millions of men and women.¹⁰

This introduction does not seem, at first glance, to be very different from those previously examined. Like the other narrators, Cossutta expresses uncertainty regarding the meaning of what he is about to narrate. He rejects the role of historian of the self and of communism in a manner similar to the previous writers and, like them, presents himself as a modest narrator without particular pretensions: the book is a simple 'chronicle' that recounts the 'personal experience' of its writer.

The specificity of this opening passage lies in the overall architecture of Cossutta's preface. Unlike in the previous examples, his declaration of modesty is not placed at the very beginning of the text, but instead appears approximately twenty pages in to a rather detailed introduction.¹¹ The account opens suddenly on 23 February 1943. Empidonio Chendi, a worker at the Falck steel plant in Milan, is accompanying a seventeen-year-old boy to face a Wehrmacht squad that will shoot them both. The scene unfolds in the courtyard of Monza prison, not far from Milan. The execution is revealed to be just a set-up: the boy is none other than Armando Cossutta himself, while Empidonio Chendi, we are told, is deported to a German concentration camp, where he soon dies. The author then takes a big leap and offers a quick account of the history of the PCI by discussing its key figures, from Togliatti to Berlinguer – all of whom fell ill or died due to the stress of politics – and concludes the section with the dissolution of the party in 1991 and the subsequent controversies.

The reservation alluded to in the declaration of intent at the start of the autobiography is, therefore, mitigated by the historical frame of reference presented by Cossutta. His 'chronicle' may indeed be 'little', but it is rooted in his participation in the Italian Resistance, the historical experience that – though not explicitly mentioned in the document – enabled the country's constitution to be drafted, as alluded to through reference to work as the foundation of the Republic and the anti-Fascist nature of the latter.¹² In a certain sense, the problem of offering 'a communist history' in the absence of communism is resolved, at least, in part, by embedding the latter directly into the institutional substructure of the Italian state, and, specifically, its constitution, by way of the Resistance and Cossutta's participation in it.

A sacrificial argument is also put forward to further support the validity of writing a communist autobiography. According to this theory, great communist leaders had sacrificed themselves to end the circle of violence in the country, enabling the emergence of Italian society, as we know it today. The allusion to the anti-Fascist resistance here is once again followed by reference to a form of violence – which might more correctly be referred to as self-violence – at the heart of the national institutions.[13]

We are presented, then, with a common problem – 'why write what one wants to write?' – expressed in different ways and addressed using different solutions. Can the difficulties faced by this group of authors as they embark on writing their autobiographies be exactly pinpointed?

> Experience shows that in no instance does domination voluntarily limit itself to the appeal to material or affectual or ideal motive as a basis for its continuance. In addition, every such system attempts to establish and to cultivate the belief in its legitimacy. But according to the kind of legitimacy which is claimed, the kind of administrative staff developed to guarantee it and the mode of exercising authority will differ fundamentally.[14]

What does this classic Weber quote have to do with the communist political autobiography? Let me return briefly to an observation made at the start of the book. Autobiography is characterized by the shared identity of the author, narrator and character, but these three figures are united by a power relationship that variously favours one of these over the others. In the communist case, the default configuration for militant and cadre autobiographies seems to be the subordination of the character to the narrator. The self-narratives examined in this chapter, meanwhile, enable a more accurate definition of the power and subordination dynamics experienced by the figures in the autobiographical narrative.

In the party autobiographies considered in the first chapter, *not only did the narrator occupy a dominant position in relation to the character, its dominance also enjoyed a legitimacy that guaranteed its unchallenged operation*. The narrator figure ruled over the character because it had the support of the party, whose officials presided over the legitimate forms of autobiographical production. In other words, the autobiographical narrator had ultimate authority over the meaning of the account in which it also appeared as a character, because its role was guaranteed by a figure that, deep down, occupied the position of true narrator – what I would call the 'master narrator' – that is, the party.[15] The latter defined the parameters of the communist self-narrative, establishing the ceremonial forms of self-enunciation – to be engaged in at the time of joining or during cadre courses – and providing an audience for those stories.

What appeared unquestionable in the first decade of the PCI's history is no longer so half a century later. The demise of the party had destroyed the legitimizing space within which communist autobiographies could be presented and unfolded without challenge. In the self-narratives written after the end of communism, the narrator figure finds itself in a state of ruling without legitimacy. Naturally, it still has the power to set the biographical account in motion and drive it forward: without a narrator, of course, there is no narrative. In these later texts, however, the latter serves merely as a sort of official tasked with the ordinary administration of the account, lacking the authority to take it in a specific direction. It can, of course, seek to gain power and attempt to transform that into narrative legitimacy, using the author figure to its advantage. The narrator's right to recount the autobiographical story derives from the celebrity of its author counterpart. Legitimacy achieved in this way, though undeniable, is not political in nature. The resulting artefact, then, is no longer *a communist autobiography* – in the sense of those penned by the militants in chapter I – but rather the *autobiography of a communist*, which draws its legitimacy from how interesting and successful that person's life was, rather than from an organized political phenomenon.

As such, the issue of narratorial legitimacy remains problematic. And, as we saw previously, when faced with a paradoxical autobiographical injunction – as occurred in both the communist and feminist spheres – the only solution is to attempt to circumvent it. The response to the crisis of autobiographical legitimacy, then, inevitably takes the form of a stopgap, consisting of a series of remedies that conceal the problem without resolving it. From this perspective, it seems that the narrator figure has just two options: either abandon the autobiographical space – by writing an autobiography that is not an autobiography – or immerse oneself fully in that space. Beyond metaphors, the legitimate right of the narrator to narrate may have either epistemic or existential foundations, the first of which is discussed here below.

> Before writing these pages, I wanted to reread the two pieces in the *Il Ribelle e il Conformista* magazine published in early 1955, which I hadn't looked at for quite a while. I don't think I risk being presumptuous if I say that it was not merely a juvenile magazine, but instead represented the most politically (and in some ways culturally) sophisticated material that could be produced in the Christian Democratic sphere at that time. It is no coincidence that, for a long time, *Il Ribelle e il Conformista* remained an essential point of reference for anyone wishing to trace the history of the DC left in the 1950s. [...] The first issue was published at the end of January. Carlo Leidi was the editor, working with Lucio and I as the publication's core editorial team.[16]

Giuseppe Chiarante was a contemporary of Rossana Rossanda, Emanuele Macaluso and Armando Cossutta. The trajectory of his political background, however, was different: as a left-wing Catholic, he started out as a Christian Democrat, only joining the PCI in 1958. He lived out the rest of his political career with the party, until its dissolution. This alternative path gives rise to a different style of first-person account, resulting, perhaps, from having followed a less linear course than those who began their political careers as communists without making that critical daring leap from DC to PCI.[17]

Here, the power play between character and narrator comes down firmly in favour of the latter, but takes a different form to the communist *Bildungsroman* discussed previously. There is no pursuit of the narrator by the character, here: their coincidence is presented as a given, something that does not require justification. And, in fact, the only real action featured in the above passage is not performed by the character, as an autonomous figure, but by the narrator, who is the only true character in the memoir: he reads back over an old political magazine (*Il Ribelle e il Conformista*) before beginning to write – or rather to recount – the words that we read. Chiarante, furthermore, is open about his intentions right from the beginning of the text.

> I did not conceive of this book as an autobiography in the true sense, but rather as a generational testimony. It strikes me as not an uninteresting undertaking – at a distance of fifty years from those events – to seek to contribute to the reconstruction of the cultural and political climate in which the generation of young people that entered public life after the end of the Second World War found itself making its decisions.[18]

Chiarante is not tormented by doubts like Ingrao or Rossanda; he does not wish to write a 'little chronicle' like Cossutta and, unlike Macaluso, he works from documents that he has saved and rereads. Why? Because he has chosen not to write an autobiography, but rather what he calls 'a generational testimony', an ambiguous concept that we will encounter again in the feminist autobiographical sphere. It represents a compromise that enables a departure from the autobiographical field without encroaching on historiography, which Chiarante wishes to avoid, most likely because he cannot occupy the position of authority reserved for the third-person historian who recounts events in which he did not participate. Despite this limitation, the author's decision is abundantly clear. The character in the story merely serves to support the plotting activities performed by the narrator, whose motivation is epistemic in nature: to know what happened, and to read back over documents that he has read before in order to grasp their meaning and decipher aspects of the past that remain obscure.[19]

This decision results in a sober text, with reflexive tendencies, that leaves little space for the character, his actions and sufferings. It is no coincidence that, unlike all of the self-narratives discussed previously, Chiarante's does not feature a family background or childhood stories. The text opens abruptly on 16 July 1954 – when the author was already twenty-five years old – with a visit to the Rome-based headquarters of the DC to participate in a national party council meeting. Little or nothing is revealed of the character's private life, which is employed merely as a prop for the narrator to engage in political reflections over the course of the story. This policy of absolute discretion as regards the private self is infringed on just one occasion, which is, however, worthy of note. In his 'advisory to readers', Chiarante mentions that he is reviewing the draft of his book under 'somewhat difficult circumstances'. He has suffered a stroke caused by a cerebral ischemia, resulting in partial sight loss that makes 'reading' and 'writing' extremely challenging. This insight into his state of health is followed by an expression of heartfelt thanks, not only to friends and family, but also to the 'medical and healthcare staff at the Forlanini Hospital in Rome', to his GP and his niece, 'a highly gifted cardiologist at the "Gemelli" University in Rome'.[20]

His revelation regarding his health is touching, in human terms, and conveys the author's profound suffering – as evinced by the list of medical staff and healthcare institutions deserving thanks. It is interesting to note, however, that it is the author, rather than the character, who is affected by this situation, tasked with preparing the book for print and ensuring the accuracy of the account. This circumstance reinforces the fading of the character in favour of the other figures in the autobiography, while at the same time alluding to another method of legitimizing one's memoirs.

Not only does Chiarante define himself by the acts of reading and writing, he also, crucially, links his intellectual pursuits to his distress at the hands of his illness. In other words, his apparent attempt to ascribe a quasi-historiographical legitimacy to his self-narrative conceals a much stronger draw towards mythological legitimacy. Chiarante is, to all effects, a hero of knowledge because he has attained his insight through pain, according to the Greek *topos* of *pathein mathein* – learning through suffering. He has survived the descent to Hades, and resurfaced, armed with a greater understanding of the way of things.[21]

Seeking legitimacy to recount one's communist story on existential grounds provides a counterpoint to the epistemic approach.

> From Civitavecchia, we were soon brought back to Rome, to one of the large barracks on Via delle Milizie. And things seemed to improve a bit, although now it was the extremely adept bedbugs that assailed our young, naked bodies – I don't know how they lowered themselves from the ceilings of the barracks to the rows of coarse mattresses in those rooms, where we spent our infinite slumbers, and where, when we awoke at dawn, we compared the generous erections of our young members, sniggering.[22]

I have already discussed Ingrao's fondness for emphatic writing. Here, however, his passion for hyperbole crosses the line into shamelessness. Exaggeration after exaggeration: the bedbugs do not merely bite, instead they are 'extremely adept' and 'assail' the young soldiers; the latter sleep 'infinite' slumbers and do not laugh, but sneer. Ingrao describes the erections of the soldiers' 'young members', which he cannot help but describe in superlative terms as 'generous'.

A simple case of poor literary taste? I think not. The quoted passage is taken from a chapter entitled *La guerra totale* ('Total War'), which opens with a reference to the Nazi German attack on the USSR, recalling the courage of the Red Army who sought to slow the invaders' progress 'with acts of tragic courage and inconceivable extinguishment of lives'.[23] The progression from war on the Soviet front to the erections of a group of infantrymen in Rome – over the course of less than two pages – is astonishing but by no means accidental.

Ingrao resolves the issue of the legitimacy of his autobiography by literally matching the figure of the narrator to the profile of the character. This is not to say that the narrator does not feature in the text, raising questions about situations that affect the character or making thoughtful observations on events. Rather, it means that the narrative converges entirely on the character, endorsing his humours and analysing his most minute actions, including his erections. If we take the militant autobiographies of the 1940s and 1950s as a yardstick, Ingrao's self-narrative is certainly the account of a communist, but it is not a communist account. Whereas the former is characterized by a tension experienced by the character towards the narrator, the latter is defined by the attraction of the narrator to the character. It is not the character who is required to conform to the expectations of the narrator, here, but rather the narrator who must adapt to the actions of the character.

The leap from grand narratives of battles and death to infinitesimal accounts of the sexual palpitations of a group of young Italian males – and likewise Ingrao's fascination with the material bodily stratum[24] – are consequences of this alternative dynamic between the narrator and character. In short, the narrator retains its power to organize the account and seek meaning in it, but it derives its legitimacy from the character, whose qualities and experiences are absolutely foregrounded. A number of tendencies are clearly identifiable in this new direction taken by the post-communist autobiographies, according to which the difficult pursuit of the meaning of life is arranged. Nietzsche's distinction between three kinds of history – antiquarian, monumental and critical – is rather useful in this regard.

> The small and limited, the decayed and obsolete receives its dignity and inviolability in that the preserving and revering soul of the antiquarian moves into these things and makes itself at home in the nest it builds there. The history of his city becomes for him the history of his self; he understands the wall, the turreted gate, the ordinance of the town council, the national festival like an illustrated diary of his youth and finds himself, his strength, his diligence, his pleasure, his judgment, his folly and rudeness, in all of them.[25]

The antiquarian historian – or antiquarian autobiographer, in our case – recalls that which has been forgotten because it is deemed of little importance in the greater context of human history. He loves villages rather than metropolises and, when he looks back on the past, he sees town corners rather than great city architecture.

> One day I arrived late to a committee meeting of the Turin Youth Federation in Via Monte di Pietà, and sat at the back. I took off my jacket and was wearing braces underneath. Luciano Rossi, the provincial secretary, was discussing the need to be able to speak to young workers, starting with clothing. At a certain point he saw me and said: 'For example, I find it difficult to imagine how comrade Novelli could speak to the workers while wearing braces.' I got to my feet and responded: 'Comrade Rossi, this is why I wear braces ....' Then I unfastened them and let my pants fall.[26]

Diego Novelli's account perfectly captures the antiquarian approach to recounting one's communist past, starting with the title of his collection of autobiographical notes: *Com'era bello il mio PCI* (*Oh, How Wonderful Was My PCI*). Here, the party does not exist as a mass mobilization organization, as an Italian centre of an international movement or even simply as a political player in parliament. The PCI is, first and foremost, 'my PCI': the text presents Novelli's acutely personal experience of it, of the militants he encountered, of the party practices he took part in. This personal experience is best captured in the presentation of minor episodes, anecdotes of little importance that the power of hindsight has imbued with meaning, and that Novelli recounts with nostalgic pleasure. The story of the unfastened braces is a perfect example of this: an incidental detail of an irrelevant episode that is laden with value for the narrator.[27]

Despite the build-up of adjectives and hyperbole that weigh down Ingrao's writing, his basic narrative style is identical to Novelli's. The former's autobiography does not feature the sort of anecdotes that the latter takes pleasure in – Unity Festival celebrations with comrades preparing stuffed pasta, the distribution of the party newspaper every Sunday, games between party workers and cadres etc. Ingrao's antiquarian passion for 'the small' and 'the limited' is instead channelled into the magical territory of his youth. In this space, which seems extraordinary when viewed through the lens of his recollections, the Roman barracks with bedbugs dropping down from the ceiling, the coarse mattresses and the dormitory full of nude male bodies make up the 'illustrated diary of his youth', the comfortable nest where he finds himself and the lost meaning of his life.

This nostalgia for lost youth, looked back on with the indulgence of an antiquarian self-historian, manifests in the temporal articulation of the text. Taking 1948 – a terrible year for Italian communists, who were defeated in the first republican elections and suffered an (unsuccessful) attack on their secretary, Palmiro Togliatti – as a point of reference, a cursory examination of the texts considered here yields some interesting results. Armando Cossutta spends two chapters out of fourteen – equal to around thirty pages (out of approximately two hundred and sixty) – reaching that moment. Emanuele Macaluso gets there in six out of thirty-one chapters, totalling around fifty pages (out of two hundred and forty). Rossana Rossanda places 1948 in her seventh chapter out of seventeen, approximately one hundred and thirty pages in to the text (out of approximately three hundred and eighty). It takes Pietro Ingrao, meanwhile, twenty-eight chapters out of forty-seven – totalling nearly two hundred out of approximately three hundred and seventy pages – to get around to recounting the attack on Togliatti. I have, of course, excluded Giuseppe Chiarante from this survey, both on account of the different focus of his memories and due to the different course of his political career compared to the other writers.

The weight placed by Ingrao on the story of his youth is clear, and the argument that he is ten years older than the others is not relevant: of significance here is how much space the narrator dedicates, in constructing the plot, to the years furthest from the present in which it recounts its story. The different emphasis placed by the writers on their respective youths indicates their varying degrees of interest in this phase, and the range of methods used to confer legitimacy on their narratives.

A strong emphasis on youth rather than adulthood or old age may, in fact, be employed in an even more radical way, shedding further light on the elements underpinning this strategy of establishing legitimacy.

Luciana Castellina[28] takes the solution adopted by Ingrao to another level, pushing back the timeline of the account further still: the communist leader, born in 1929, focuses exclusively on the years between 1943 and 1948, that is, the period before she joined the PCI in October 1947. The result is a sort of little *Bildungsroman*, the significance of which is established in the foreword written not by Castellina herself, but by her daughter, Luciana Reichlin.

> Fourteen years old in 1943. My mother, a girl, is tottering towards adulthood in a world that suddenly shows itself to be larger and more intricate than the one she has learned about on the cramped, stifling school benches of Fascist Italy. […] As in all coming-of-age stories, the pages tell of a will to shake the confines of an over-familiar environment to be a player in life and no longer just a spectator.[29]

Luciana Castellina's autobiographical account is, therefore, a voyage of discovery of the world, during which she encounters communism among other things; it is certainly not a journey facilitated by communism that brings her into contact with the world. The title, *Discovery of the World*, meanwhile, leaves little room for doubt regarding the significance of the work. Considered in light of the introduction by her daughter – an economist who held various significant posts in Italian and European economics institutions – what emerges is a coming-of-age novel nestled within a family story that is, in turn, an intergenerational success story. It is, in essence, the story of a character who becomes a communist, rather than of a communist who becomes a character. In order words, the narrator is not the bearer of independent – communist – meaning, which informs the life of the character. The communist significance of the character's life, meanwhile, is but one element of a broader, existential meaning, which emerges through the account of the vicissitudes experienced by the character over time. Yet again, then, it is not the narrator that confers meaning on the life of the character, but rather the character that reveals, to the narrator, the meaning to be ascribed to her actions.

Although extensive reference to one's youth tends to coincide with the antiquarian style – as a fondness for one's own distant past equates to a love of mythical youth, forever lost, but to which no specific chronological structure can be assigned[30] – it is not synonymous with the latter. It also features in self-narratives that interpret the events of one's life from a critical perspective. Let us refer once again to Nietzsche.

> He must have the strength, and use it from time to time, to shatter and dissolve something to enable him to live: this he achieves by dragging it to the bar of judgement, interrogating it meticulously and finally condemning it – for that is how matters happen to stand with human affairs: human violence and weakness have always contributed strongly to shaping them.[31]

In this case, the narrative attitude to the past is not one of nostalgic reverence towards the buried treasures of youth; instead, it is that of a critical historian, who casts a judgemental eye over everything that has happened, 'interrogating it meticulously and finally condemning it'. An example of this autobiographical posture can be found in the following passage.

> Every time I thought of sharing some sadness or other with my companion, he reminded me to think about what was objectively necessary, and I had convinced myself that he was right. But even we were wearing each other out with our indefatigable friendship; that friendship would never end, but it caused us unspoken sadness, and first we began to spend our days apart, then to live apart, and finally we severed the legal ties to which we had never attached any importance. I began to wonder whether being the woman that I wanted to be meant that I had lost out somewhere. And then came other doubts. A lot of doubts, as numerous as the changes in the environment around us. Doubts about what we in the PCI were doing. I had none about socialism, and none about USSR, with which I was already disenchanted. But even in 1956 I was thinking over what my party was.[32]

In terms of presentation and content, Rossana Rossanda's account resembles Pietro Ingrao's, in its intertwining of large-scale historical events and smaller personal episodes. Rossanda opens the page from which the above passage is taken with the death of her mother, followed by her waning relationship with her sister and finally the end of her marriage. These personal events, however, are tinged with a specific tone arising from the doubt that clouds all things in this work. Self-doubt, as evident from the above passage, quickly followed by uncertainty over the situation in Spain, where she was sent by the PCI in 1962 to make contact with the anti-Franco opposition. We are then told of her misgivings regarding the PCI and its ability to move with the tide in the Italian political and economic sphere of the 1960s, marked by major national economic growth and the first centre-left government, formed by the Italian Socialist Party (PSI) and the DC.

As mentioned, Rossanda gives over ample space to narrating her youth and the years of the war. And, like Ingrao, she ends her account well before the international crisis suffered by communism, concluding it with her expulsion from the PCI in 1969. Such similarities are superficial, however, as Rossanda's primary interest is not in evoking the elusive beauty of days gone by, but rather in passing judgement on what was done, what could have been done differently and what absolutely should not have been done. Ingrao's antiquarian passion is matched by Rossanda's desire for critical understanding. The former's aestheticization of the past is replaced by the latter's unyielding moral – and political – judgement of it.

Let us turn, now, to the final variant of the existential legitimization strategy applied to the autobiographical account, and our final reference to Nietzsche.

For his commandment reads: what once was capable of magnifying the concept 'man' and of giving it a more beautiful content must be present eternally in order eternally to have this capacity. That the great moments in the struggle of individuals forms a chain, that in them the high points of humanity are linked throughout millennia [...] this is the fundamental thought of the faith in humanity which is expressed in the demand for a *monumental* history.[33]

This monumental quality is already evident in Armando Cossutta's chain of communist secretaries and great union leaders who died or were left seriously disabled as a result of their political engagement, referred to above. It is Emanuele Macaluso, however, who fully realizes the potential of the monumental autobiography. Whereas Cossutta mainly focuses on sacrifices made by great communist leaders, Macaluso concentrates on the heroic deeds of the series of great men that he encountered over the course of his communist militant career. The contents section of his book alone presents a procession of personalities – not limited to PCI secretaries – and the author dedicates a chapter to each, accompanied by a title summarizing its content: 'Palmiro Togliatti: The Reasons behind His Decisions', 'Emilio Sereni: A Dramatic Figure', 'Giancarlo Pajetta, the Intelligence and the Obsession of the PCI', 'Luigi Longo: An Undervalued Secretary', 'Enrico Berlinguer, The Most Beloved Secretary' and so forth.

This approach has certain things in common with that taken by Giuseppe Chiarante, but with one essential difference. In Chiarante's work, the character is subordinate to a narrator who has a tendency towards impersonal scientific enunciation, stepping outside of the autobiographical territory. In Macaluso's case, on the contrary, the character is firmly rooted in the account, even if the self-narrative does not hinge exclusively on what the minor and major events of the story mean to that character, as in Ingrao's text. Macaluso has more in common with the figure of Ishmael, to whom I referred previously: he is a witness – who is, however, neither silent nor detached – to a past greatness that, though it existed long ago, must continue to be remembered. Below is an excerpt from his section on Giancarlo Pajetta – one of the PCI's most prestigious members, who experienced exile in France, Fascist jails and the partisan struggle.

> Pajetta was a great help to me in getting to know the PCI, at the centre and in the federations. His harsh judgements of people and things, separated from his ironic quips, congeniality and obvious idiosyncrasies, got to the heart of things. Giancarlo had an extremely sharp mind, extensive cultural knowledge, an extraordinary critical capacity in relation to what he read, saw or heard: and his response was often a piercing but insightful quip. An accomplished and sarcastic speaker, the crowds loved him. He was the most listened to and feared voice of the 1950s and beyond.[34]

The centrality of character over narrator is evident here again, but manifests in an entirely different form compared to the previous example. Here, the narrative focus shifts from the character that coincides with the narrator to other characters encountered by the former, of whom he provides personal portraits and political assessments. Taken together, they form a 'chain' of the sort described by Nietzsche, encapsulating the 'high points' of communist humanity, whose exploits are recounted by Macaluso as though to provide a warning to contemporaries. If the main feature of Ingrao's autobiography is the aestheticization of his past, then, and Rossanda's focus is on passing critical judgement without compromise, it seems that Macaluso's interest is primarily pedagogical in nature. Indeed, the fundamental trait of the monumental history is the idea that 'the great which once existed was at least possible once and will again be possible sometime'.[35] The portraits presented by Macaluso are not mere funereal effigies, then, but instead serve as examples that remain relevant, because they encourage the reader to emulate them – the most primitive, yet effective form of pedagogy – so that the great communist political spirit can once again inspire the contemporary political scene.

This discussion of Emanuele Macaluso's memoirs brings my examination of communist autobiography in the post-communist era to a close. The most significant distinction between this later autobiographical space and that of the original autobiographies is not the different cultural capital at the disposal of the writer, or the specific audience to whom the autobiographies are addressed (that is, no longer the party, but a largely well-educated general public). The key shift lies, instead, in the loss of legitimacy previously enjoyed by the communist narrator, resulting in that figure no longer being able to produce self-narratives that rely on communism for their horizon of significance. The result of this delegitimization is the breakdown of the communist autobiographical space. This manifests, on the one hand, in an exodus to a domain of enunciation that borders the autobiographical space, but that is separate to it: this is the case with Giuseppe Chiarante's non-autobiographical autobiography. On the other, it sees the narrative figure being drawn to the sphere of action inhabited by the character, resulting variously in the antiquarian, critical and monumental autobiographical strategies. As noted previously, the ultimate effect of this is the production of a collection of autobiographies of communists, but no communist autobiographies in the original sense of the term.

The question, of course, is not whether these self-narratives are worse or better than the writings of militants who opted to become PCI members after the Second World War. From a literary perspective, my strong preference is for the latter, for the unbiased and often unexpected use of language, compared to the anodyne editorial perfection of the former. Such an opinion is, of course, disputable, but the reasons behind it seem less open to debate. Whereas the autobiographies of militants are living texts, struggling to address the paradoxical injunction that made their existence possible, the later memoirs of more or less well-known communists, despite their cultural status, read as elegies[36] to a time that is long past and, when considered together, form a sort of Spoon River of Italian communism.

Late feminist autobiographies: The journey towards legitimacy and normality

The feminist autobiographical universe that emerged in the wake of the season of social movements – that is, the 1970s – is entirely different to its communist counterpart. The communists had lost their political battle, and wrote to make sense of that defeat and celebrate the greatness of their efforts. The feminists, on the other hand, found themselves on the right side of history. Certainly, one could argue that they had not engendered the revolution hoped for in the 1970s. Their movement, however, enjoyed great public esteem, and they did not face the sort of major spectres battled by the communists: Stalinism, the twentieth century as a period of unregulated clashes between equal but opposite totalitarian systems in the form of communism and Nazism etc.

It is not, therefore, surprising that feminists who penned their autobiographies at decades' remove from the height of the movement's activism did not obsess over the legitimacy of what they were writing. Late feminist self-enunciation is not marked by a crisis of narrator similar to that experienced by the communist narrator figure. In some ways, feminists faced the opposite quandary: of what significance was the public legitimacy that they had undeniably achieved to their personal lives? Or, to put it more simply still, how best to manage their public victory? This overarching question then triggers others: was it truly a victory? And if so, what was won? And what was lost to that victory?

If we accept that this is the main point around which the feminist autobiographies discussed in this chapter pivot, there is little point in expecting the sort of discursive experimentation described in the previous chapter. Early neo-feminist self-enunciation does not focus on the issue of managing feminist success. Instead, it is concerned with talking about the self in alternative terms, from a political perspective, compared to male discourse. As such, the new feminist success stories certainly feature familiar self-narrative strategies and a series of discursive forms that we encountered previously but, in the main, such similarities are merely superficial.

Elements that resurface from the past no longer carry the same meaning that they held in the earlier context. The discursive traits that had seemed to represent the only possible route for feminist self-enunciation are no longer employed as tools in the clash against the male power of words. Instead, they emerge as objects of remembrance. In a certain sense, it is as though these autobiographies served as narrative machines by way of which to pursue the normalization of that which had originally prided itself on its abnormality. They are devices used to legitimize something that was initially illegitimate and that had consciously resisted legitimacy, because legitimacy was seen as synonymous with male social power. At their roots, these self-narratives hinge on this contradiction – which, however, no longer takes the form of the paradoxical injunction employed creatively in the past – and seek, in some way, to rectify it.

The most accomplished document, in my opinion, which features the shifts mentioned above, is *Autobiography of a Generation* by Luisa Passerini,[37] a scholar who enjoys international acclaim for her work on oral history and, more recently, on the concept of Europe and affective historiography.[38] Odd and even chapters in the book serve different functions. The latter are essays presenting the results of the historian's research, in the 1980s, into the generation of 1968, conducted through interviews with protagonists of the movement and life stories. The former, meanwhile, are diary excerpts. These chapters revisit the diary kept by the author between 1983 and 1987, combined with a series of autobiographical writings mainly published during the 1970s in new-left and Italian feminist publications, including *Sottosopra*.[39] From this perspective, if the main focus of this work, as alluded to in the title, is 1968 and its protagonists, the use of the diary form, together with the materials incorporated into the text, enable its unquestionable classification as a feminist memoir. Even the fact that the original edition of *Autobiography of a Generation* was published in 1988 – distinguishing it from the other works examined here, all of which were written after the close of the twentieth century – represents not a problem, but an opportunity. Indeed, a comparison between the first and latest Italian editions facilitates a clearer identification of the transformations experienced by late feminist enunciation.[40]

Passerini herself provides the starting point for the analysis, on the first page of the diary section of the work; this is the only section dealt with here, as the historian's interpretation of the generation of 1968 is not of direct relevance to my work.

> January. I conducted my first interviews with the protagonists of '68. The interviews plunge me into my own past: as I listen, the film of what I was doing at the time unreels. Memory redoubled this way is hard to bear; it seems to me that until now no one has wanted to take on this burden, sometimes not even those who tell their stories. The mirror I see my image reflected in is opaque.[41]

In a January that seems not to belong to any specific year, but instead to a sort of metaphysical winter, Luisa Passerini muses thoughtfully on the meaning of her ongoing research. Or rather, she loses herself in the hall of mirrors that she herself is constructing. 'The mirror I see my image reflected in is opaque,' she declares, as her opening statement in the chapter entitled Mirrors. In effect, the scholar, as narrator, recounts the story of herself as a character listening to other characters who are their own narrators. Furthermore, the stories of those other characters are also her own story, because the generation she is researching – that of 1968 – is her own. As such, she narrates the story of characters who narrate her own narrative. The vertiginous quality of this reflexivity seems inevitable, and the image of the mirrors is extremely apt. The text operates as a *mise en abyme*, wherein the work duplicates itself, becoming the account of an account – or rather the account of many accounts – in which the characters are self-narrators and the self-narrator is the only true character.[42]

This explains the absence of dates in the diary entries that the scholar alternates with theoretical chapters. The months, without years and without days, specified at the beginning of her autobiographical writings – with the exception of a very small number of significant dates, such as 25 December – do not, in fact, form a chronological account. Rather, they are manifestations of a purely interior calendar, wherein the past loses its substance to be arranged within the absolute present – a reversal of the 'absolute past' of the epic – of the consciousness that evokes it. And so diary excerpts from the 1970s and 1980s happily coexist, blending into one another with no discernible borders. The mirrors to which Luisa Passerini refers, then, are clearly the speakers who tell their stories. As such, they are little more than reflections that offer an image of the narrator that is not entirely satisfactory – Passerini's mirror is 'opaque' – because the narrator has had to duplicate herself to produce her character and those that surround the latter, and this subtle distance between the two autobiographical figures is a constant source of disturbance. Eliminating the chronological element, then, serves to bridge the gap between story and discourse, reducing characters and events to a condition of absolute narratability – that is, to their purely intrinsic and, crucially, timeless, significance.

These narrative decisions are quite familiar. Luisa Passerini's chosen method of self-enunciation in *Autobiography of a Generation* is similar to that adopted by Carla Lonzi in *Diario di una femminista*. It is an example of the paranoid self-narrative strategy, in which the character is entirely subordinate to the narrator and its pursuit of meaning within the story. Carla Lonzi recounts the story of herself and her relationships with her feminist group, made up of women who write about themselves and exchange autobiographical artefacts, while Luisa Passerini narrates the story of herself listening to the protagonists of the generation of 1968 narrating their stories. The manner in which these two texts double back on themselves is also the same: both recount accounts that recount themselves. As noted by Todorov, to whom I referred extensively in the previous chapter, the paranoid approach is that favoured by critics, philosophers and researchers. In this sense, Passerini's choice of paranoid discourse is, to some extent, inevitable, given her profession as a historian.

As noted before, however, the repetition of something – in this case a form of self-enunciation – never produces the same result twice. And indeed, the similarities in form between Carla Lonzi and Luisa Passerini's texts are significantly less important than the divergence in substance that separates the two works. The former, of course, pursued a paranoid strategy to challenge the legitimate male power of words. Everything was said in order to be oneself and free oneself from the discursive monopoly enjoyed by men over women.

If adopting such an approach represented an existential decision for Carla Lonzi, for Luisa Passerini it is a methodological choice. Her diary is a tool to facilitate historiographical comprehension. This is not to say, naturally, that it is devoid of existential dimensions and political considerations. Rather, it implies that the latter are subordinate to the epistemological horizon that is of primary concern to the historian. Viewed through a Goffmanian lens, the relationship between the autobiographical and historiographical chapters is characterized by a set of negotiations that produce the role distance at the heart of Luisa Passerini's textual identity: she is a historian, certainly, but a feminist historian who combines the rigour of a scientist with the passion of a woman. It is the former, however, that makes the latter possible, and not the contrary.[43]

Carla Lonzi's diary, then, is a 'wild' work, whereas Luisa Passerini's is a historical text, the legitimacy of which is rooted precisely in this classification. The clearest example of the distance between the two texts lies in their treatment of the dream-like material, and the presence of the figure of the psychoanalyst therein. Let us begin with Luisa Passerini.

> I talk to G. again about the old dream about 'zoerrosis', loss of life, to tell him that such a malady has struck my heroic identity, currently moribund. G. responds that in the past that identity itself represented a loss of life. Connections between the heroic part and rigid notions of reason on one side, of passion on the other. 'But I am not capable of putting on the red dress of passion.' 'Who says? In the dream it suits you perfectly.'[44]

G. is the author's psychoanalyst in the account, to whom she confides her anxieties regarding the possibility of finishing the book in which he himself appears as a character. It is impossible to know much of his personality: his existence consists entirely of commenting on the historian's dreams and worries, requesting payment and increasing the fees for her sessions.

In Carla Lonzi's diary, meanwhile, there is no trace of a psychoanalyst. One appears in a rather negative form in a dream, and is banished without delay.

> I am in a hotel: two couples engage in group psychotherapy. There is a psychoanalyst among them, I actually think of asking him to explain my dreams; but then I don't. One of the women near me is writing, I ask if she's writing a dream. She says yes, she does so every so often, then she starts knitting. They are all mysterious, there is a strange understanding among them, one gently licks the other's toe.[45]

Carla Lonzi too uses the narrative mechanism of duplication: she wants to ask the psychoanalyst who appears in her dream to interpret her dreams – in a paradoxical circularity – but she decides not to, without explaining why. Also because the figure tasked with receiving dreams is a woman, who does not listen to them – like Passerini's psychoanalyst – but rather transcribes them. Though the text is not extremely clear, the dream expert is placed in the subordinate position of licking the woman's toes.

And so, while psychoanalytical authority is the subject of surreal mockery in Carla Lonzi's text, Luisa Passerini embraces it fully, with the exception of normal moments of tension that are part of the dynamics of transference and countertransference. Likewise, dream-like materials emerge in very different forms in the two works. In *Taci, anzi parla* they are mainly transcribed without interpretation. They are textual islands that allude to a different method of self-enunciation – the schizophrenic approach discussed previously. In *Autobiography of a Generation*, however, dreams are not presented as transcripts;

instead, they are integrated into the narrator's interpretation or the often-oracular observations delivered by G.

Such distance is also evident in the conclusions of the two works. The last words written by Carla Lonzi prior to the dream that effectively ends the text are strikingly brief compared to her usual plethoric writing style: 'I'm free.'[46] Luisa Passerini's concluding passage, however, is very different.

> The ego breathes a sigh of relief and regret simultaneously, its adventure is over too. It behaved with courage, accepting sorrow and joy, the cowardly part and not just the rebellious part of this undertaking. The id is quietly, sly, it sends little riddle-dreams, hints at unforeseen solutions. All together, like a merry group of actors, we are reasonably well disposed to accept what will come, the next piece of writing, for as long as we can.[47]

Carla Lonzi has succeeded in freeing herself and, in so doing, has managed to reconcile with her lover and her friend Piera. *She freed herself and therefore she reconciled herself.* Luisa Passerini seems to express the same ultimate feeling of relief, but she walks the path between freedom and reconciliation in reverse. *She reconciled herself, and in so doing, she freed herself.* It is no surprise, then, that the conclusion of Carla Lonzi's work is open-ended, and that the ultimate attempt at reconciliation with herself takes the form of a funeral dream: being oneself is only possible in death, but this final condition can only be experienced as a fantasy, that is, as a dream. What will the Carla Lonzi from the diary do after writing her last page? Nobody knows. Luisa Passerini, on the contrary, is very clear as regards her future. She will 'accept what will come', or, more specifically, 'the next piece of writing'. As she said herself a few pages earlier: 'This book is finished. I can begin once more to do serious things, like methodological essays with footnotes and copious bibliographies. I am content to return to my trade, I have various projects in mind.'

Ultimately, Carla Lonzi finds freedom in life, whereas Luisa Passerini discovers the theatre of life or life as theatre – she herself is nothing more than a 'merry group of actors'. Life experienced as the theatre of life is certainly one of many *mise en abyme* featured in her work; it also, however, represents the discovery that allows her to reconcile herself with the social world that, deep down, is merely a large stage on which everyone is required to perform.[48] Only by way of this insight, acquired without sadness, is the author finally free and definitively able to be herself. The distance between these two conclusions reflects the long journey travelled by the feminist autobiography from the field of illegitimacy to that of legitimacy.[49]

It is possible, however, to venture further along this path. The year 2003 saw the publication of *Baby Boomers*, a book featuring the autobiographies of four Italian feminists: Serena Sapegno, Annamaria Tagliavini, Roberta Mazzanti and, the most famous of all, Rosi Braidotti.[50] The work's subtitle is rather ambitious: *Vite parallele dagli anni Cinquanta ai cinquant'anni (Parallel Lives from the '50s into our 50s)*.[51] The Plutarch reference is not only obvious but also justified: just as the lives of the Greek and Latin figures presented by the ancient writer are only comprehensible by way of the element that links them, so too must these four autobiographies be read together for their true significance to emerge. The choice of subtitle also arguably alludes to another objective pursued by the Greek writer in his biographical accounts: to present the reader with paradigms of virtue and vice to be honoured or deplored.[52] *Baby Boomers*, obviously, does not feature models of vice, but focuses instead on feminist virtue, though the authors do not openly declare this as an intention.

What these writers do clearly affirm is the underlying unity of their four autobiographies.

> With *Baby Boomers*, instead, we wanted to experiment with a hybrid of private and collective writing. We met every two months, more or less, to discuss the broad strokes of our accounts; then everyone returned to their writing, individually but interwoven with the others' work, thanks to regular e-mail exchanges. Wonderful dinners, laughs and discussions were ingredients that proved just as important as the processes of remembering and writing.[53]

At first glance, the sociable evening meetings described in this passage may seem like a throwback to the small feminist groups of the past, where women talked and told their stories. Yet again, however, the key issue is the discursive treatment of this content. Suffice to recall one of the feminist collective transcripts featured in *Sottosopra* and presented in the previous chapter. No literary form, except the bare minimum required for the rambling series of contributions to be legible. Voices linked only to a name, expressing themselves without the guardianship of a narrator.

In *Baby Boomers*, the situation is reversed. We do not hear the four protagonists' voices. Their exchanges are not reported directly, but are instead referred to by the narrator. As such, their dialogues are transformed into 'narratized speech': the evening conversations become an event that can be recounted, presented in a form that guarantees the maximum distance between the character – and her words – and the surface level of the text, administered by the narrator.[54] We are thus presented with the repetition of a repetition. The four authors' dinners are a repetition of the collective activities of feminists in the seventies, and the narrator repeats that repetition by presenting it as an event rather than a dialogue with first-person speech by the characters. The pathos of the absolutely personal voice that characterized the reports of collective meetings in *Sottosopra* is lost forever. The setting seems the same, but the women's voices have been tamed by the narrator as agent of order.

This discursive operation appears similar to that performed by Luisa Passerini in relation to her dreams and psychoanalysis. Ultimately, the best approach to autobiographical normalization is to entrust the account to a narrator who enjoys a position of absolute public legitimacy, unlike in the communist sphere. Indeed, though the authors' claim to have been inspired by *Autobiography of a Generation* may be true,[55] they have, in any case, gone significantly beyond that model. While the anguish of the past continues to haunt the pages of Luisa Passerini's diary, here, the operation of distancing oneself from one's political youth is much more radical. Before even considering the texts, an examination of the covers of the two books – the 2008 Italian edition, in Passerini's case – provide an interesting insight.

Autoritratto di gruppo features a black-and-white photo by Ted Streshisky of a young couple smoking – probably under the influence of LSD – at the Merry Pranksters' Acid Test Graduation.[56] In the foreground, a girl with hair down to her shoulders smiles in the direction of the camera. The image is authentic – in the sense that it portrays an event that actually occurred – but its content is filtered through the nostalgia of black and white, which softens the descriptive acuity of the image in favour of its evocative potential. In essence, the cover sums up Luisa Passerini's narrative agenda: a melancholic reconstruction of the past, the referential content of which is mediated through an oftentimes anguished memory.[57] Very different design decisions have been applied to *Baby Boomers*. The cover is divided into four rectangular sections that occupy equal space below the title. Each features one of the authors' faces. Here, too, the images present real content: the face of each of the four women, presumably captured before they turn fifty, as referred to in the subtitle. The key difference lies in the treatment of the image.

Instead of the evocative black and white, we have a Warhol-style cover. Rather than a realistic backdrop, each portrait is presented against a single block of colour, which varies from one face to the next, except in Roberta Mazzanti's case, where the ochre is accompanied by aquamarine. It is a curious choice: the women's pictures ought to allude to the autobiographical stories contained in the book, but what stands out most is the de-historicization of the faces. One might be forgiven for thinking that the objective of this decision is to achieve an 'epiphany of the face',[58] with the abstract background serving to offer future readers a face-to-face encounter with the authors. This is not so. The four women's features are given the same pop-art treatment as their faces. Broad strokes of colour outline their lips, hair, eyebrows and chins, producing an overall effect reminiscent of Warhol's Marilyn Monroe. The resulting images appear entirely two-dimensional, more akin to icons than photographic portraits.

The significance of such a design choice is not entirely clear. On the one hand, it suggests that the old concept of the feminist collective, alluded to in the introduction, can easily be translated into such a seriation – a thing is repeated, but it differs with each repetition. Certainly, given Rosi Braidotti's inclusion among the authors, such an interpretation would seem consistent, to some extent, with her concept of nomadic subjectivity. On the other hand, the decision to be portrayed as two-dimensional icons, beyond any religious reference, indicates a prioritization of mere surface considerations to the detriment of depth.[59] We are a long way here, from the pathos of distance characterizing Passerini's writing and her sense of loss of the past, the significance of which she recovers through the patient practice of deciphering.

Should we conclude, then, that the four *Baby Boomers* are – or rather, want to be – pop-art icons? Their joint introduction leads one to suspect that this is the case. I provide their self-introduction here below, as it is rather interesting.

We are the '50 year-old girls' described by Marina Piazza, protagonists of that profound change brought about by the so-called women's revolution, the only twentieth-century revolution that, according to Eric Hobsbawm, was successful and victimless. We are part of a generation that experienced the transition, at great speed, from a pre-modern and pre-industrial past to a future of technological revolutions, the new economy and globalization.[60]

The text is perfectly consistent with the expectations raised by the cover, or at least this is my impression. It is only thanks to the lack of depth deliberately signposted by the cover design that the authors can adopt the label of '50 year-old girls'. This description paints them as both young and middle-aged at once, a combination more commonly reserved for the realm of advertising. Likewise, we discover that the authors have not travelled from the 'pre-modern' and 'pre-industrial' past into the present – as logic would suggest – but instead have arrived directly in the future. As well as a resistance of depth – and its temporal articulation in the form of past, present and future – there is another element at play here that is rather typical of twentieth-century Italian culture, specifically a fixation with the historical backwardness of the country, which gives rise to a celebration of the future. It is no coincidence that Italy's twentieth-century avant-garde movement took the form of futurism.

In this same vein, the future inhabited by our authors is characterized by 'technological revolutions, the new economy and globalization'. These women, then, have lived through a revolution – the feminist revolution, to be precise – only to find themselves faced with numerous others, as part of a frenetic, ceaseless life. This quote – together the subsequent paragraphs that I have omitted here – would not be out of place in a self-marketing text, as part of a personal brand-building exercise. In short, the reader should infer that these are excellent lives – as already suggested by the Plutarch reference – the extraordinary nature of which is verified by the enthusiasm with which the protagonists of these inimitable existences look to the future.[61]

One might, of course, argue that such an inference cannot reasonably be drawn simply by glancing at the cover of a book and reading its introduction. To assess the accuracy of such a conjecture, then, let us delve into the text. For reasons of brevity, I will focus solely on the autobiography of Rosi Braidotti, the most famous author featured in the book. The most interesting section of her autobiography is not the account of her Friulian origins – Braidotti was born in Latisana, in the province of Udine, in the North-West of Italy – but rather her description of her experience as an immigrant. Indeed, the philosopher, whose research focuses on nomadism, left Italy for Australia with her family in 1970. There, she stood out for her surprising academic achievements. She ranked fifth in the state exams – out of thousands of students – despite barely having any English. This drew interest from the press, and she was lauded as an 'exemplary emigrant'. She then received 'many offers to various Australian universities' and opted for a scholarship to study at the country's most prestigious university in Canberra.[62] There, she was one of the 'very first' European immigrants to become a member of the country's academic elite, to the amazement of the professors, one of whom commented, condescendingly: 'My God! [In English in the original edition] But she's come from one of the country's worst secondary schools.' The passage that immediately follows this observation is worth examining in more detail.

> Landing in Canberra in 1973, I had the distinct feeling that I had finally arrived in Australia. And so I became staunchly feminist. Despite continuing to fight for my cultural identity, working to educate the children of local Italian emigrants, my political horizon broadened and was updated. [...] I decided that the time had come to focus on myself.[63]

Rosi Braidotti offers no reaction whatsoever to the welcome she received from the Canberra academic world, no sarcastic response to its implicit racist classism. Her assertion that she felt she had truly 'arrived' in Australia is devoid of any subtext: it is a mere observation, a form of protocol statement. What she does, instead, is become a feminist. The correlation between arriving in Canberra as a brilliant Italian scholar and becoming a feminist is not clear, except insofar as it relates to Italian emigration to Australia.

> When I returned to 'Little Italy' in Melbourne for the holidays, I had the opportunity to gauge the ground gained and the distance that was opening up between me and 'them'. But by now I had made my choice: my political field was feminism and my existence as a woman in the world: I had become a female intellectual, who expressed herself in English by choice.[64]

Though it may be narratively coherent, this argument makes no logical sense: being an immigrant and a feminist need not be mutually exclusive. For Rosi Braidotti, however, her decision to be a feminist means turning her back on her experience of immigration – represented by Melbourne's 'Little Italy'.[65] On the one hand, choosing feminism is simply a consequence of the colonial violence imposed by the colonized subject on itself: no longer wishing to express herself as an immigrant, Rosi Braidotti resolves to speak as a feminist, in English. From this perspective, the philosophy of nomadism is the ultimate, euphemizing result of this violent transaction that the Italian philosopher engages in with herself, whereby the sufferings of the migrant – and the double absence of the latter[66] – are replaced with the joys of the nomad. On the other hand, from reading these pages, Braidotti's feminism seems to be the most (supposedly) illegitimate of the legitimate products of the English-speaking academic sphere: an innocent transgression that may be consummated with the absolute approval of one's professional audience. Is this an exaggeration? I think not.

> A fundamental element of my feminism has always been a passion for doing and finding a link between theory and practice. The transition to institutions provided a perfect outlet for this impulse, and I stayed there until the end of the 1980s, November 1987 to be precise. [...] At the age of thirty-three, following a

lengthy selection process, I was awarded a Women's Studies professorship with the Utrecht Humanities Department. Since then, I have been engaged in the challenge of trying to mould the institutional structures to align with my vision of nomadic, multicultural, efficient and outward-looking feminism. [...] Doing this work, and therefore becoming a professional feminist, I have learned many things.[67]

For reasons of brevity, I have omitted the long list of academic programmes launched by the philosopher. Here, too, the superficial linearity of the self-narrative glosses over a series of logical inconsistencies. In what way does a university position provide the 'perfect outlet' for combining theory and practice? The more traditional, perhaps slightly outdated, image of an impulse as primal energy that seeks freedom from its shackles is replaced with that of an impulse towards institutions, and so an institutional impulse, I would say, which is such because it emerges already institutionalized. And indeed, meritocratic discourse, with its profoundly ideological dimensions, is never criticized but, instead, is always the object of appreciation, because it is a tool of self-appreciation: Rosi Braidotti, in fact, specifies that the selection process that led to her employment at Utrecht was 'lengthy'.[68]

It is no surprise, then, that she refers to her feminism as 'efficient'. How so? Is it because it helps the organizations run better and increases productivity? The implicit response would seem to be affirmative, as we are told, at the end of the passage, that Rosi Braidotti has become a 'professional feminist', something that implies that it is not, perhaps, the institutions that have bent to the will of feminism, but rather the other way round. Of course, just as there are professional communists – many of whom we encountered in the previous paragraph – so too can there be professional feminists. Such a status merely involves administrative activities that have little to do with revolutionary pursuits. The point, then, is not to refrain from celebrating one's successes, but rather to grasp their authentic nature, particularly in the context of sincere self-narratives.

Here too, we witness the descent of autobiographical writing into the realm of business jargon. A struggle to adapt the self-discourse is a consequence of the precarious status of the autobiographies in this volume. The purpose of these autobiographical performances, in fact, is to lay claim to a contradictory legitimate illegitimacy – a distant shadow of the pragmatic paradox underpinning feminist self-enunciation of the 1970s. This issue presents itself in full force at another point in Braidotti's account.

> There were Sapphic nights, inundated with pleasure, when we both experienced divine metamorphoses: her marine body sought to transform me into pure sex, the coveted and adored object of her overwhelming desire. Her caresses set chain reactions in motion deep down inside of me, reawakening primitive mechanisms and unknown sensations. An elementary passion, whereby all our lips spoke with the unspeakable slowness of internal accelerations that halt the breath and illuminate body and mind in a single stroke. She made me tremble

right down to within my spinal cord, before bounding forth like a dolphin, crazed with joy in the most obscure channels of my brain.[69]

The page proceeds to roll out further sea- and water-based metaphors: Braidotti's 'sluice gates' burst open and the philosopher 'moored gratefully in the glow of an immense happiness, ancient as the sea, active as the mouths of volcanoes'. The best way to analyse this sex scene is through comparison with another.

> She pushed on my hips, an order that thrust me in. I entered her. Not only my prick, but the whole of me entered her, into her guts, into her darkness, eyes wide open, seeing nothing. My whole body had gone inside her. I went in with her thrusts and stayed still. While I got used to the quiet and the pulsing of my blood in my ears and nose, she pushed me out a little, then in again. She did it again and again, holding me with force and moving me to the rhythm of the surf. She wiggled her breasts beneath my hands and intensified the pushing. I went in up to my groin and came out almost entirely. My body was her gearstick.

This quote is taken from Erri de Luca's *The Day before Happiness,* and describes a sexual encounter between a girl with supernatural powers and an orphan. Significantly, it is the text that won the Bad Sex in Fiction Award 2016,[70] a contest run by the *Literary Review* since 1993 to honour 'the year's most outstandingly awful scene in an otherwise good novel'.[71] The pelagic context is the same, except here, instead of dolphins, marine glow and the mouths of volcanoes – not necessarily by the sea, though the text alludes to a maritime setting – we have the surf. In place of De Luca's experience of release, meanwhile, Braidotti offers us an image of refilling, in the form of the inundation of pleasure to which she surrenders.

As the *Literary Review* editors note, it is difficult to write a good sex scene. The issue lies not with recounting what happened in bed or elsewhere, but rather with employing a style characterized by 'euphemism, confusion about what's actually going on, clumsy use of language, metaphor, and hyperbole'.[72] To this list, I would also add unintended comedy – the dolphins 'crazed with joy', leaping around in one's brain, or reducing oneself to a mere 'gearstick' – and trite images, such as the marine glow or the obscurity of sex.

Braidotti's linguistic missteps in the context of sex are particularly striking given the philosophical centrality that she places on desire and the body, and her repeated claims that writing is her home, her chosen space. Such stumbles seem to me, however, to be the price paid by the writer for her consecration. If Ingrao's emphatic writing is a tribute by old age to youth, where everything is bigger and more beautiful, Rosi Braidotti's is the consideration exchanged for becoming the pop-art icon of her cover.

The story of her existential hyperbole becomes an account built on hyperbole, wherein everything is described in excessive terms: being an exemplary immigrant, selection through a very difficult process, or attending Australia's worst secondary school. It is natural, then, that such hyperbole also extends to the sexual sphere. And as this is the story of an extraordinary life, it stands to reason that it should include accounts of excellent sex. Unfortunately, hyperbole and grandiose metaphors represent the most pedestrian and clumsy means employed to describe the intimacy of sex and the closeness of bodies.

Among the exaggerations mobilized to construct a pop-art style aggrandizement of the self is the relationship between Braidotti and psychoanalysis. We noted previously that Luisa Passerini's text features G., her psychoanalyst, thus endorsing the legitimacy of the practice. Her relationship with G. remains a source of anxiety, however, arising from the cost of the sessions and the therapist's financial greed. Psychoanalysis is treated entirely differently in Rosi Braidotti's autobiography.

> Psychoanalysis has had an impact on our lives both in intellectual and affective terms. Many of us have undertaken pilgrimage-like expeditions to Bergasse in Vienna and Hampstead in London, to pay tribute to Freud. I believe that he had a heart as big as his head, and a soul riddled with holes, through which the wind of history whistled, in a momentous encounter with the sidereal storms of the unconscious.[73]

The writing style here echoes that used in the previous sex scene. It features the same emphatic tone, and the same inaccuracies in its description of the subject. It is less jarring, here, because the subject is not sex. The image of Freud in whose soul 'the wind whistles, the storm rages' – a reference to the Italian partisan song *Fischia il vento*, written by Felice Cascione to the music of the Russian popular song Katyusha – is, nevertheless, no better than that of the dolphins, inebriated with joy, prancing around in the author's brain. Over the course of the following pages, Rosi Braidotti piles exaggeration on top of exaggeration, informing us that: (a) she is engaged in a 'Pascalian wager' with respect to her 'psychoanalytical fate'; (b) she visited a Parisian psychoanalyst three times a week for seven years, from 1981 to 1988; (c) the initial cost was 50 francs per session and by the end she was paying 200 francs a session.[74] If we still had any doubt as to the extraordinary nature – including in financial terms – of this experience, the author reserves the following appeal for her psychoanalyst:

> Oh Great Unknown One! I beg you, do not amputate my suffering as though it were an external cancer, easy to access, because such anguish artfully enshrines the essence of me. [...] And so what do I ask of you? To teach me to find methods and times befitting my intensity, so that I may better live it and manage it.[75]

Here we have ventured into territory far beyond the placement of feminism and its characteristic features – including an interest in the unconscious and psychoanalysis – within a horizon of normality, as performed by Luisa Passerini in her *Autobiography of a Generation*. The Piedmontese historian employed duplication techniques and mirror games within an epistemological-style framework – knowing history to know oneself and knowing oneself to know history – thus removing the feminist paranoid self-enunciation strategy from its politically radical origins to become a critical tool for understanding the world.

Rosi Braidotti, however, no longer feels the need to justify her self-narrative in epistemological terms. All of the complexity and intellectual endeavours engaged in by Passerini are let fall by the wayside, enabling her autobiography to become an unapologetic celebration of herself and her story. The text is a hall of mirrors that reflect and distort the image of the writer. Her appeal to the psychoanalyst – or to psychoanalysis in general – can be summarized as follows: Braidotti invokes a subject without a name – the 'Great Unknown One' – whose existence is defined by absence: her psychoanalyst has made the unconscious (the void at the heart of our existence as human beings) her profession and a means of making money. The gap created by this system of absences, each reflecting the other, is filled by the gigantic figure of the author herself, who commands a degree of magnitude equal to her own – though Braidotti prefers to speak of 'intensity' and not of magnitude.

Do the accounts offered by Braidotti and her co-authors represent the only possible path for late feminist autobiographies? In fact, the journey towards legitimacy need not take the form of a triumphant parade of self-celebration. For other feminists – perhaps because they lack the charisma of office afforded by an academic career – normalization of feminism is presented in much more darker terms, and reconciliation with the world is achieved at the cost of painful internal wounds.

> For me, always inclined to submit beyond all measure, it was the collapse. The collapse of an entire world. Because the woman who had taken her life in the French capital, our friend Adriana to whom we went to say our final goodbyes, had introduced me completely – me, who had come from Palermo – to a strongly politicised North. […] Those oft-reminisced-over 1970s were split in two for me, from that moment: the time up until that dramatic death, and the time after it. But if that had been all, it would have simply been my personal affair. What took it beyond the limits of the private sphere, I believe, is that a relationship like ours could only exist in that period in which the 'personal' and 'political' were so closely linked.[76]

This quote is taken from the work of Maria Schiavo, a rather complicated figure in intellectual and political terms. She was involved in the neo-feminist movement, cultivating a political consciousness from the perspective of her own lesbian experience. She was also an essayist and fiction writer.[77] Unlike Passerini and Braidotti, she did not have an academic career. The lack of any specific institutional shield is acutely evident in the opening pages of her autobiography. Maria Schiavo faces a problem that neither Luisa Passerini nor the four feminists who contributed to *Baby Boomers* had to address. Why write about her life?

Luisa Passerini does not need to justify herself because hers is a history book, albeit an eccentric one, which weaves her personal story with more traditional historiographical writing. The scientific nature of her work, then, makes such a question redundant: the diary is where it is – in odd chapters – because it serves the scientific pursuit undertaken by the historian. Rosi Braidotti and her co-authors raise the question explicitly – 'why write about your existence, particularly as a group of four?' – without resolving the matter. They simply assure us that they will not commit the sin of 'modesty', and that the interesting aspect of their work is that it was written as a group of four.[78] The number of self-narrators makes justification superfluous and provides legitimacy to the autobiographical activity, as though by dint of the age-old notion of *consensus gentium*, whereby if enough people believe or do something, it is true, right or legitimate.

Maria Schiavo, however, not only poses the question, but also seeks to respond to it, in a linear fashion and according to the criteria imposed by neo-feminism. Precisely because the personal is political, the self-narrative is never entirely private, but is, instead, of general interest. As such, her autobiography is arguably of universal value, justifying its introduction to a wider audience. Such a pretext for legitimacy is obviously open to discussion, but her logic is linear and irreproachable.

The content of the self-narrative granted legitimacy in this way is essentially funereal in nature, and is, therefore, closer in style to the communist narratives than the feminist texts examined above. The account opens with a bereavement: the death of her beloved friend Adriana, of whom a passionate and painful portrait is provided. Maria Schiavo travelled to Turin – from Palermo – to be closer to the woman she loves who, however, lives in Paris. Meeting Adriana at school – both women were teachers – marked her initiation into political activism, in a sphere that went beyond the traditional working-class context and its demands. Adriana is at once ascetic and extraordinarily full of life. She eats very little, consuming food almost exclusively to meet her physiological needs, and detests restaurants. She is wary of books and hardcopy culture, but is irresistibly drawn to political activism, to the homosexual and feminist groups emerging in those years and to co-living experiments.

Above all, the author and Adriana – who identifies as a lesbian, like the author, despite having relationships with men – are two halves of a whole: 'Adriana and I were almost like two prototypes, we were attracted to each other like two somewhat complementary beings.'[79] As such, Maria Schiavo died along with Adriana. And as Adriana was politics personified as a woman, her death also represents the symbolic death of the political activity she embodied. Schiavo's autobiography thus takes the form of a lengthy exploration of mourning for the 1970s, rather than a celebration of erotic and academic successes like that presented by Braidotti, beating the drum of her life story. The omnipresent spectre of death manifests as an omen of the end.

> There too was that same mad channelling of sexuality into casual latrine encounters, a mainstay for the gays, alongside the rare ability, in certain cases, to maintain very long-lasting, tender couple relationships, solid alliances, still or no longer dependent on sex. Gays represented the extreme, the excess of sexual practice. In Aahrus, however, the steady transition from revolution of desire to consumption was already evident. […] In Aahrus, these circumstances were already clearer, lively consumption could already be perceived, in glimpses, beneath the apparent revolutionary drive.[80]

Maria Schiavo is recounting her attendance at a Sex Festival in Denmark, at the University of Aarhus near Copenhagen in 1972. Her description of the event is interesting. First, the author laments the lack of women – and that those there were in the company of a man or group of men – and then claims that such a civil, North European gathering of bodies would not have been possible without the revolutionary zeal of the movement of those years. Finally, she arrives at the grim observations contained in the passage above. Signs of the political irrelevance of homosexual sex are not merely grasped by the narrator retrospectively. Rather, they manifest in the character's present moment, as the Sex Festival is unfolding. They do not belong to the realm of critical reconstruction of events by the subject, transforming the latter into a text to be interpreted, but rather to the sphere of the objective destiny of things that crops up in the least expected of places. They are, in fact, omens of an obscure fate awaiting the political season of free sex.[81]

From this perspective, the end of the autobiography is by no means surprising.

> I still remember an encounter in Milan, at a restaurant, with Maria Gregorio and Sylvie Coyaud, an agent for Feltrinelli at the time, on the occasion of Luce Irigaray's visit to Italy. During the conversation, the French philosopher asked me what I was writing, and given that, at the time, in the early 1980s, I was fumbling around attempting, in various ways to mark that painful passing, I responded without being understood, and without wishing or being able to better explain: 'I write about voice'. 'About what?!' they asked again. 'Voice, *la voix*', I tried to make myself understood, I stammered. But my response was met with silence.[82]

The above encounter in Milan is a funereal parody of the old consciousness-raising meetings of the 1970s. The unmediated exchange among women had evolved into a professional meeting between publishing house representatives and their authors – Luce Irigaray's early works are all published by the Milan-based Feltrinelli. Maria Schiavo seems to be there almost by chance, and the question posed to her by the French philosopher most likely arises more from courtesy than genuine interest. Indeed, her first response was not understood and her subsequent attempt to explain herself gets lost in her stammering and the silence of those around her.

The Italian women's movement's passage into the 1980s is perfectly symbolized by this – ultimately marginal – episode in Schiavo's autobiography. It is the transition from the feminist experience to professional feminism, as referred to by Rosi Braidotti. Maria Schiavo is thus faced with the choice of turning her back on language – no longer capable of expressing anything, characterized by an aphasia that manifests as the 'civil inattention'[83] of a group of literary professionals – in favour of voice, the site of the pure presence of the self, where what has lost may finally be recovered. Her retreat to voice is, in any case, problematic. A few pages later, in fact, the writer defines her experience of institutional feminism of the 1980s in terms of a 'loss of voice',[84] for which she prescribes a rereading of Carla Lonzi's *Taci, anzi parla*. Her proposed solution, then, is immersion in a text presenting the lived experience of speaking the unspeakable or, from Maria Schiavo's perspective, giving voice to that which is voiceless. An analogous experience of lacking acknowledgement and encountering silence can be found, in almost identical terms, in Daniela Pellegrini's work.

> At times I am struck by the unease of identifying in women the inherent sign of their cancellation and perfect compliance, particularly when they claim 'womanness' within this culture, which in turn has conferred 'this womanness' upon them. [...] Sometimes I am struck by the painful perception of being an outsider even among women. These women who, for many long years, were my sole point of reference, in whom I invested my love and thought, making me dependent. [...] These writings say little of what might be said if, in fact, one wanted to write about living. This book, in truth, was not written to become a book.[85]

Daniela Pellegrini shares the disappointment expressed by Maria Schiavo: feminism has culminated in a 'womanness' with which even she does not identify. And, as in Schiavo's case, the thread of continuity with the past is maintained by way of a reference to Carla Lonzi, albeit an implicit one here. In her introduction to *Vai pure* – discussed in the previous chapter – the latter speaks of a book that, though it was published, was not specifically intended for publication. A work that, in fact, is not a work because what it wants to say is never up to the task of capturing what should be said. This is the feeling expressed by Daniela Pellegrini when she states that her book 'was not written to become a book'.

And just as Carla Lonzi's brief comment alludes to a self-enunciation strategy – of a schizophrenic nature – that differs from the main, paranoid approach pursued in *Diario di una femminista*, Daniela Pellegrini constructs an autobiography essentially based on the former, rather than the latter, feminist self-narrative approach. Whereas Maria Schiavo's account takes the form of a memoir, in which events are almost always mediated through the retrospective interpretation of the narrator, Daniela Pellegrino opts to significantly curtail the latter's role. Her text takes the form of a collection of documents belonging to different genres – pages from old diaries, notes, poems, articles for feminist magazines and essays for conferences – arranged chronologically starting in the 1970s. Many are preceded by an introduction that ought to function as a caption, but that very often explains very little. The resulting impression is of being presented with a palimpsest. A text from the present is superimposed on a text from the past, producing a layered discourse, which cannot be interpreted in a linear manner; this is the opposite to a caption, which is not superimposed but rather subordinate to the text it captions, providing a commentary on the latter.

Within the sphere of schizophrenic self-enunciation, the quashing of the narrator's prerogative corresponded to the emancipation of the character in the form of the dream-like self-narrative. Here, however, this second element seems to be entirely absent. At most, then, we might speak of partial employment of the schizophrenic approach, deprived of one of its essential elements. We should remember, however, that, like Maria Schiavo, Daniela Pellegrini is engaged in recounting the death, rather than the life, of feminism. In this context, then, releasing the character from the guardianship of the narrator to restore her vital force and freedom would be inappropriate. Instead, the only possible option is to collect traces – almost like relics – of that past in which the character lived and operated, gathering documents without truly treating them as documents. From this perspective, then, these writings do not form a book, as they are not part of a whole that determines their interpretation. As with previous examples of schizophrenic self-enunciation, we find ourselves still within the realm of the dream-like self-narrative. Except that these are dead dreams, in which action has dissolved and meaning is trapped in an abstract form, which no comment can revive. If the schizophrenic self-discourse experimented with by Italian feminism could be placed in a museum, it would take the form of Pellegrini's book that is not a book.

The end of the work presents the culmination of its funereal essence.

> I write my contribution almost easily, at an odd emotional and intellectual 'distance'. Like a true professional! And I submit it. Title: 'Identity in movement: politics of women. [...] Almost at the same time, Luciana Percovich, having read my piece on money, asks me to give 'a course' (which I refuse, obviously) on this subject at the University of Women. I risk having a career! Also, why would I finally have decided to publish this book? Because I think that offering a testimony will liberate my life.[86]

We are a very long way, here, from Rosi Braidotti's pursuit of the professionalization of feminism. Teaching feminism, or teaching as a feminist, are regarded by Pellegrini as bewildering prospects, to be steered clear of with a certain sense of self-deprecation. Beyond the grim notion that one's autobiography is nothing more than a testimony, Daniela Pellegrini also seems to reject the notion of assuming a teaching role and having students: her legacy is not for anyone's benefit. Rather, it is akin to being relieved of a burden.

And so the journey towards legitimacy is not necessarily a triumphant march. For some, certainly, personal success in an institutional context serves to endorse one's political past, but for others – who have not enjoyed the same fate – the relationship between one's past revolutionary aspirations and the mundane normality of the present becomes the problematic subject of uncertain reflection. This dissatisfied documentation of the past serves as a counterpoint to the celebratory self-narrative. Naturally, from the latter standpoint – that occupied by Rosi Braidotti – we might say that some won because they deserved to win, while others did not because they did not deserve to. Just as a distinction between deserving and undeserving poor has never made sense, however, such a separation between meritorious and non-meritorious feminists is equally fallacious. Some may have won and others lost, but the dividing line is not one of merit, but rather of chance and, probably, aspiration.

Echoes of the origins: The autobiographies of Giorgio Napolitano and Laura Lepetit

I have chosen to dedicate a separate section to the accounts of Giorgio Napolitano and Laura Lepetit because they seem to offer a resolution to the issues underpinning late communist and feminist autobiographies. In the former case, as mentioned earlier, this involves a transition from legitimacy to illegitimacy following the disbandment of historical communism, whereas for the latter group the transition is reversed following the public success of feminism. Stating that these works offer a solution to the questions at the root of these autobiographical contexts is not to say that they are better or more interesting than those examined previously. Rather, it suggests something simpler and more radical: that the problem – the relationship between legitimacy and illegitimacy – that served as a driving mechanism for the texts analysed thus far, literally vanishes. This occurs in opposite ways – with the subject sinking into the world, in Napolitano's case, and the world dissolving into the subject, in Lepetit's text – but in a manner perfectly consistent with the respective political spheres. Paradoxically, in fact, such an elimination is produced by way of the very features that originally defined the communist and feminist autobiographies.

Giorgio Napolitano: The man who made himself an institution

In keeping with the order adhered to thus far, I will begin by examining Giorgio Napolitano's autobiography. Here, we are not merely dealing with the autobiography of a communist. As well as enjoying a very long career with the PCI, in which he held various distinguished positions, and an equally long parliamentary career – being elected for the first time in 1953 – Napolitano also became president of the Republic of Italy in 2006. He was the first member of the former PCI to occupy this role, and the first to be re-elected by the parliament for a second term in 2013. He stepped down two years into his second seven-year term, however, citing his advanced age as a reason.[87] Naturally, then, an interpretation of his autobiography must necessarily take such a *cursus honorum* into account, although it should also be noted that the text was published in 2005, before he became president.

Napolitano's self-narrative opens in 1942 when he, born in 1925, was already sixteen. The childhood memoirs that feature in almost all previous communist autobiographies are omitted entirely. Napolitano enters his own story as he is completing his classical school-leaving examinations and enrolling at university. His work contains no recollections of life in the barracks, as in Ingrao's case, no reminiscing on the drama of the Resistance, as in Cossutta's text; it should be noted, in this regard, of course, that Napolitano embarked on his university career in Naples, and, therefore, would not have experienced the partisan struggle, which was an eminently Northern phenomenon. Very little information is offered on his family, aside from a brief portrait of his father: a liberal lawyer, initially rather lukewarm towards Fascism and the anti-communist movement, and subsequent supporter of the PCI as a means of upholding constitutional values. Napolitano emphasizes the exemplary nature of his father by underlining that 'he rigorously applied himself to his work – treating his profession as a mission'.[88]

Aside from this personal digression, Napolitano informs us that, while in Naples, he encountered the local GUF (Fascist University Group) organization, which revolved around the *XI Maggio* weekly publication, to which he contributed as a theatre and cinema critic. Thus begins the reader's introduction to this experience.

> The Neapolitan group that I became involved with drew talented figures destined to become leading national players in a variety of fields, including literature, entertainment, journalism and politics: Raffaele La Capria, Luigi Compagnone, Francesco Rosi, Giuseppe Patroni Griffi, Antonio Ghirelli, Maurizio Barendson, Tommaso Giglio, Massimo Caprara. It was an extremely intense group experience: we met nearly every day, in one of our houses or boarding rooms, to discuss what we had read and our first literary or artistic endeavours; these turned into discussions on all sorts of matters.[89]

This description of what ought to be the youths' lively – 'extremely intense' – cultural life is anything but fervent. The protagonists of these 'discussions on all sorts of matters' do not exist as characters capable of action, with individual profiles that make them recognizable. Such matters are of no interest to the narrator. His focus, instead, is on their grouping as a coherent set consisting of directors, journalists and writers, whose common feature is not what they are and what they do, but rather what they will be and what they will do – their 'becoming leading national players in a variety of fields'. Napolitano's account is characterized by a sort of past tense loaded with potential, which looks towards the future. The characters that he parades in his account are incapable of action because they have already acted, and their names alone conjure a complete destiny – with which, it is assumed, the reader is already familiar – in its ultimate completeness, thus requiring no further explanation. This is at the heart of the sense of detachment that seems to characterize Giorgio Napolitano's writing: page after page, he invokes faces and stories that have already been concluded, the only enduring feature of which is their celebrity, at least in Italy.

In other words, the characters in Napolitano's life are entirely static. Their inclusion in the story rarely involves mentioning an act they performed, or quoting them using direct speech. And while free indirect speech is never used – probably regarded as excessively literary and better suited to fiction than autobiography – indirect speech also rarely features. Instead, characters disappear beneath the admiring description provided by the narrator, whose celebration of these exceptional men means sacrificing their life-blood, in the form of unforeseen events, indecision and ambiguity.

> It is a device that makes us see society like a gigantic Foucaultian *tableau*, where an implacably detailed and yet conspicuous taxonomy confines every individual

to his slot for life. It is a decidedly pre-modern vision, 'a seemingly "feudal" hierarchy of class and ranks'.⁹⁰

Franco Moretti's observations on the English novel are perfectly applicable to Giorgio Napolitano's autobiography. Above all, though it may seem surprising for one who has been a Communist for most of his political life, the world he conjures up – more so even than pre-modern – is a sort of stone garden, where everyone is assigned to a category that they cannot escape, however much they may wish to. The opposing portraits presented of Mario Alicata, an intellectual and communist leader, and Salvatore Cacciapuoti, a worker, party cadre member and strict adherent to Stalinism, are telling in this regard.

> Alicata, who also worked for Luchino Visconti on the concept for a film about *I Malavoglia* (released, years later, as *La terra trema*), spoke of 'love and the practice of the truth' and also, as an already established historian and literary critic, studied the relationship between literature and truth, literature and life. [...] following the liberation of Rome, he joined the municipal council in the area of urban cleaning. [...] In late autumn 1944, however, Alicata left that particular role and, together with socialist Nino Gaeta, was appointed director of the *La Voce* daily newspaper, published in Naples.⁹¹

Giorgio Napolitano, in turn, became a theatre critic with *La voce*. He encountered his old friend Eduardo Vittoria on the editorial team there, whom he immediately specified 'would later go on to become a brilliant architect and university teacher'. He also met Paolo Ricci, who, though he did not work in academia, had a studio in the 'beautiful Villa Lucia del Vomero' – the Neapolitan bourgeois district – where he hosted Pablo Neruda and other 'cultural figures' over the course of the 1950s.⁹²

Cacciapuoti's profile is much more sombre.

> A worker from Silurificio di Baia (Naples), Cacciapuoti was arrested and convicted in 1936 as a communist agitator with the communist trade union movement and was only released from prison after 25 July 1945. A man of unquestionable intelligence and instinctive prudence and shrewdness, in spite of his impressive self-learning efforts while in prison, he never attained more than a basic level of cultural acumen and the intellectual complexities of his national leaders, Sereni and Amendola, eluded him. His strength lay in the common ground that he shared with the working-class from which he came and of which he continued to bear the stigmata.

There is no reason, of course, to doubt that Cacciapuoti, as a person, had a 'basic level of cultural acumen', or that he was astute and intelligent. What stands out, however, is that his long career with the PCI – he remained with the party until its dissolution – is entirely glossed over, and his role as a leader is reduced to the fact that he belongs to the working class and continues to bear its 'stigmata' – that is, the resulting 'stigma', a negative personal attribute.⁹³

Napolitano's treatment of Cacciapuoti is in keeping with the approach reserved for the working class in general, to whom less-than-marginal space is dedicated in the autobiography. It first features in the form of the 'terribly poor common folk' who thronged to the air-raid shelters during the Second World War bombings,[94] and later as the monarchist 'common folk' that attempted to storm the headquarters of the communist Federation in Naples after the constitutional referendum in 1946, following the collapse of the Italian monarchy. Actual members of the working class finally make an appearance, in the form of a rather long list of names of workers involved in the communist party. This recognition of the working class as individuals – albeit certainly not destined for celebrity – occurs in reverse compared to the treatment of the famous men encountered by Napolitano over the course of his life. Whereas the latter are individuals first and foremost – despite their statue-like immobility – and then communists, the former are primarily members of the working class, and then workers with a name and surname. The list of names to which I refer is preceded by two clarifications, apparently of little relevance, but that unequivocally cement such subordination. Between 1948 and 1951, in his capacity as a party official, Napolitano immersed himself in the rural social climate and the 'factory world'. No reference is made to this experience, aside from an observation that, though trivial, is, nevertheless, quite significant. 'Attending the working class school' might seem like a dated slogan, we are told, but not for the young Neapolitan leader: mixing with the common people 'translated, for me (and others) into a genuine experience of personal growth'.

The relationship with the working class, then, is not expressive in nature – 'the party and its cadres reveal the proletarian truth' – and nor is it instrumental – 'the party and its cadres are means by way of which the proletariat can mobilise politically'. More ambiguously, the relationship that unites party and class is a pedagogical one. Not, however, in the sense that any actual power of instruction is ascribed to the latter; rather it represents the teaching material for a lesson that the party teaches itself. It is not, then, the party that owes its pedagogical existence to the class, but rather the contrary. Napolitano's excursion into the depths of the lower tiers of society, therefore, becomes an opportunity for 'personal growth'. Members of the working class, then, exist in relation to his existential and political journey. This initial 'functional' subordination is accompanied by its 'logical' counterpart. Before emerging as individuals, these figures are presented as 'types'. More specifically, they can be divided into two categories: the 'extrovert, communicative fundamentally cheerful and positive' type and the type that is 'sombre, speaks little, is reflective and bitter, if not downright pessimistic'.[95] Our first encounter, then, is with what the working class means for the author, before moving on to the types of workers with whom he came into contact, and only then meeting flesh and blood workers, complete with names and surnames.

Napolitano's autobiography, therefore, presents a social space where the popular masses exist in amorphous terms – as 'common people' – or in an abstract form – as the working class from which to derive useful political lessons. Politics, in turn, becomes a long series of meetings, conferences and national and international encounters, while the people who inhabit this lifeless scene resemble statues in a mausoleum. From this perspective, Napolitano's self-narrative resembles Macaluso's, but differs in one fundamental detail. The latter's is certainly a monumental autobiography but, despite their exemplary excellence, the characters he discusses are alive. Not so much because he grants them direct speech and dedicates space – not often, but occasionally – to their idiosyncratic actions and reactions, which can never be fully reconciled with the sobriety of a monument.[96] Rather, it is primarily because the chain of great examples presented in Macaluso's text engages in a dialogue not only with the character, but also with the narrator, who interrogates it for answers regarding his own past and the political present.

The process of monumentalization engaged in by Napolitano, however, is different. He perfectly polishes his statues and commemorative medals before presenting them to the reader, enshrining his characters within their successes or condemning them to their irrelevance although, in the latter case, such figures get lost in abstraction, as seen with the example of the working class. His characters have nothing to say because they have already said everything, and the narrator cannot communicate with them in any way, because to do so would suggest a dialogue between living subjects. In this sense, Napolitano's statement that this is not the story of himself or of Italy – because it does not seek to offer 'historical exhaustiveness or systematic presentation' – is truer than even he realizes.[97] Not so much because his is an autobiographical, rather than a historical text, but because the task of the historian consists of 'lengthening the list of questions he will able to ask his documents'.[98] Napolitano, on the contrary, has nothing to ask of his characters and, as a consequence, does not expect any response. In some ways, his account is not a history, but nor does it have a story. Is it possible, though, to have an autobiography without a story, similar to the situation, discussed in Chapter 2, of a narrator without characters?

In a certain sense, it is. The issue simply lies in identifying the unusual narrative object in question. Let us refer once again to Max Weber.

> The domination of a spirit of formalistic impersonality. *Sine ira ac studio*, without hatred or passion, and hence without affection or enthusiasm. The dominant norms are concepts of straightforward duty without regard to personal considerations. Everyone is subject to formal equality of treatment that is, everyone in the same empirical situation. That is the spirit in which the ideal official conducts his office.[99]

The ideal official of Weberian bureaucracy operates in an entirely impersonal way. This impersonal status is doubled: it extends to the person before him – who is transformed into a mere case to be processed according to office rules – and to himself – given that he does not exist as a person, but as a function that performs official tasks. The actions performed by the official, then, are repetitions by way of which universal bureaucratic rules are applied to individual cases. They do not form a story, because the latter is made up of individual, qualitatively unrepeatable events. Likewise, the cases that he handles are defined by their legal status and are in no way attributable to an independent subject as the expression of its freedom and lived experience.

When Giorgio Napolitano writes his autobiography, he is writing as a Weberian ideal official. The impersonal nature of his account derives from this initial decision, of which everything else noted thus far is a consequence. Napolitano begins his self-narrative at sixteen years of age, because officials do not have childhoods. At most, he underwent technical training – in the form of secondary school and university – which granted him access to the profession, and to which he can reasonably refer as an official. The characters celebrated in his account are lifeless because they only exist as cases within the bureaucratic consciousness, and their greatness tells us nothing of them, but instead signals to us that we are in the presence of a first-rate official. The protagonist himself is also blurred: he lacks a childhood or an adulthood beyond the official domain he inhabits. And so we have a bureaucratic narrator who, while intending to tell his story, instead replaces it with a simulacrum: he narrates his career, made up of more or less standard promotions, granted based on length of service – from the PCI to European socialism, as the title of the work states.

In this sense, Napolitano is the author of an autobiography without a story. It is no surprise, then, that unlike all of the other communist memoirs examined here, his bears no traces of historical changes and the end of communism. Napolitano's account is not the victim of a crisis of legitimacy, because it lacks an autobiographical subject to experience that crisis. As an ideal official, he is not a person, but rather the personification of a bureaucratic system – at least in a Weberian sense, given that real administrative systems do not function as described by the German sociologist.[100] In short, if an institution could write its autobiography, it would take the same form as Napolitano's.

In a curious roundabout fashion, then, we have returned to our starting point, to the autobiography of Maurice Thorez, the secretary general of the PCF, first written in 1937 and most recently edited and republished in 1960. What has led us here is certainly not the themes recounted by Thorez, all of which focus on Stalinism and the related proletariat mythology. The link between Napolitano's work and that of Thorez – written almost seventy years earlier – lies in the 'impersonal personality' and bureaucratic identity featured in both works.[101] A continuity of form that is rather interesting given the different historical periods and party cultures in which the two works were produced. Might we conclude from all this that, in spite everything, Napolitano remains a communist? I do not believe such an inference can be drawn. Rather, I would say that, while emerging from communism as an historical experience may be painful and leave traces of doubt regarding one's past, communism as an organizational and bureaucratic experience need not be abandoned. Or, to put it better, the substance of communism may be left behind while still preserving its institutional form in a manner that is readily compatible, without particular strain, with new bureaucratic contexts and official duties. This is demonstrated by Giorgio Napolitano's autobiography and by the political career he built after the text's publication: President of the Republic, a key player in maintaining good political relations between Italy and the United States, and an advocate within Italy for the binding nature of the European Union's economic requirements.

Laura Lepetit: Feminism as distraction

Laura Lepetit belongs to the same generation as Carla Lonzi[102] – who is one year her senior – and Maria Schiavo, Daniela Pellegrini and Luisa Passerini – all of whom were born between the early 1930s and the early 1940s. One might suppose that the dividing line of the Second World War explains the shift in tone and significance in feminist autobiographies. Autobiographies penned by those born in the earlier period sees neo-feminism's journey towards success cast as an object of critical reflection and varying degrees of suffering, coupled with disillusionment. The advent of the baby boomers, meanwhile, sees a complete change of tone, as exemplified by Rosi Braidotti's self-narrative.

This impression of a linear progression towards reconciliation with the broader social context and unquestioning celebration of one's success is, however, undermined by Laura Lepetit's autobiography. Despite carefully avoiding any trace of triumph or naive self-commemoration, the latter does not exude the suffering characteristic of *Autobiography of a Generation*, the subdued pain of Maria Schiavo's account, or the confused, ultimate awareness that marks the end of Daniela Pellegrini's account.

> In books that talk about old age, women always have a slightly apologetic air, as though seeking to justify their continued presence in the world. But instead it is a new season, almost like a gift, because previously, people died very early, growing old was rare, and the long lives of Leonardo da Vinci or Queen Elizabeth I were exceptional. It is a season that has its peculiarities, yet to be understood. It strikes me that it is similar to adolescence, a period of waiting for something unknown. In adolescence, we were waiting for life, in old age we are waiting for death, another change, uncharted ground that we must venture into without knowing when and where.[103]

Laura Lepetit published her memoir – *Autbiografia di una femminista distratta* (*Autobiography of a Distracted Feminist*) – in 2016, at the age of eighty, with a successful life behind her: she was one of the owners, in the early 1970s, of the Milano Libri bookshop, a hub of Milanese cultural life. She made the Charlie Brown comics available in Italian, and took advantage of this experience to launch *Linus*, one of Italy's longest running publications. She founded the La Tartaruga publishing house in the 1970s, which played a central role in promoting and disseminating women's literature, boasting a catalogue made up entirely of Italian and international women's writers. The opening passage of her work is reminiscent of a sort of feminist *De Senectute*, with the author reflecting at length on the passing of time, the dissolution of things and awaiting death. The first page reads like an introduction to a reflection on life as a journey of loss.

> Disillusion is the chief characteristic of old age; for by that time the fictions are gone which gave life its charm and spurred on the mind to activity; the splendours of the world have been proved null and vain; its pomp, grandeur and magnificence are faded. A man has then found out that behind most of the things he wants, and most of the pleasures he longs for, there is very little after all; and so he comes by degrees to see that our existence is all empty and void.[104]

In truth, the autobiography never presents the sort of disillusionment described by Schopenhauer, experienced as the discovery of the 'empty and void' nature of existence. Or rather, Laura Lepetit perfectly captures the futility of things, but this is not accompanied by any sense of disenchantment with the world, either in a conscious form – through meditation on the passing of time – or in emotional reflections on the vague sadness of the experience. This is because the reference to old age, here, is a trick used by the narrator to toy with the reader,[105] preventing an unambiguous interpretation of the text. As the narrator of her own story, Lepetit is entirely unreliable and makes no effort to pretend otherwise.

> Having written almost everything that I remember, it seems it is time to reach a conclusion. […] I have been asked, every so often, to write my story. I didn't know where to begin, because I didn't think I had anything special to recount, aside from having a poor memory. […] And so one fine day I sat down at my computer, and this is my life as I remember it. I apologise to all those who I have forgotten, but they certainly also have a place in my heart.[106]

Having reached the end, the narrator thinks that she should conclude, but does so without any real conviction; more out of a sense of duty or boredom than because the internal dynamics of her story require it. Not only, however, is the ending arbitrary, the narrative content is also questionable, given that it is 'nothing special' and probably also full of gaps – she has a poor memory, after all. The unreliability of the narrator, however, is not an epistemic issue. Despite Laura Lepetit claims about herself, it does not result from an objective problem – the irrelevance of the material, which would make it difficult to provide the account – or from subjective inadequacies – a memory that is not up to the task in question. The unreliability is, instead, a positive trait that identifies the author – in keeping with her chosen title – as a 'distracted feminist'. Distraction is an existential state of diversion in which a certain cultivated carelessness is combined with amused pleasure at such carelessness. The story of how she arrived at the name for her publishing house is rather interesting in this regard:

> When asked why I called the publishing house, which only publishes books for women, La Tartaruga [The Turtle] edizioni, I give a different answer every time. In truth, while trying to find a name for the publishing house, I happened to read a short article in a magazine that said: 'the turtle is a nice little animal, it moves slowly, carries its home with it and is happy with a few salad leaves.' Oh, I thought, that's me. I like moving slowly, I eat a lot of salad and I always carry my home with me.[107]

This is immediately followed by the clarification that an encounter with a real turtle did not live up to that charming description, as the creature 'ate huge quantities of everything, always seemed to be late and very hungry.' This relegation of the turtle in her estimation is not, however, accompanied by an indication of whether her affinity with the reptile remains. This omission goes entirely unnoticed – though I will return to it later – mainly because, in a show of pragmatism that does not seem particularly in keeping with the spirit of a distracted feminist, Laura Lepetit goes on to state that, in choosing her name, she also considered that 'one day I will be fed up with women and their cause.' Best, then, to choose an 'ambiguous and adaptable' name. This discordance between amused levity and a somewhat coarse dose of pragmatism permeates her work.

> The war that took away our terrible Fräulein was, for us kids who went to a convent school to become good, marriageable girls, a period of great freedom and fun. Nobody bothered with us, the adults had other things on their minds, and we scampered freely through the streets of Rome, without a car in sight. Playing in the courtyards, bike races, climbing trees and gates, everything was possible. [...] Today, with this prolonged crisis and constant scarcity, we need a barter economy, with no money. They should open a place where goods or services are bartered. But to earn something from it. Otherwise I feel like all the avenues around me are blocked off and I feel trapped.[108]

The Fräulein in question is the author's German teacher, who disappeared during the Second World War – it is not clear whether she died or followed the Germans in their retreat northwards. The more or less unhappy fate of this governess aside, we move, as is common in her autobiography, from the 1940s to the economic crisis of 2008 in the space of a page. In both cases, we are offered singular perspectives on these events. The allied bombings, German searches and Italian deaths are entirely absent from her account of Rome. All that remains are empty streets where children can finally play, free from oppressive adult supervision. The 2008 financial crisis receives similar treatment: no foreclosures on homes or unemployment. Just 'prolonged scarcity.' In response to which, with a certain nonchalance, the author hopes for a return to 'the barter economy' which might set in motion a vague undefined trade in 'goods and services' that would make it possible to 'earn something from it'. This final clarification does not help us to determine whether Laura Lepetit is more interested in commercial activity, with its spaces and rituals, or the gains she hopes to make in this new age of barter.

The elimination of history and its violence[109] and a fondness for market dynamics reduced to the exchange of goods among people – without the alienating medium of money[110] – form a combination that is difficult to defend, however, even with the practiced nonchalance of the narrator. The latter may be a perfect approach to everyday life, but when applied to such significant events, one inevitably risks descending into the realm of bad taste. And indeed, a few pages later, following a series of reflections on cats, humans and animals, she offers a clear stance on herself and the world.

> It is often said that there comes a moment in your childhood when you lose your innocence and encounter reality. In various ways: losing faith in adults, in your parents, discovering cruelty, injustice and so forth. I think, though, that there are people who never lose their innocence. Like me, for example, always trusting everyone, never suspecting that I have been deceived, believing in tarot, astrology, in signs and chance encounters. I have not lost my innocence and I see children as my peers.[111]

Laura Lepetit did not notice the bombing of Rome, then, and failed to perceive the suffering brought by the economic crisis because she is still a child, and has not experienced hardship. It is this childlike innocence that affords her such nonchalance and that explains the whimsical structuring of her narrative, wherein large situations and small anecdotes are presented in no particular order, dictated by the freedom of the narrator to conjure up events at her discretion. But is Laura Lepetit truly innocent? Her passion for commerce – even in the money-free form of barter – and her skill in choosing a name for her publishing house would suggest not. This question cannot, however, be answered directly, without some further considerations.

> 'You in fact honestly accept a law as existing in and for itself [it says to others]'; 'I do so, too, but I go further than you, for I am also beyond this law and can do this or that as I please. It is not the thing [Sache] which is excellent, it is I who am excellent and master of both law and thing; I *merely play* with them as with my own caprice, and in this ironic consciousness in which I let the highest of things perish, I *merely enjoy myself*.'[112]

Quoting Hegel in the knowledge that Carla Lonzi incited women to spit on the old German philosopher may seem inappropriate. This is not a feminist book, however, but rather a book that deals with feminism, among other things. Thus I believe that taking such a liberty is, if not justifiable, at least comprehensible. Furthermore, I am not interested in Hegel from a philosophical perspective, but because he offers a useful description. His representation of the ironic consciousness of romantics – personified, in his eyes, by Friedrich Schlegel – perfectly sums up the attitude of the self-narrator in *Autobiografia di una femminista distratta*.

Laura Lepetit is not a child. She can claim to be so because she enunciates her story from the position of supreme detachment offered by irony, which masters 'both law and thing'. The innocence and senility of which she speaks are, in fact, merely figures of that separation. And, starting from the ironic distance that the narrator establishes from the events that she recounts, small appears large and large appears small, the accidental seems essential and the essential accidental. The war and the economic crisis may be reduced to little or nothing, and the reader can be subject to good-natured teasing, because what really counts is not the story that is being told or the audience that it is addressed to, but the solitary sovereignty of the narrator, in whose presence everything else is irrelevant.

The primacy of the narrator tirelessly pursued by Carla Lonzi is repurposed by Laura Lepetit in a more radical form, to curiously more traditional effect. The former's obstinate search for meaning, rummaging through life events in the hope of discovering the definitive, constantly elusive, answer about herself is no longer necessary. Seeking to arrange things in order, to find an approach that gives them meaning is, in Lepetit's eyes, futile. Everything comes together by chance, everything is equally relevant and irrelevant. The greatness of the act of narrating the self lies not in the pursuit of an evasive meaning, but rather in recognizing that no such meaning exists. Only then can the narrator celebrate its detachment from everything and everyone and, irony of ironies, from male discourse as well as feminist counter-discourse. The purity of self-enunciation no longer means absorption of the character by the narrator – as in Carla Lonzi's case – but rather its abandonment, together with its actions and relevant events, to itself, without any regret. Should we, therefore, conclude that Italian neo-feminism has found its ultimate incarnation – in chronological terms – in a form of feminist romanticism?

Not quite. Or rather, Laura Lepetit's irony resembles its romantic counterpart, criticized by Hegel, but emerges in a context that is by no means romantic. If it is true, in more general and philosophical terms, that the ironic subject is indifferent to the object and that, in the autobiographical account, the narrator is indifferent to the character and his or her world – and that this sublime indifference is at the root of the superiority of both – the opposite is also true. And so, just as the subject is indifferent to the world, so too is the world indifferent to the subject, in an opposite and symmetrical balance. How does all this manifest in *Autobiografia di una femminista distratta*? Essentially, in the acceptance of the world as it is: the frivolity of our narrator allows her to move freely from one event to another, moving from the world of cats to the publishing sphere, without ever touching upon the deeper power relations that make this kaleidoscopic series of events possible. Also because, for the author, *freedom from the world* is *freedom in the world*, a stance that enables her to establish this comfortable relationship of reciprocal indifference.

> What does it mean to live one day to the next? Is it a good thing or a bad thing? I don't know. I have grown fond of this city house, where I live, and I like being here, whereas at the beginning I hated it and found it boring, suffocating and overly middle-class. And yet so-called middle-class values are interesting in their own right, they have the best of things by a long shot. A home, family, relatives, flowers, good education, life's little luxuries, money. I never paid it much attention, I frittered everything away, thinking that the abundance would never end.[113]

Ironic distance from existence, then, requires non-ironic belonging to the middle-class world. It is an unpleasant truth that should be concealed, though the author is not overly committed to her disguise – it is, in fact, incompatible with the narrative distraction on which the autobiography is built. And so, in her ode to good old middle-class values, 'money' is placed at the bottom of the list, with a certain distaste, like a negligible, secondary detail. And the author immediately distances herself from it: she has frittered it all away, without any interest. This aesthetic – rather than political – aversion to money was previously alluded to in her fantasy of a barter economy, where it would be possible to earn without resorting to money. In any case, it is an unresolved and unresolvable relationship. Rejection of money is not, in fact, anti-middle-class, but rather the means by which the middle-class consciousness distances itself from the feral foundations – the struggle for social survival – on which it is built.

This difficult relationship with the obscure and unpleasant aspects of the world underpins Laura Lepetit's ambiguous relationship with her mascot, the animal that symbolizes her social success: the turtle. The author identifies with the latter's pacifist, vegetarian image, but then discovers that the amiable reptile is in fact a tense and hungry beast and, at heart, an opportunist: the choice of name arises from the desire not to be tied to the feminist movement, which sooner or later would come to an end. Which of the two turtles is the writer? Certainly the first, but probably also the second, given that she does not explicitly distance herself from its voracious temperament. Like money – the superfluous nature of which she makes sure to emphasize – the obscure side of middle-class virtues is only mentioned to be silently cast aside.

From this perspective, it is no surprise that some of the objects that we have encountered in the feminist autobiographical universe reappear here, but in an entirely different way. The Turicchi rural retreat, to which Carla Lonzi escapes in search of peace, corresponds to Laura Lepetit's country house. However, whereas Turicchi is the secret garden where the Tuscan feminist's innocence is discovered and emerges free from urban deceit, the Milanese editor's pastoral dwelling is, more prosaically, a second home where she can get away from the stresses of modern life and enjoy the pleasures of being among flowers and plants, with her cats.[114] Laura Lepetit's victim of choice, however, is psychoanalysis.

> And anyway, in the crisis years, around middle age, when everyone flocks to that idol, a psychoanalyst, I got my first horse, Paco, a veteran, and he and all the others who followed, thankfully taught me how to live much better than any analyst.[115]

With princess-like indifference, Laura Lepetit recommends buying a horse rather than visiting a psychoanalyst. Psychoanalysis is regarded – with her usual middle-class pragmatism – as a remunerative profession, the value of which does not even merit discussion: 'My psychoanalyst friends have tonnes of work and tonnes of clients. Good for them.'[116] In two lines, she tears down psychoanalysis, the feminist idol par excellence, reducing it to a mere commercial phenomenon.

As such, Laura Lepetit draws on a series of key elements of the feminist self-narrative, but changes their meaning entirely. The primacy of the paranoid narrator figure is occupied by a loquacious and unreliable narrator, the countryside, previously a sphere of innocence, is transformed into a retreat from one's entrepreneurial labours, the world of psychoanalysis is no longer the domain of dream-like experiences, but is presented as a purely commercial practice. Italian feminist self-enunciation, therefore, takes on its ultimate form – at least from a chronological perspective: feminist snobbishness. Snobbishness that is so snobbish it is, perhaps, no longer even feminist. Deep down, for the distracted feminist who wrote her autobiography, feminism was little more than a distraction.

Of these terminal forms of feminism, which is preferable: Rosi Braidotti's feminist professionalism or Laura Lepetit's snob feminism? There is no right answer to this question. All we can say is that, hiding beneath the shade of the feminist autobiography are narrative subjects whose gender – or sexual difference or otherness – does not suffice to explain the forms taken by their self-narratives. Underneath gender and sexual difference, indeed, there lies another difference, one of class and standing, which may explain why the Italian immigrant in Australia has an anxious desire for recognition, while the successful Milanese businesswoman is satisfied with the company of her cats.

CONCLUSIONS

Having reached the end of this journey, what else is there left to say? Not much, truth be told. All that remains is to make a few general observations.

The first concerns the distance between the self-narratives of the old left and those of the new left. The way in which the relationship between author, narrator and character is handled in communist and feminist self-enunciation – beyond their basic shared identity, which guarantees that what we are reading is an autobiography – is easily distinguishable and gives rise to two rather distinct autobiographical cultures. The classic, first-person *Bildungsroman* structure adopted in the communist sphere is in contrast to the narrative innovation employed by the feminist movement, that used psychotic forms of self-discourse – producing paranoid and schizophrenic autobiographical accounts, coupled with the silence of catatonia – in an effort to liberate women's expression from the discursive power of men.

Such a finding, broadly speaking, is neither surprising nor unexpected. Given the different political profiles of the old and new left, one might predict that communist and feminist forms of self-enunciation would present specific morphological features that, to some extent, are mutually incompatible. The most important contribution of this book, then, is not that it presents such an obvious conclusion, but rather that it offers a series of more precise descriptions of what happens in the respective autobiographical fields. How do communist and feminist autobiographical paradoxical injunctions operate? What do we mean when we talk about an accomplished communist autobiography? To what extent does the concept of allegory and repetition apply to the PCI militants' self-narratives? How is the breakdown of discourse pursued in the feminist context? What autobiographical opportunities are offered by the feminists' dream reports, and how can one escape the clutches of the narrator, as an agent of order, when embarking on a feminist self-narrative?

All interesting questions, worthy of scholarly investigation: their value is that they enable us to explore not so much *why* men and women declared themselves communists or feminists, but rather *how* they can make such a declaration when speaking about themselves. To use a classic distinction, then, the key focus of my research is not the – communist and feminist – soul, but the – autobiographical – forms by way of which that soul materializes and is expressed.[1] An extensive corpus of research exists on the former issue, but very little seems to have been written on the latter.

I do not, of course, believe that the approach taken here represents the only way to gain an insight into the discursive methods of constructing the communist and feminist autobiographical self. Analysing the dynamics between author, narrator and character seemed, however, like a good starting point, because it facilitates an investigation into the narrative treatment of the pragmatic dimensions of the self-enunciation act, that is, the paradoxical injunction underpinning communist and feminist self-expression. That said, a more strictly rhetorical analysis, for example, would also be extremely interesting. Is there a metaphorical apparatus, a system of *topoi* and, more generally, specific methods, for justifying one's allegiance to the communist or feminist causes? This is one possible example of the 'lengthening of the list of the question' discussed by Paul Veyne – to which I refer in the third chapter – that defines the work not only of the historian, but also of social scientists in general, from sociologists to anthropologists.

From my perspective, however, much more significant than the previous question are the forms of discontinuity evident within the two autobiographical traditions considered. These separate the original autobiographies from their later counterparts, enabling some more general theoretical considerations to be posited, particularly as regards the Italian feminist context. As mentioned previously, while communist self-enunciation moved from the field of legitimacy to that of illegitimacy, its feminist equivalent performed the opposite transition. Surprisingly, however, the more problematic shift is not that engaged in by the former group but rather by the latter.

The loss of legitimacy suffered by the communist autobiography with the decline of the twentieth-century movement manifested in the bewilderment of former militants and leaders, who no longer had the means to clearly define the meaning of their previous political lives. As we saw, such a scenario offers few solutions. Some chose to abandon the autobiographical field and use the first person to present a personal spin on what are, essentially, historiographical accounts. Others engaged in self-narratives with a view to reliving their lost youth, or reminiscing about the beauty of a small world of customs lost forever. Still others used autobiographical enunciation to filter old communist politics and their militant past through the lens of criticism, or to erect a small narrative monument to an era that, though over, has not lost its greatness. Finally, of all of the authors of communist memoirs, one – the former president of the Italian Republic – offers a self-narrative in which his own, appropriately reinterpreted, communist past, becomes a mere foreshadowing of his institutional present. In other words, he presents a figural reading of his membership of the PCI that enables it to be viewed as preparation for his ultimate moment of glory, in which man and communist becomes state and institution.

In all of these instances, notwithstanding the prestige of the late communist memoirs' authors, the communist autobiographical tradition retains a recognizable narrative identity. The dynamics between narrator and character in the party autobiographies of the 1950s are, in fact, more or less the same as those found in the communist and ex-communist works published at the start of the new millennium. The political tradition wanes, old certainties evaporate, the tone is no longer triumphant, but the narrative processes underpinning the self-narrative resist erosion.

It is no coincidence that Giorgio Napolitano's autobiography takes the same impersonal approach, and strategy of quashing the human element, that characterizes Thorez's text from seventy years earlier. This can be attributed, in part, to the use of broadly conventional narrative forms, which are naturally less exposed to the premature ageing processes to which avant-garde innovations are prone. In part, at least as regards the impersonal self-narrative, it also comes down to a desire to transform oneself into an institution. Not, however, in the sense of assuming a single, exemplary and unforgettable personality, but rather in the literary sense of depriving oneself of one's empirical individuality in favour of a superior system of universality – in the form of class, party or state. And so, while the paradoxical injunction to be active that inspired the original party autobiographies no longer applies, the corresponding narrative forms continue to operate, though they no longer serve the objective of transforming the subject into a communist militant.

The feminist case is notably different. While the communist autobiographical tradition waned, its feminist counterpart underwent a clear break. In other words, the distance separating Carla Lonzi's diary from Maria Schiavo or Rosi Braidotti's autobiographies is greater than that between Simone B. and Pietro Ingrao's *Volevo la luna*. The culture of feminist experimentation revolving around self-enunciation – of which *Taci, anzi Parla* represents a sort of pinnacle – simply disappears. The sole exceptions to this demobilization of feminist autobiographical technologies are represented by Luisa Passerini – who revives them in an academic context, employing them as scientific research tools – and Daniela Pellegrini who, instead, inhabits a heightened state of awareness of the definitive loss of a previously living, creative world.

In terms of narrative procedures – but not, obviously, in terms of themes – the other late feminist autobiographies are much closer to their communist counterparts published in the same period than to the forms of self-enunciation experimented with by Italian feminists in the 1970s. Indeed, the discontinuity is such that the observation made regarding the later communist accounts – that they are autobiographies of communists, but not communist autobiographies – is even more applicable to the feminist memoirs: these are memoirs written by feminists, but they are in no way feminist memoirs. Such an assertion may seem exaggerated, but its aptness would seem to be demonstrated by the example of Rosi Braidotti, whom I have already discussed at length, but who deserves further, brief consideration.

In *Nomadic Subjects*, the academic states that her works draw on the interaction between her autobiographical experience and her theoretical interest in nomadism.[2] A nomadic mindset is, in a certain sense, the philosophical manifestation of her existential experience. She also adds that, if she were ever to write an autobiography, she would write one like Luisa Passerini's.[3] Yet her self-narrative cannot be compared in any way to *Autobiography of a Generation* because, unlike the former, it contains no trace of the feminist enunciation strategies of the 1970s.

The latter, instead, is nothing more than the success story of an Italian immigrant in Australia who finally received the recognition she deserved from the anglophone academic world. A success story presented in the anthology of the lives of successful women that is *Baby Boomers*. As mentioned previously, the problem is not with presenting the account of one's life in self-congratulatory terms. Indeed, panegyric writing is an ancient, glorious and somewhat diverting genre. The issue, instead, is whether this mode of self-enunciation, within the framework of analysis used in this text, can be considered a feminist autobiography.

My response is no. Or rather, to clarify my position, when Rosi Braidotti writes about herself, despite the stylistic difference and disparate existential experiences, she writes exactly like Giorgio Napolitano. Just as Napolitano is a communist turned state, Braidotti is a feminist turned university. Perhaps this makes it easier to understand the choice of Laura Lepetit's autobiography over Rosi Braidotti's as an example of late feminist self-narrative that remains true to its political roots: Lepetit, with characteristic bourgeois detachment, continues, in an ironic way, to reject the world and its institutions.

Of interest here, however, is not merely the handing-down of narrative procedures from one generation of feminists to another; nor is it the trite observation that Rosi Braidotti does not write like Carla Lonzi. The problem, rather, is of a more inherently political nature. If, indeed, in Carla Lonzi's diary, the coincidence of the personal and political on which second-wave feminism is founded is immediately effective – by way of the enormous effort to say everything about oneself in the first person, so as to leave no space for male discourse – it is unclear, in Rosi Braidotti's autobiography, how these two worlds are connected. If the Italian philosopher is indeed a nomad, we might, at most, say that hers is the account of a nomad, but certainly not a nomadic account.[4] Even by applying Davidson's principle of interpretive charity to its fullest potential, it seems difficult to imagine how a success story can be regarded as a nomadic autobiography. Framed differently, Braidotti's feminist political activities are indisputable, but this does not give rise to a specific and recognizable strategy of self-narration, which is the only level on which I consider her autobiography here.[5]

From this specific perspective – that is, that of analysing Italian feminist autobiographical artefacts produced from the 1970s onwards – even the standard distinction between first-, second- and third-wave feminism implies a continuity of theoretical perspectives and political stances, albeit with an evolution of key themes, that makes the specific quality of ties that link and separate the various generations of feminists imperceptible.[6] For me, the journey from Lonzi's diary to Braidotti's autobiography seems more comprehensible if considered through the lens of the distance between Greek myth and Hellenistic mythology.

> All of this changes in the Hellenistic period. Literature is intended to be learned. Not that this is the first time that literature has been reserved for an elite (Pindar or Aeschylus were not exactly popular writers), but it demands a cultural effort

from its audience that excludes the amateurs. Myths then give way to what we still call mythology and which will survive until the eighteenth century. The people continued to have their tales and superstitions, but mythology, now a matter for the learned, moved beyond their reach. It took on the prestige of the elite knowledge that marks its possessor as belonging to a certain class.[7]

The distancing described by Paul Veyne[8] is the same movement that defines the evolution of the feminist self-narrative. The feminists' previous autobiographical experiments – dream-like reports, paranoid self-enunciation, criticism of psychoanalysis – cease to be experimental experiences engaged in by the women in the first person, and become objects of commemoration by subsequent feminist scholarship. At the end of this journey of detachment, we find Rosi Braidotti's autobiography that focuses, reflexively, not on the feminist past as the object of scholarship, as in Luisa Passerini's, but on that scholarship itself, on the journey of self-construction – that is, how the scholar became a scholar – and, ultimately, on how Rosi Braidotti transformed herself into a world-renowned 'professional feminist'. The ancient feminist *mythoi*, then, are replaced by the science of those *mythoi*, and the feminist activist is supplanted by a scientist of feminism.

Rosi Braidotti's Alexandrian feminism is thus defined by a lack of potential for interaction between her lived experience – as recounted in her autobiography – and the radicalism of her nomadic philosophical stance. The personal, then, is no longer political. A very brief autobiographical note that appears in *Nomadic subjects* further confirms these observations.

> Once, landing at Paris International Airport, I saw all of these in between areas occupied by immigrants from various parts of the former French empire; they had arrived, but were not allowed entry, so they camped in these luxurious transit zones, waiting. The dead, panoptical heart of the new European Community will scrutinize them and not allow them in easily: it is crowded at the margins and nonbelonging can be hell.[9]

Rosi Braidotti arrives in Paris, sees the non-European immigrants who cannot cross the French border and, faced with that scene, muses that 'nonbelonging can be hell'. She does not protest, she does not run to offer them solidarity, or even express minimal indignation. She sees what is unfolding and, most likely, leaves the airport. Faced with the denial of freedom of movement and the right to migrate, then, her sole reaction is *theoretical*, not *practical*.

From this perspective, Braidotti's[10] Hellenistic feminism runs deeper than may seem at first glance and, in fact, would seem to account for a significant portion of contemporary feminist theory. As power increasingly slips away from individuals and becomes progressively more difficult to control using traditional liberal democratic tools, men and women's capacity to act steadily diminishes. As in the Alexandrian era, all that is left for individuals is to engage in self-improvement, which no longer takes a stoic or epicurean form, but instead translates into practices of manipulation or self-manipulation of one's body. The insistent focus by many contemporary feminists on sex, desire and corporeal materiality is merely the inevitable response to an entirely asymmetric political challenge, tipped in favour of the great international economic, state and military powers. Nomadic or eccentric subjects,[11] or the politics of parody,[12] do not, therefore, seem to be a proportional response to contemporary conditions of oppression.[13] The peaceful coexistence of Rosi Braidotti as the autobiographical subject of an absolutely ordinary life – integrated into the legal space of our society – and Rosi Braidotti as a nomadic subject, offers a good indicator of the ultimately innocuous character of such political proposals.[14]

This leads me to my final consideration, which concerns a political sphere other than feminism: specifically that discussed by Ernesto Laclau in *On Populist Reason*.[15] The central tenets of this work are fairly widely known. They can be summarized as the notion that – more so even than a historical phenomenon that is difficult to define – populism represents the 'royal road to understanding something about the ontological constitution of the political as such',[16] and that 'the people' is a discursive concept, constructed by way of a linguistic performance that unifies the various demands. Laclau's work is fascinating and rather complex, in conceptual terms. It fails, however, to properly address a question that is pertinent to this work: who controls the performance of the people and, therefore, produces the political? Reading *On Populist Reason* might give one the impression that a political leader manifests as a sort of necromancer, holding a magic formula to invoke political power in the form of the people. Naturally, a leader only possesses the political mana because he is possessed by it. In a certain sense, then, politics is a sort of obscure power that emerges spontaneously almost without the need for human intervention – and this mythical and impersonal aspect of politics, which derives directly from Sorel, is not immediately apparent due to the Lacanian linguistic blanket that shrouds Laclau's work.[17]

The Italian situation and, more specifically, the autobiographical issues considered in this text seem to offer interesting insights into the limitations of such a theoretical perspective. In keeping with Italy's longstanding tradition as a political laboratory, in fact, the best application of the model described by Laclau is the Five Star Movement. The latter, indeed, owes its existence to pure discursive performance. At its origins is the significant 'Vaffanculo!' (Fuck off!) pronounced by Beppe Grillo, the movement's founder, on the occasion of the V-Day (Fuck off Day) event that he organized on 8 September 2007 across Italy, himself appearing in a Bologna piazza. Subsequent iterations of the event took place on 25 April 2008 and 1 December 2013. Beyond the specific political proposals presented on any given occasion, the primary objective of these events is to allow Beppe Grillo to establish his 'people' as 'people who say fuck off' – to traditional parties, to political corruption, to parliament as a den of crooks and *mafiosi*.

Not only, then, does Grillo produce the significant void discussed by Laclau – the 'people', specifically – he also expresses its main feature in brutal and vulgar terms: a rejection of the existing system of generally accepted social demands. This translates into a resounding 'fuck off', emphatically repeated by the Genovese comic. Worth noting here, is that Grillo's movement was originally constructed not only around this utterly populist speech act, but also in eminently discursive terms, revolving first around Grillo's own blog and subsequently around the Rousseau platform, which serves as the 'operating system' for the Five Star Movement. Here, then, exemplifying Laclau's populist model nearly to the letter, the political and organizational planes merge almost completely with the discursive plane: the Five Star Movement is nothing more than the discourse engaged in by the Five Star Movement about itself via its leaders.[18]

The very fate of this political formation, however, reveals the weakness of the political phenomenon outlined by Laclau and highlights the ongoing relevance of the autobiographical issue addressed, in different ways, by communism and feminism. Having received more than 32 per cent of the vote in the national elections in 2018, the movement failed to secure much more than 17 per cent in the European elections the following year, a figure comfortably surpassed by the Northern League. Electoral flows are obviously not the only means of measuring the power of the populist Five Star party. They do, however, point to a certain challenge in conferring stability on the populist discursive performance that, moreover, just as it appears from nothing – conjured by the linguistic magic of the great politician – may as easily return to nothing, because the political magic formula, transient as it is, offers no certainty as to success.

I would, therefore, propose that any emancipatory political project should, as a condition for its success, offer the opportunity to write alternative self-narratives that fall outside of the sphere of traditional models. Only by having the chance to tell one's narrative, repeat that narrative and avail of an audience that offers legitimacy to that narrative performance – unlike that normally accepted by existing institutions – can an alternative political solution take root and grow stable. In this sense, the communists – albeit very partially – and the feminists, more so, grasped the need for autobiographical politics: the subject is reinvented in narrative terms, by way of interactions between narrator and character, opening up channels for new political possibilities. And this operation seems to me, in 'ontological' terms to take priority over the discursive creation of the 'people' by a great politician; it cannot, in other words, be regarded merely as a tactical option within a strategy of populist construction of a new political hegemony.

I do not, obviously, wish to suggest that recounting oneself in a different way produces a different world. This would be grossly reductionist and naive. Rather, I would posit that, faced with the choice between a demiurge – whose discursive formulae serve to unite the disunited and disunite the united, creating a new world – and the capacity of individuals to produce unforeseen meaning, which manifests in the way they express themselves and in what they do, as a condition of a world that is even marginally different from that in which we live[19] – I would opt for the latter mode of political action.

NOTES

Introduction

1   In the context of these groups, the women's narratives were not merely means of self-expression, but also served as tools to enable recognition of the self and of others as women. See Adriana Caravero, *Relating Narratives: Storytelling and Selfhood* (London and New York, 2000), p. 91.
2   The distinction between the features of the old and new left is clearly expressed by Herbert Marcuse, *The New Left and the 1960s. Collected Papers*, trans. Douglas Kellner (London and New York, 2005), pp. 57–8. See also Alastair J. Reid, 'The dialectics of liberation: the old left, the new left and the counter culture', in D. Feldman and J. Lawrence (eds), *Structures and Transformations in Modern British History* (Cambridge, 2011), pp. 261–80 and Daniel Geary, '"Becoming International Again". C. Wright Mills and the emergence of a New Global Left', *The Journal of American History* 95/3 (2008), pp. 710–36.
3   Mauro Boarelli, *La fabbrica del passato. Autobiografie di militanti comunisti (1945–1956)* (Milan 2007).
4   Andrea Possieri, *Il peso della storia. Memoria, identità, rimozione dal Pci al Pds (1970–1991)* (Bologna, 2007), p. 111.
5   Chiara Sebastiani, 'I funzionari', in A. Accornero, R. Mannheimer and C. Sebastiani (eds), *L'identità comunista. I militanti, la struttura, la cultura del PCI* (Rome, 1983), pp. 79–178.
6   Anna Rossi-Doria, 'Ipotesi per una storia del neo-femminismo italiano, in A. Rossi-Doria, *Dare forma al silenzio. Scritti di storia politica delle donne*l (Rome, 2007), pp. 234–65.
7   Judith A. Hellman, *Journeys among Women. Feminism in Five Italian Cities* (Cambridge, 1987).
8   See Chiara Martucci, *La libreria delle donne a Milano. Un laboratorio di pratica politica* (Milan 2008), p. 26, note 26.
9   Marcel Detienne, *Comparing the Incomparable* (Stanford, 2008), p. XIII.
10 Kevin Morgan, 'Comparative communist history and the "Biographical Turn"', *History Compass* 10/6 (2012), pp. 455–66. See also Kevin Morgan, Gidon Cohen and Andrew Flinn (eds), *Agents of Revolution: New Biographical Approaches to the History of International Communism in the Age of Lenin and Stalin* (Oxford, 2005).
11 Mary Fulbrook and Ulinka Rublack, 'In relation: the "social self" and ego-documents', *German History* 28/3 (2010), pp. 263–72.
12 Erving Goffman, *Encounters: Two Studies in the Sociology of Interaction* (Harmondsworth, 1972), pp. 88–93.
13 See Urs Marti, 'Techniques de soi, techniques de domination et pratiques identitaires dans la culture stalinienne. Remarques sur la valeur analytique d'un concept de Foucault', in B. Studer and B. Unfried (eds), *Parler de soi sous Staline. La construction identitaire dans le communisme des années trente* (Paris, 2002), pp. 35–45. Naturally,

the primary theoretical reference here is to Michel Foucault, 'Technologies of the self', in Luther H. Martin, Huck Gutman and Patrick H. Hutton (eds), *Technologies of the Self: A Seminar with Michel Foucault* (Amherst, 1988), pp. 16–49.
14 See Harold Garfinkel, *Studies in Ethnomethodology* (Englewood Cliffs, 1967), pp. 18–24. The questions can be found on p. 20.
15 Ibid., pp. 35–6.
16 Philippe Lejeune, *On Autobiography* (Minneapolis, 1985), pp. 3–30. This definition, though appropriate to my work, has been challenged, at least in part, by the proliferation of digital autobiographical practices. On this topic see Arnaud Schmidt, 'From autobiographical act to autobiography', *Life Writing* 15 (2018), pp. 469–86.
17 In fact, Lejeune states that the author is 'represented at the edge of the text by his name'. Ibid., p. 21.
18 Ibid., p. 23.
19 Carla Lonzi, *Taci, anzi parla. Diario di una femminista* (Milan, 1978).
20 I refer here, in particular, to the 'Dream' notebooks spanning from 1966 to 1970 located in Folder 1, file 2 and file 3, Archivio Lea (Maddalena) Melandri, Fondazione Badaracco, Milan. For a general overview of the figure of Lea Melandri in the context of Italian feminism, see Graziella Parati and Rebecca West, 'Introduction', in G. Parati and R. West, *Italian Feminist Theory and Practice: Equality and Sexual Difference* (Madison, 2002), pp. 13–28.
21 See Alessandro Ferrara, *La forza dell'esempio. Il paradigma del giudizio* (Milan, 2008).
22 See Paul Watzlawick, Janet H. Beavin, and Don D. Jackson, *Pragmatics of Human Communication: A Study of Interactional Patterns, Pathologies, and Paradoxes* (New York, 1967).
23 Ibid., p. 212.
24 Ibid., pp. 211–13.
25 The idea – that I have repurposed in fairly liberal terms – of using the 'paradoxical injunction' in a political sense is attributable to Alessandro Dal Lago in 'L'infanzia interminabile', in *aut aut* 191–192 (1982), pp. 27–48.
26 On this topic, see David E. Leary, 'William James on the self and personality: clearing the ground for subsequent theorists, researchers, and practitioners', in W. James, M.G. Johnson and T.B. Henley, *Reflections on The Principles of Psychology: William James after a Century* (Hillsdale, 1990), pp. 101–37.
27 In reality, even the logical distinction between the self as a subject and the self as an object, in relation to which the former acts, or that the former knows, seems to hold little water. As Vincent Descombes observes in *Le parler de soi* (Paris, 2014), p. 132, the existence of an objective self is, indeed, only possible if 'someone other than me may be subject to this consciousness of which I am the object (like a doctor can be treated by a colleague). It would also be necessary to be able to shift my consciousness of myself to something other than me (just as the doctor is able to provide patients other than himself with the treatment he received)'. In other words, the relationship between the self and the self cannot be conceived of in transitive terms.
28 Research based on the same archive has been carried out by Mauro Boarelli in *La fabbrica del passato*. An analysis focusing on women's autobiographies was also previously performed using this material by Paola Zappaterra in 'Autobiografia e tensione alla politica nelle comuniste bolognesi', *Storia e problemi contemporanei* 20 (1997), pp. 49–62.
29 On this subject, see Alessandro Dal Lago and Emilio Quadrelli, *La città e le ombre. Crimini, criminali, cittadini* (Milan, 2003), p. 24.

30 Howard S. Becker, *Tricks of the Trade: How to Think about Your Research While You're Doing It* (Chicago, 1998), pp. 96–151.
31 Anders, Günther, *Die Antiquartheit des Menschen. Über die Seele im Zeitalter der zweiten industriellen Revolution* (Munich, 1961), p. 15.

Chapter 1

1 As Igal Halfin states in *Red Autobiographies: Initiating the Bolshevik Self* (Seattle, 2011), p. 3, 'to discover the self, to change the self, to perfect the self – the Soviet regime took these as its most essential duties after 1917'.
2 S. Fitzpatrick, *Tear Off the Mask! Identity and Imposture in Twentieth Century Russia* (Princeton, 2005), p. 31.
3 Claude Pennetier and Bernard Pudal, 'La volonté d'emprise. Le réferentiel biographique stalinien et ses usages dans l'univers communiste (éléments de problematique)', in C. Pennetier and B. Pudal (eds), *Autobiographies, autocritiques, aveux dans le monde* communiste (Paris, 2002), p. 18.
4 Fitzpatrick, *Tear Off the Mask!*, p. 35.
5 More specific details on the structure and composition of this biographical volume of the Granat Encyclopaedia can be found in the *Introduction* to the English translation of the volume. See Georges Haupt and Jean-Jacques Marie (eds), *Makers of the Russian Revolution: Biographies of Bolshevik Leaders* (London and New York, 2017). The first English language edition of this text was published by Cornell University Press in 1974.
6 In the years between the October Revolution and the civil war, membership increased sevenfold, totalling 576,000 by the end of that period. On this point, see John A. Getty, *Origins of the Great Purges: The Soviet Communist Party Reconsidered. 1933–1938* (Cambridge, 1985), pp. 38–40.
7 The purge procedure is described in Oleg Kharkhordin, *The Collective and the Individual in Russia. A Study of Practices* (Berkeley, 1999), pp. 140–2.
8 Penntier and Pudal, 'La volonté d'emprise', p. 26.
9 This distinction is discussed in Oleg Kharkhordin, 'By deeds alone: origins of individualization in Soviet Russia', in B. Studer and B. Unfried (eds), *Parler de soi sous Staline. La construction identitaire dans le communism des années trente* (Paris, 2002), pp. 125–45.
10 Ibid., p. 129.
11 In *The Collective and the Individual in Russia*, p. 173, note 31. Kharkhordin claims that emphasizing the 'revelation' over the 'deed' is an incorrect interpretation of what occurred during the Great Purge. In his opinion, the point is that the 'deeds' discussed in sessions aimed at vetting party cadres were void of stable points of reference, and were gradually redefined over the course of the investigative processes. From my perspective, this simply means that it is not the subject's autobiography, but rather the act of autobiographical enunciation, that counts in Stalinist biographical assessment procedures. Or, to reframe it slightly, of primary relevance is the performance of the autobiographical subject of enunciation, while what the autobiographical subject of utterance recounts about himself is only of secondary importance.
12 Krilenko and Vyshinskii's assertions are referred to in Igal Halfin's 'Looking into oppositionist's soul: inquisition communist style', *The Russian Review* 60/3 (2001),

p. 318. Halfin's analysis of the construction of the self during the Stalinist era favours the concept of a hermeneutics of desire over that of revelation of the subject through actions as discussed by Kharkhordin, to which I have referred extensively herein. As the unit of analysis of interest here is autobiographical self-enunciation – in the context of which actions and desires are but two different potential types of content of telling the truth about oneself – such a distinction is of less importance.

13 Nor, in this case, would the 'protocol sentences' to which the autobiography is reduced be statements, but rather simple signals, that fall outside of the scope of the discursive field. On this point, see Rudolf Carnap, 'On protocol sentences', *Noûs* 21 (1987), pp. 457–70.

14 According to Pascal, confession gives rise to one's culpability just like praying and kneeling down generate faith. On the performative nature of the ritual act of prayer, see Slavoj Žižek, 'Introduction: the spectre of ideology', in S. Žižek (ed.), *Mapping Ideology* (London, 1997), pp. 1–33.

15 Igal Halfin, *Stalinist Confessions: Messianism and Terror at the Leningrad Communist University* (Pittsburgh, 2009), p. 9.

16 Joseph V. Stalin, 'Against vulgarising the slogan of self-criticism', in J.V. Stalin (ed.), *Works*, Vol. 11 (Moscow, 1954), p. 133.

17 During his lectures at Sverdlov University in 1924, Stalin referred to 'criticism and self-criticism' as one of the four fundamental principles of Leninism. Cf. Joseph V. Stalin, 'The foundations of Leninism', in J.V. Stalin (ed.), *Works*, Vol. 6 (Moscow, 1953), pp. 71–196.

18 Stalin, 'Against vulgarising the slogan of self-criticism', p. 135.

19 Ibid., p. 137.

20 See John A. Getty, '*Samokritika* rituals in the Stalinist central committee', *The Russian Review* 58/1 (1999), p. 52.

21 And so Kharkhordin, in *The Collective and the Individual in Russia*, emphasizes the penitential construction of Stalinist society, considered to be a legacy of the Orthodox tradition, while Roland Boer, in *Stalin: from Theology to the Philosophy of Socialism in Power* (Singapore, 2017), pp. 88–94, believes that it is the moment of confession and repentance that is central, beyond any distinction between Catholicism and Orthodoxy.

22 Émile Durkheim, *The Division in Social Labor*, trans. George Simpson (Glencoe, 1960) pp. 108–9.

23 Émile Durkheim, 'Two laws of penal evolution', *Economy and Society* 2/3 (1973), pp. 285–308.

24 On this matter, see Larry Portis, 'Les fondements politico-idéologiques de la sociologie durkheimienne', *L'homme et la societé* 84 (1987), pp. 95–110.

25 On this topic, see Michel Foucault, in 'The subject and power', in H. L. Dreyfus and P. Rabinow, *Michel Foucault: Beyond Structuralism and Hermeneutics* (Chicago, 1983), p. 209, on the two European 'diseases of power', that is, Fascism and Stalinism, which 'in spite of their own internal madness […] used to a large extent the ideas and the devices of our political rationality'. The 1970s and 1980s also saw a 'revisionist' turn in the historiography of the Soviet Union, with the categories of analysis typical of liberal societies being successfully applied to the Soviet Union. On this point, see Sheila Fitzpatrick, 'Revisionism in soviet history', *History & Theory* 26/4 (2007), pp. 77–91.

26 Brigitte Studer, *The Transnational Word of the Cominternians* (Basingstoke, 2015), p. 73.

27 Around 1,000 foreign communists had enrolled in courses at the Communist University of the Minorities of the West by 1936. The International Lenin School had around twice that number of students between 1926 and 1938. See Brigitte Studer, 'L'être perfectible. La formation du cadre stalinien par le "travail sur soi"', *Genèses. Sciences sociales et histoire* 51 (2003), p. 95.

28 On the International Lenin School and its peculiarities compared to the other educational institutions for foreign communist cadres, see Serge Wolikow and Jean Vigreux, 'L'école léniniste internationale de Moscou: une pépinière de cadres communiste', *Cahiers d'histoire* 79 (2000), pp. 45–56.

29 See Claude Pennetier and Bernard Pudal, 'La "verification" (l'encadrement biographique communiste dans l'entre-deux guerre)', *Genèses. Sciences sociales et histoire* 23 (1996), pp. 149–51.

30 See Claude Pennetier and Bernard Pudal, 'Le questionnement biographique en France (1931–1974)', in C. Pennetier and B. Pudal (eds), *Autobiographies, autocritiques, aveux dans le monde communiste* (Paris, 2002), p. 136.

31 For an example of the questionnaire presented to militants, see Pennetier and Pudal, 'La "vérification"', pp. 154–5.

32 Pennetier and Pudal, 'Le questionnement biographique en France (1931–1974)', pp. 142–51.

33 Claude Pennetier and Bernard Pudal, 'Les mauvais subjects du stalinisme, in B. Studer and B. Unfried (eds), *Parler de soi sous Staline. La construction identitaire dans le communism des années trente* (Paris, 2002), p. 92.

34 Its objective was to defend communist parliamentarians from disparagement by political adversaries arising from their low level of formal education. On this point, see Bernard Pudal, *Prendre parti. Pour une sociologie historique du PCF* (Paris, 1989), pp. 211–15.

35 An extensive and accurate presentation of Togliatti can be found in Aldo Agosti's *Palmiro Togliatti: A Biography* (London, 2008).

36 For a detailed description of Togliatti's return to Italy, see Paolo Spriano, *Storia del Partito Comunista Italiano. La resistenza. Togliatti e il partito nuovo*, Vol. V (Turin, 1976), pp. 282–313.

37 Palmiro Togliatti, 'I compiti del partito nella situazione attuale', in P. Togliatti, *Opere*, ed. Luciano Gruppi (Rome, 1984), p. 86.

38 Ibid., p. 102.

39 This opinion is shared by Giuseppe C. Marino in *Autoritratto del PCI staliniano* (Rome, 1991), p. 20, who believes that 'it is acceptable to have doubts regarding the end of Bolshevism [...] and the suggestion that it can be taken for granted that the cadre system was overcome certainly does not stand up to scrutiny'.

40 The political opinion on Togliattism, however, is more complex. The progressive democratic strategy was founded on the notion of mass participation in national political life, mediated by the large parties: not only the PCI, but also the Italian Socialist Party (Partito Socialista Italiano – PSI) and the Christian Democrats (Democrazia Cristiana – DC). Consequently, at the centre of communist action was an alliance with the large political organizations, which lasted until May 1947, when the DC formed a new government that excluded the socialists and the communists. Nevertheless, this indicated a lack of true desire to reform the state, its systems and its methods of functioning. For a balanced analysis of Togliatti's actions, see Marcello Flores and Nicola Gallerano, *Sul PCI. Un'interpretazione storica* (Bologna, 1992), p. 88.

41 The data on PCI membership trends can be found in Gianfranco Poggi (ed.), *L'organizzazione partitica del PCI e della DC* (Bologna, 1968).
42 The Bologna questionnaire has a similar structure to that used in Novi Ligure, in Piedmont. It is probable, then, that it is a standard format used by the PCI. On the Novi Ligure communists and their *Biografie del militante*, see Cecilia Bergaglio, '"Sono comunista dall'età della ragione". Il PCI a Novi Ligure attraverso i questionari biografici dei militanti. 1945–1946', *Quaderno di storia contemporanea* 55 (2014), pp. 31–49.
43 Andrea A., born in 1911, *Biografia del Militante* (1945). Article XVIII of the Provisional Regulations for Organisation of the PCI clearly addressed the issue of Fascist membership by communist militants: 'given that PNF membership was imposed on entire categories of workers and citizens, who simply by joining the PNF had the opportunity to find work or practice a profession, those who joined the PNF before 25 July but who never held positions, or performed Fascist activities, may be accepted as candidates', in Patrizia Salvetti, 'Il Partito Comunista Italiano', in Carlo Vallauri, *La ricostituzione dei partiti democratici (1943–1948)* (Rome, 1977), p. 770.
44 Loretta A., born in 1915, *Biografia del Militante* (1945).
45 Giacomo A., born in 1925, *Biografia del Militante* (1948).
46 Amadeo Bordiga was a founding member of the PCd'I and its first secretary. He was expelled from the party in 1930 for having defended Trotsky. Bordiga's politics, however, were not identical to Trotsky's and Bordigism is not synonymous with Trotskyism. For a discussion on Bordiga, see Andreina De Clementi, *Amadeo Bordiga* (Turin, 1971).
47 Giorgio S., born in 1928, *Biografia del Militante* (1950).
48 In the case of Simone S., born in 1911, who spent his younger years during Mussolini's twenty-year reign, his arrest was almost certainly the product of anger accumulated over years of Fascist oppression. When asked if he was arrested under Fascism, he responded: 'no. I was arrested during the Badoglio period, because on 27 July 1943 I gave the ex-secretary of the Fascist group a serious beating' (*Biografia del Militante* (1949)). Apparently, two days after Mussolini fell from power and the Fascist regime began to crumble, Simone S. settled a score – which had most likely remained unresolved for many years – with a small local Fascist leader.
49 Simone S., 1949 autobiography.
50 Enrico F., born in 1929, *Biografia del militante* (1950). Enrico F. joined the party in 1945 but, unlike other militants, he remained a basic member for three years without holding any specific positions, probably due to his personal and employment problems.
51 Mario Spinella, 'La scuola centrale di partito', *Rinascita* 8 (agosto 1948), p. 345.
52 Pietro Secchia, *Il partito della rinascita. Rapporto alla conferenza nazionale di organizzazione del Partito Comunista Italiano* (Rome, 1947), p. 8.
53 Alberto C., born in 1923, *Biografia del Militante* (1950).
54 Paolo C., born in 1924, *Biografia del Militante* (1948).
55 Antonio B., born in 1923, *Biografia del Militante*, no date.
56 Pietro Secchia, 'Rafforzare le organizzazioni di massa, rafforzare il partito', *Quaderno dell'attivista* 6 (15 marzo 1951), p. 178.
57 Pietro Secchia, 'L'operosità nel lavoro e la democrazia nel partito', *Quaderno dell'attivista* 16 (15 August 1952), p. 483.
58 Secchia, *Il partito della rinascita*, pp. 49–50.

59 The pedagogical slant of the communist organizational bond is well articulated by Secchia: 'it is preferable that a task not be completed one hundred percent, but that a new cadre is challenged in a role of responsibility, and gains experience for his or her future'. Ibid., p. 49.
60 On pastoral power as a sacrifice, see Michel Foucault, *Security, Territory, Population: Lectures at the Collège De France, 1977–78*, trans. Graham Burchell (London, 2007), pp. 115–90. As Foucault himself notes, however, pastoral power does not correspond directly to a pedagogical relationship.
61 Pietro Secchia, 'L'arte di organizzare', *Rinascita* 12 (dicembre 1945), p. 543.
62 Pietro Secchia, *Più forti i quadri, migliore l'organizzazione* (Rome, n.d.), p. 34.
63 Ibid., pp. 24–5: 'stronger, better discipline is essentially achieved through better training of our cadres. [...] We must activate all comrades, we must entrust each of them with a concrete job to perform'.
64 *Pragmatics of Human Communication*, p. 217.
65 Michel Foucault, *On the Government of the Living: Lectures at the Collège de France (1979-1980)*, trans. Graham Burchell (London, 2014), p. 230.
66 Carl Schmitt, *Political Theology: Four Chapters on the Concept of Sovereignty*, trans. George Schwab (Chicago and London, 2005), p. 13.
67 Pietro Secchia, in 'Che cosa è la cellula', *Quaderno dell'attivista* [The Activist's Notebook] (October 1946) p. 43, states that the cell, as a base unit in a party 'is not simply a subdivision of the organisation to make placement of the mass members of the Party easier, and nor is it an entity conceived of to facilitate the collection of fees. It is, first and foremost, an entity that engages in discussion and development of the Party's political line'. Shortly thereafter, while confirming that the cell is the heart of the party's political activity, the author adds that 'cells also engage in great politics'.
68 As an impossible task, the politicization of the organizational act translated, in practical terms, into communication of the political line from top to bottom, while adopting a posture of paternalistic bonhomie, taking care to ensure that comrades understood the soundness of the political decisions – made by others – that they were required to implement. Thus 'learning from lower-level comrades' bizarrely came to mean 'knowing those comrades' thoughts: whether they understand the political line, whether they have grasped the reason for a particular political move. It means knowing how to correct those who are wrong in a fraternal way, without silencing or humiliating them' (in 'La democrazia nel partito' in *Quaderno dell'attivista* [October 1946], p. 44).
69 Pajetta made this comparison in conversation with a Jesuit. The anecdote is reported in an interview conducted by Oriana Fallaci with him in 1974 for *L'Europeo*. The text of that interview is now available in Oriana Fallaci, *Intervista con il potere* (Milan, 2009), pp. 398–431.
70 On the interpretation of Weber's ideal type in terms of example, see Ahmad Sadri, *Max Weber's Sociology of Intellectuals* (New York, 1992), pp. 20–1.
71 Simone B., born in 1921, *Autobiografia*, written in 1952.
72 For a discussion of Rousseau's *The confessions*, see Jean Starobinsky, *Jean-Jacques Rousseau: Transparency and Obstruction*, trans. Arthur Goldhammer (Chicago, 1988), pp. 270–9.
73 The significance of this guilt carried by Simone B. is easier to understand in light of the table of vices and virtues of a communist militant found in Marino, *Autoritratto del PCI staliniano*, p. 80.

74 Peter Brooks, *Troubling Confessions: Speaking Guilt in Law and Literature* (Chicago, 2001), p. 22.
75 From this point forward, my analysis of communist autobiographies will focus specifically on their narrative aspects. With regard to the linguistic dimensions of the didactic products that emerged from the party schools – including the autobiographies of those who attended the courses – see Andrea Pozzetta, 'Italian Communist Party Schools: Writing Practices and Linguistic Analysis' [1st Conference of the European Labour History Network – Workshop: Workers' Writing in Europe. A Contribution to the Cultural History of the Worlds of Work. Turin, 14–16 December 2015].
76 Carlo C., born in 1914, undated autobiography.
77 Enrico C., born in 1909 autobiography undated, but written in response to a request from the Activists' Commission from 22 December 1949. Probably to clarify the reasons for his previous membership of the PNF, which, he claimed, was only because it was required to attend university.
78 The reference, here, is to the idea of 'chaotic enumeration' developed by Spitzer in *La enumeraciòn caótica en la poesía moderna* (Buenos Aires, 1945).
79 On Homeric cartography, see the impressive site curated by a group of scholars from the University of Virginia, *Mapping the Catalogue of Ships*, available at http://ships.lib.virginia.edu/ (accessed 11 October 2018).
80 Giovanna C., born in 1931, 1949 autobiography.
81 I found many of the autobiographies that I read interesting from a literary perspective, not so much due to their narrative form, imposed upon them from an organizational perspective, but more because of the linguistic inventions they contain. In many instances, this is the result of having the opportunity, for the first time, to write in a context, other than state administration, that justified such an act of writing. This gives rise to a creative mix of bureaucratic formulae, party jargon, linguistic structures typical of spoken language and school memories, blended together in the pursuit of one's own communist voice. And so Giovanna C.'s obsession with description is not dissimilar to Robbe-Grillet's, but the latter is literature whereas the former is not, because the social framing – the set of valid paraliterary enunciations, ranging from specialist criticism to pages on literary scandals contained in magazines and newspapers – surrounding these texts is different. On the social construction of the work of art, see Howard Becker, *Arts World* (Berkeley, 1982) and Alessandro Dal Lago and Serena Giordano, *Mercanti di aura. Logiche dell'arte contemporanea* (Bologna, 2006).
82 Peter Brooks, *Reading for the Plot: Design and Intention in Narrative* (Cambridge, MA, 1992), p. 22.
83 Luca C., born in 1925, 1951 autobiography.
84 Franca A., born in 1929, undated autobiography.
85 Patrizio G., born in 1930, undated autobiography.
86 Patrizio G., born in 1930, 1951 autobiography.
87 Paolo A., born in 1923, 1949 autobiography.
88 Hatred is a frequent theme in communist autobiographies, but it is always neutralized by being ascribed to the militant's past, to their childhood or youth. 'This led even at just 7 years of age to instilling a hatred and resentment in me for those who commanded with force and cruelty', says Carlo O. (born in 1928, 1964 autobiography). Serena M. (born in 1933, 1955 autobiography), on the other hand,

remembers that 'at 12 years of age I started work at a dressmaker's and it was the contrast between my family's poverty and the wealth of the bourgeois ladies who bought our services, together with the constant humiliation we received from these ladies and from the owner that gave me a deep hatred for the rich'. Likewise, Carola D. (born in 1936, 1949 autobiography) recalls her own experience of Fascism: 'I recognised the injustice of what Fascism was doing, I hated it just as wicked men – and not as political men. I hated war, the injustice that there were rich people and poor people.' It is also worth adding here that hatred has a specifically political dimension, as observed by Walter Benjamin, who criticized German Social Democracy for having made the working class forget 'hatred' and the 'spirit of sacrifice', which are both 'nourished by the image of enslaved ancestors, rather than that of liberated grandchildren' (in 'Theses on the philosophy of history', in W. Benjamin, *Illuminations: Essays and Reflections*, trans. Harry Zhon (New York, 2007), p. 260).
89 Franco Moretti, *The Way of the World. The Bildungsroman in European Culture*. New edition, trans. Albert Sbragia (London, 2000), pp. 45–6.
90 See Gérard Genette, *Narrative Discourse: An Essay in Method*, trans. Jane E. Lewin (Ithaca, 1980), pp. 226–7.
91 Carlo O., born in 1928, 1954 autobiography.
92 Patrizio U., born in 1925, *Cosa mi aspetto dalla scuola*, undated.
93 Erich Auerbach, 'Figura', in E. Auerbach, *Scenes from the Drama of European Literature*, trans. Ralph Manheim (Minneapolis, 1984), p. 47.
94 Ibid., pp. 52–4.
95 Benedetta R., born in 1930, undated autobiography.
96 In general terms, we could say that the communist autobiography tends toward – but does not achieve – the radical form of repetition between narrator and character that Goethe engages in at the end of the seventh book of *Wilhelm Meister's Apprenticeship*. Here Wilhelm, having gained access to the secret rooms of the Society of the Tower, discovers that his story, that is, *Wilhelm Meister's Apprenticeship*, has already been written and preserved in a scroll. Wilhelm's story, then, repeats the plot presented by the narrator who is recounting it – the Society of the Tower. On this, see *The Way of the World*, p. 22.

Chapter 2

1 For a brief, but clear interpretation of the history of Italian neo-feminism and its various stages of development, see Anna Rossi-Doria, 'Ipotesi per una storia del neo-femminismo italiano', in A. Rossi-Doria (ed.), *Dare forma al silenzio. Scritti di storia politica delle donne* (Rome, 2007), pp. 243–65. For an English-language discussion, see Maud A. Bracke, *Women and the Reinvention of the Political: Feminism in Italy, 1968–1983* (New York, 2014), and the less recent, but nevertheless excellent, Hellman, *Journeys among Women*.
2 Manuela Fraire, *Lessico politico delle donne. Teorie del femminismo* (Milan, 2002), p. 59. The original edition of this text was published in 1978. *Lessico politico delle donne* is a sort of encyclopaedia of Feminist knowledge that includes five more volumes in addition to *Teorie del femminsmo*, covering subjects ranging from law to medicine.

3   The consciousness-raising practice seems, in any case, to have had Italian roots of sorts, given that the Catholic association groups also engaged in similar practice. On this, see Luisa Passerini, *Storie di donne e di femministe* (Turin, 1991), p. 143.
4   Consider that unlike the English term 'consciousness-raising', the Italian '*autocoscienza*' (literally, 'self-consciousness') 'stresses the self-determined and self-directed quality of the process of achieving a new consciousness/awareness' (in Paola Bono and Sandra Kemp, 'Introduction: coming from the South', in P. Bono and S. Kemp (eds), *Italian Feminist Thought* (Oxford, 1991), p. 9). Overall, the two authors very clearly define the points of affinity and divergence between Italian feminism and its French and English counterparts.
5   Carla Lonzi was one of the most influential Italian feminists. On her work, see Margrit Brückner, 'On Carla Lonzi: the victory of the clitoris over the vagina as an act of women's liberation', *European Journal of Women's Studies* 21/3 (2014), pp. 278–82 and Francesco Ventrella, 'Carla Lonzi's artwriting and the resonance of separatism', *European Journal of Women's Studies* 21/3 (2014), pp. 282–7. For an Italian-language discussion, meanwhile, see Maria Luisa Boccia's two pieces on Carla Lonzi: *L'io in rivolta. Vissuto e pensiero di Carla Lonzi* (Milan, 1990) and *Con Carla Lonzi. La mia vita è la mia opera* (Rome, 2014).
6   Carla Lonzi, 'Significato dell'autocoscienza nei gruppi femministi', in C. Lonzi (ed.), *Sputiamo su Hegel. La donna clitoridea e la donna vaginale e altri scritti* (Milan, 1974), p. 143.
7   Alma Sabatini, 'Il piccolo gruppo. Struttura di base del movimento femminista', in *Effe* (January 1974). Available at http://efferivistafemminista.it/2014/07/struttura-di-base-del-movimento-femminista/ (accessed 3 December 2018).
8   See, for example, Herbert Marcuse, 'The obsolescence of psychoanalysis', in H. Marcuse (ed.), *Collected Papers of Herbert Marcuse* (London and New York, 2011), pp. 109–21. For a discussion of Adorno's critique of revisionist psychoanalysis, on the other hand, see Nan-Nan Lee, 'Sublimated or castrated psychoanalysis? Adorno's critique of the revisionist psychoanalysis: an introduction to "The Revisionist Psychoanalysis"', *Philosophy and Social Criticism* 40/3 (2014), pp. 309–38.
9   In the transcript of a discussion between Nadja and Valeria, two women involved in the labour and feminist movements, they discuss how they came to consciousness-raising: '**Valeria**: Our problem was: what to do? We thought we were practising consciousness-raising, but we didn't know what it was ... **Nadja**: We imagined ourselves, you sit there, bring up a diagram and discuss it ... decide what to discuss – but actually it's nothing like that ...' ('Un anno di esperienza tra autocoscienza e lotta di fabbrica', in Anonymous A, 'Un anno di esperienza tra autocoscienza e lotta di fabbrica', in *Sottosopra. Esperienze di gruppi femministi in Italia* (1974), pp. 187–8.
10 In her description of how the consciousness-raising groups operate, Luisa Passerini (in *Storie di donne e femministe*, p. 168) states that the first person to contribute is the one 'with the greatest urgency to narrate'.
11 Anonymous B, 'Vedrai che dopo cambierà', *Sottosopra. Esperienze di gruppi femministi in Italia* (Milan, 1974), p. 35.
12 Liliana, 'Capi e segretarie: ovvero il sesso in azienda', *Sottosopra. Esperienze di gruppi femministi in Italia* (Milan, 1974), p. 37.
13 Anonymous C, 'Storia d'ufficio', *Sottosopra. Esperienze di gruppi femministi in Italia* (1974), p. 32.
14 These are the 'ten winters' discussed by Franco Fortini in *Dieci inverni. 1947–1957. Contributi a un discorso socialista* (Macerata, 2018). For a brief introduction to

Fortini, see Matteo Soranzo, 'Franco Fortini (Franco Lattes)', in G. Marrone, P. Puppa and L. Simigli (eds), *Encyclopedia of Italian Literary Studies* (London and New York, 2007), pp. 759–62.

15　Paul Ricoeur, 'L'hermeneutique du témoignage', in P. Ricoeur (ed.), *Lectures* 3 (Paris, 1994), pp. 114–15.

16　The intention of my reconstruction of the feminist self-narrative is purely descriptive, from a sociological perspective. Adriana Cavarero, in *Relating Narratives: Storytelling and Selfhood*, trans. Paul A. Kottman (London and New York, 2000), on the other hand, offers a philosophical interpretation of this scenario focused on the concept of a 'narratable self' that emphasizes not only the act of self-narration but also the fact that the self is fundamentally 'narratable' by others.

17　On the literary fortunes of Scheherazade as a feminist princess, see Fedwa Malti-Douglas, 'Shahrazād feminist', in R.G. Hovannisian and G. Sabagh (eds), *The Thousand and One Nights in Arabic Literature and Society* (Cambridge, 1997), pp. 40–55. Adriana Cavarero also offers an interpretation of Scheherazade in *Relating Narratives*, pp. 119–28.

18　On this point, and for an interesting reading of *Arabian Nights*, see Abdelfattah Kilito, *L'oeil et l'aiguille. Essais sur Les Milles et Une Nuits* (Paris, 1994).

19　Anonymous D, 'E continuavamo a chiamarci femministe', in *Sottosopra. Esperienze di gruppi femministi in Italia* (1974), p. 241.

20　This sense of tiredness was also recorded in Milan Women's Bookstore Collective, *Sexual Difference: A Theory of Social-Symbolic Practice*, trans. Patricia Cicogna and Teresa de Lauretis (Bloomington, 1990), p. 45: 'Actually, by now the practice of autocoscienza was producing a feeling of impotence for the simple reason that it had exhausted its potential. It was a limited political practice which could not be prolonged after it succeeded in making women conscious of being a separate sex, a sex neither subordinate nor assimilable to the male.' This explanation of the exhaustion of consciousness-raising experiences is, naturally, internal to the Italian feminist movement itself and differs from my interpretation according to which the categories used by Italian neo-feminism are discursive objects to by analysed rather than explicative concepts that explain the feminist movement.

21　Lea Melandri, *Una visceralità indicibile* (Milan, 2000), p. 55.

22　On the methods according to which denunciation and indignation work, see Luc Boltanski, *Distant Suffering: Morality, Media and Politics*, trans. Graham Burchell (Cambridge, 2004), pp. 57–66.

23　See Leigh Gilmore, *The Limits of Autobiography: Trauma and Testimony* (Ithaca, 2001).

24　Georg Simmel, *The Sociology of Georg Simmel* (Glencoe, 1950), p. 344.

25　When I speak of aphasia I am not referring to *ontic* silence, making somewhat free use of heideggerian language, but rather to *ontological* silence. As such, the subject is not simply silent, because even in this case he would not stop saying anything – as noted by Paul Watzlawich, Janet Beavick and Don D. Jackson, in *Pragmatics of Human Communication*, p. 49, 'no matter how one may try, one cannot *not* communicate. Activity or inactivity, words or silence all have message value.' And so being silent, in this case, does not mean putting on a pair of dark glasses, which allow the expression of something – my sad state of mind – through its concealment, that is, they continue to say something even if they seek to say nothing: 'the power of language: with my language I can do everything: even and especially *say nothing*' (in Roland Barthes, *A Lover's Discourse: Fragments*, trans. Richard Howard (New York, 2001), p. 44).

Rather, feminist enunciation is oriented towards absolute silence, which interrupts the possibility of speaking and communicating. This, however, is an impossible task – at least as long as there is a desire to enunciate. Consequently, as we will see in this chapter, the slide from ontological to ontic silence in inevitable.

26 Watzlawich, Beavick and Jackson, *Pragmatics of Human Communication*, p. 212.
27 Tzvetan Todorov, 'Le discours psychotique', in T. Todorov, *Les genres du discourse* (Paris, 1978), pp. 78–85. I refer here to the French edition, because the English version – *The Genres in Discourse* (Cambridge, 1990) – does not include this essay, along with various others that appear in the original text.
28 Todorov, 'Le discours psycotique', p. 78.
29 Ibid., p. 85.
30 According to Maria L. Boccia (in *Con Carla Lonzi*, p. 15), there is profound consistency between Carla Lonzi's theoretical works and *Taci, anzi parla*. They are all based on the same 'incessant recording of movements between the self and reality, between public and private events and consciousness'. I have no reason to challenge this interpretation: suffice to say that, given the nature of my research, I am much more interested in the narrative form than in the theoretical content.
31 For a summary of these events in the context of Italy in the 1970s, see Paul Ginsborg, *A History of Contemporary Italy: Society and Politics 1943–1988* (Basingstoke, 2003), pp. 348–406.
32 Rivolta Femminile was not the first feminist group to emerge in Italy. Indeed, the mid-1970s saw the establishment of Demau in Milan (an acronym of 'Demistificazione dell'autoritarismo patriarcale' [Demystification of patriarchal authoritarianism]), which published its *Manifesto Programmatico del gruppo Demau* in 1966. See Bianca Beccalli, 'The modern women's movement in Italy', *New Left Review* I/204 (1994), p. 94. Rivolta Femminile and Carla Lonzi's theoretical writings, however, represent the beginning of Italian neo-feminism as 'feminist practice intended to change the relationship with the world starting from an analysis of oneself' (in Passerini, *Storie di donne e femministe*, p. 179). For a discussion of Demau and Rivolta Femminile, see also Milan Women's Bookstore Collective, *Sexual Difference*, pp. 35–40. Carla Lonzi's theoretical writings referred to in the text are collected in *Sputiamo su Hegel. La donna clitoridea e la donna vaginale e altri scritti*.
33 I will not provide the full list of names that appear in the text because in many cases it is impossible to identify a real-life independent person behind the character. And besides, the author is very clear on this point. As regards the 'necessary requirements' – which should serve to identify characters who appear in the text – she says as follows: 'the fact that I recognise them, and discern them with an accuracy that the diary reveals before my eyes as it unfolds, does not say anything definitive about those who possess those requirements or the substance thereof. I talk about relationships in the diary, not people' (in Lonzi, *Taci, anzi parla*, p. 7).
34 Tuuli Tarina published *Una ragazza timida* (Milan, 1973) under the Rivolta Femminile banner. Sara, addressing Carla, says that the latter has behaved like a 'little Hitler, first imposing the distinction between clitoridian and vaginal, and then gratifying her cadaver, the timid girl' (in Lonzi, *Taci, anzi parla*, p. 981). Sara, like Tuuli Tarina, is Finnish: 'I loved her a lot, but if she had died, disappeared to Finland forever, I would have felt relief' (Ibid., p. 1032).
35 It is no coincidence that the second manifesto by the Rivolta Femminile bears the title 'I say me' in Rivolta Femminile, 'Second manifesto of Rivolta femminile: "io dico io"', in Rivolta Femminile, *La presenza dell'uomo nel femminismo* (Milan, 1977), pp. 7–9.

36 In this case, the feminist self-narrative should operate according to a Benjamin-style spirit: 'a chronicler who recites events without distinguishing between major and minor ones acts in accordance with the following truth: nothing that has ever happened should be regarded as lost for history. To be sure, only a redeemed mankind receives the fullness of its past – which is to say, only for a redeemed mankind has its past become citable in all its moments' – in Benjamin, 'Theses on the philosophy of history' p. 254.
37 Lonzi, *Taci, anzi parla*, p. 617.
38 Ibid., p. 1146.
39 Each repetition is never a perfect repetition, given that each repeated element produces an 'accumulation of significance'. See Krystyna Mazur, 'Repetition', in R. Greene and S. Cushman (eds), *The Princeton Encyclopedia of Poetry and Poetics*, 4th edition (Princenton, 2012), p. 1169.
40 Lonzi, *Taci, anzi parla*, p. 1147.
41 Tilde Giani Gallino, 'L'amore materno è …', in *Effe*, 5/9 (1977). Available at http://efferivistafemminista.it/2014/11/lamore-materno-e/ (accessed 8 January 2019).
42 As well as being an effect of the literary mechanism characterizing the *Diario di una femminista*, the proliferation of questions also has a specific sociological purpose. Feminist confession, in its various forms, does not have an institutional foundation, unlike communist militant autobiographies that are written in response to a formal request by the party. The inclusion of questions in the text rather than outside it, then, justifies its existence. In other words, it offers meaning to this particular social phenomenon of diary writing. Motivation that, given the lack of an organizational or institutional request, must be constantly reinforced – hence the almost obsessive repetition of interrogations of the self and the world in the text. On this topic, see Charles Wright Mills, 'Situated actions and vocabularies of motive', *American Sociological Review* 5/6 (1940), pp. 904–13.
43 From this perspective, in relation to Carla Lonzi, it is worth recalling the observations made by Emmanuel Levinas in 'Phenomenon and enigma', in E. Levinas (ed.), *Collected Philosophical Papers*, trans. Alphonso Lingis (Dordrecht, 1987), pp. 69–70: 'All speaking is enigma. It is, to be sure, established in and moves in an order of signification common to the interlocutors, in the midst of triumphant, that is, primary truths, in a particular language that bears a system of known truths which the speaking, however commonplace is, does stir up and led to new significations.' The repeated questions are simply a search index for these elusive new significations.
44 As Lonzi herself says (in *Taci, anzi parla*, p. 1104), 'there is nothing to do, I feel better when I manage to find some sort of meaning in what is happening.' The possibility that the events do not in fact have any meaning would, therefore, seem to be ruled out.
45 Lonzi, *Taci, anzi parla*, p. 926.
46 The stance is deeply influenced by the attributes of Milanese feminism and its criticism of the abstract claim to the right to an abortion. On this point see Martucci, *La libreria delle donne a Milano. Un laboratorio di pratica politica*.
47 Pierre Bourdieu, *The Weight of the World. Social Suffering in Contemporary Society*, trans. Priscilla Parkhurst Ferguson, Joe Johnson and Shaggy T. Waryn (Stanford, 1999), pp. 621–6.
48 Genette, *Narrative Discourse*, pp. 228–9.
49 Anonymous E, 'Il corpo politico', *Sottosopra. Fascicolo speciale* (1975), p 10.

50 Below is a brief compendium of such 'meta-diaristic' acts: 'Sara read me a passage from her diary' (Lonzi, *Taci, anzi parla*, p. 75); 'Tito is copying part of my thirteen-year-old diary on the machine' (ibid., p. 123); 'Browsing Sara's diary (ibid., 236); 'I read with Sara what she wrote about me in the chapter entitled "Crisis with Carla"' (ibid., p. 284); 'Sara's second diary, which I've finished reading' (ibid., p. 294); 'Simone is reading my diary' (ibid., p. 325); 'Simone stopped reading my diary in the middle of the night' (ibid., p. 327); 'I feel a sense of intimacy like after a childhood episode of voyeurism, it is once again Isa's diary that leaves me feeling this way' (ibid. p. 636). Within the text, character also often exchange poems.
51 Ibid., p. 635.
52 Ibid., pp. 466–7.
53 Raymond Carver, 'Feathers', in R. Carver, *Cathedral* (New York, 1983), p. 17.
54 Lonzi, *Taci, anzi parla*, p. 467.
55 In this regard, see Daniel Just's discussion of Carver in 'Is less more? A reinvention of realism in Raymond Carver's minimalist short stories', *Critiques: Studies in Contemporary Fiction* 49/3 (2008), pp. 303–17. The way that Carver is used here to interpret Carla Lonzi's method of recounting events is based on the brilliant observations made by Just.
56 The few remaining traces of reality to be found in the text are mainly reserved for the protagonist's body, her forms of autoeroticism and the effects of the illness on her: 'at night I slept, peed, coughed and spat phlegm' (Lonzi, *Taci, anzi parla*, p. 282).
57 Peter Brooks, *The Melodramatic Imagination: Balzac, Henry James, and the Mode of Excess* (New Haven and London, 1995), pp. 40–1.
58 In this game of grandiose identification, Maria L. Boccia (in *Con Carla Lonzi*, pp. 73–4) notes that Carla Lonzi, as John the Baptist, is a prophet who announces the arrival of Christ, that is, Sara.
59 The melodramatic imagination, in its various guises, does not rule out the presence of nuanced characters with complex internal lives. On this matter, see Peter Brooks' discussion of Henry James – in *The Melodramatic Imagination*, p. 159, where Jamesian characters are also defined as 'centers of consciousness' and not simply flat characters.
60 Ibid. p. 29.
61 Ibid., pp. 56–80.
62 Lonzi, *Taci, anzi parla*, pp. 163–4.
63 The protagonist cries on 2 October 1972 (ibid., p. 114); 14 November 1972 (ibid., p. 166); 17 November 1972 (ibid., p. 168); 18 November 1972 (ibid., p. 169). Twice, in one case, she is 'on the verge of tears', while the friend she met had cried 'in the bathtub'; 23 November 1972 (ibid., p. 170; even if it is simply the admission of the possibility of crying in front of Sara); 4 January 1973 (ibid., p. 196); 17 January 1973 (ibid., p. 216); 25 January 1973 (ibid., p. 236; on the following page Nicola also cries); 9 February 1973 (ibid. p. 269); 23 March 1973 (ibid., p. 335). As regards other characters: a young man cries near an old woman on 7 February 1973 (ibid., p. 262); Germana bursts into tears on 15 November 1972 (ibid., p. 166). Sara's boyfriend cries on 26 November 1972 (ibid., p. 171); Simone cries on 4 March 1973 'without hiding his face' (ibid., p. 313). I will stop here because I believe that the number of examples, relating solely to the first part of the text, is sufficient to support my claim.
64 As Brooks notes (in *The Melodramatic Imagination*, p. 79), 'mute gesture appears a new sign making visible the absent and ineffable'.
65 Lonzi, *Taci, anzi parla*, p. 982.

66   Ibid., p. 984.
67   The text is found in Sherry Rochester and James R. Martin, *Crazy Talk: A Study of the Discourse of Schizophrenic Speakers* (New York and London, 1979), p. 106. In this transcription, I have omitted the notes that the authors use to analyse the text.
68   Carla Lonzi, *Vai pure. Dialogo con Pietro Consagra* (Milan, 2010), pp. 85–6. The original edition, published in Scritti di Rivolta Femminile, is from 1980.
69   Ibid., p. 3.
70   The presence of the recorder can result in the, more or less pleasant, awareness of being recorded. See Rosalind Edwards, Janet Holland, *What Is Qualitative Interviewing?* (London, 2013), p. 69.
71   For a definition of the 'Hawthorne effect', see Lisa M. James, Hoa T. Vo, 'Hawthorne effect', in *Encyclopedia of Research Design* (Thousand Oaks, 2010), pp. 561–7.
72   This is one of the many examples where what Luc Boltanski and Ève Chiappello – in *The New Spirit of Capitalism*, trans. Gregory Elliott (London, 2007) – define as the 'artistic critique' of capitalism is appropriated by capitalism itself and put at the service of its logics of accumulation.
73   Mikhail Bakhtin, *Problems of Dostoevsky's Poetics*, trans. Caryl Emerson (Minneapolis, 1984), p. 53.
74   Eliana, 'Andare alle radici', in *Sottosopra* (1976), p. 120.
75   Pia Cadinas, '"Ode" a Paestum', in *Effe* 5/2. Available at http://efferivistafemminista.it/2014/11/ode-a-paestum/ (accessed 8 February 2018).
76   Anonymous F, 'Viaggio attraverso un'esperienza', *Differenze* 2 (1976), cited in Federica Paoli, *Pratiche di scrittura femminista* (Milan, 2011), p. 166.
77   Ibid., p. 60.
78   Not all Italian feminist poems have a lyrical quality. See, for example, that written by B.A. Olivo, 'La canzone della bambina povera', – in *Effe* 2/6 (1974). Available at http://efferivistafemminista.it/2015/01/le-poesie-della-bambina-povera/ (accessed 8 February 2019) – it is actually a social satire song.
79   My definition of lyrical poetry is based on that offered by Emil Staiger, in *Basic Concepts of Poetics*, trans. Janette C. Hudson and Luanne T. Frank (University Park, 1991) pp. 43–96. Among the many interesting observations made by Staiger, one statement deserves to be quoted in full, because it is particularly significant in relation to the topic at hand: 'the lyric poet usually says "I." But he says differently than does the author of an autobiography. One can only speak of one's own life when an entire era lies in the past. Then, one looks at the "I" in perspective and gives it form. But the lyric poet does not "give form" to himself any more than "comprehend" himself. […] "To form" might seem appropriate for autobiographical writing, while the word "to comprehend" might perhaps seem appropriate for a diary, in which a person takes stock of a period just passed. But this material only *seems* to be more recent than that found in an autobiography, it only seems so according to time as measured by the clock. The person writing a diary makes himself the object of a reflection' – ibid. p. 76. The autobiographical I can, therefore, slide almost effortlessly to merge with its lyrical counterpart. The difference, however, lies in the reflexive distance between the I and its objects, which is present in the first instance, and absent in the second. This is why I do not include the poetry that features in *Taci, anzi parla* among the lyrical material. Not only so as to avoid weighing the book down with further texts by Carla Lonzi, but above all because the poetic materials that appear in her diary, though they are formally

lyrical elements, are instead, in substance, objects of reflection for the narrator and her pursuit of meaning.
80 For a discussion of this matter, see Giuseppe Bernardelli, *Il testo lirico. Logica e forma di un tipo letterario* (Milan, 2002), p. 146.
81 Lonzi, *Taci, anzi parla*, pp. 366–7.
82 For an examination of Lonzi's theoretical perspective, see Elena Della Torre, 'The clitoris diaries: *La donna clitoridea*, feminine authenticity, and the phallic allegory of Carla Lonzi's Radical feminism', *European Journal of Women's Studies* 21/3 (2014), pp. 219–32.
83 Genette, *Narrative Discourse*, p. 190.
84 Lonzi, *Taci, anzi parla*, p. 1300.
85 On this topic see Brooks, *Reading for the Plot*, in particular, pp. 90–112.
86 Alice Martinelli, *Autocoscienza* (Milan, 1975), pp. 67–8.
87 'Sogni' Notebooks, 10–11 November 1966, Box 1, Folder 2, Archivio Lea (Maddalena) Melandri, Fondazione Badaracco, Milan.
88 This interpretation is based on Bakhtin's observations – in *The Dialogic Imagination: Four Essays*, trans. Caryl Emerson and Michael Holquist (Austin, TX, 1981), pp. 111–29 – regarding the adventure novel of everyday life in Apuleius and Petronius.
89 Naturally, this mode of presenting the subject conjures up the not-so-simple Freudian notion of *Nachträglichkeit*. On this matter, see Jean Laplanche, *Après-coup*, trans. Jonathan House and Luke Thurston (New York, 2017).
90 The function of the author, meanwhile, and particularly the relevant legal aspects, is staunchly defended by Lonzi. This is evident from the correspondence between her and the German publishing house that published her texts without paying the relevant royalties; the Italian feminist complains of the Germans' lack of understanding of the 'real suffering of authors' and, therefore, requests 2,000 marks. See 'Corrispondenza su un furto di testo', in Rivolta Femminile, *La presenza dell'uomo nel femminismo*, pp. 159–66.
91 This would give rise to an alternative understanding of Carla Lonzi's vindictive criticism of Lea Melandri – in 'Mito della proposta culturale', in Rivolta Femminile, *La presenza dell'uomo nel femminismo*, pp. 137–54. Beyond the theoretical or ideological differences, there are entirely incompatible self-narrative strategies at play.
92 Maddalena Libri, 'Sulla comunicazione', in *Differenze* 3 (1977), eBook. Available at http://ebook.women.it/prodotto/differenze-collezione-completa/ (accessed 20 February 2019).
93 Collettivo della Pratica dell'Inconscio, 'Viaggio attraverso un'esperienza', in *Differenze* 2 (1976), eBook. Available at http://ebook.women.it/prodotto/differenze-collezione-completa/ (accessed 20 February 2019).
94 Collettivo femminista fiorentino, 'A un anno di distanza', in *Sottosopra. Esperienze dei gruppi femministi in Italia* (1974), pp. 16–17.
95 Gérard Genette, *Paratexts: Thresholds of Interpretation*, trans. Jane E. Lewin. (Cambridge, 1997), pp. 201–5.
96 Anonymous G, 'La radia', in *L' Almanacco: Luoghi, nomi, incontri, fatti, lavori in corso del movimento femminista italiano dal 1972* (Rome, 1978), p. 130.
97 Roman Jakobson, 'Closing statement: linguistics and poetics', in Thomas A. Sebeok (ed.), *Style in Language* (Cambridge, MA, 1960), pp. 353–56.
98 See Louis Althusser, 'The object of capital', in L. Althusser and E. Balibar *Reading Capital*, trans. Ben Brewster (London, 1970), pp. 71–193.

Chapter 3

1. Gian Carlo Onnis, 'La gioia di essere e il sacrificio da vivere. Autobiografie di comunisti savonesi 1945–1956', *Ventesimo Secolo* 3/7–8 (1993), pp. 101–37.
2. The difference between the two self-narratives is already evident from their titles. Pietro Ingrao (1915–2015 – a member of the left wing of the PCI, director of the party newspaper, *L'Unità* between 1947 and 1957, member of parliament from 1950 until 1992, President of the Chamber of Deputies between 1976 and 1979) wrote *Volevo la luna* (*I Wanted the Moon*) (Turin, 2007). Emanuele Macaluso (born 1924 – member of parliament from 1963 until 1992, director of *L'Unità* between 1982 and 1986) opted for the absolutely neutral *50 anni nel PCI* (*50 Years in the PCI*) (Soveria Mannelli, 2003).
3. Rossana Rossanda (born 1924 – head of cultural policy for the PCI, elected to parliament in 1963, expelled from the PCI in 1969), *The Comrade from Milan*, trans. Romy C. Giuliani (London, 2010), p. 1.
4. Eugenio Montale, *Collected Poems. 1920–1954*, trans. Jonathan Galassi (New York, 1998) p. 39.
5. The 'absolute past', as observed by Mikhail Bakhtin in *The Dialogic Imagination*, p. 15, 'lacks any relativity, that is, any gradual purely temporal progressions that might connect it with the present'. For Rossanda, refusing to be a 'legend' means rejecting the notion of her political death. That said, her refusal is ambiguous. The English translation of the work's title (*The Comrade from Milan*) is very different to the Italian original, which literally translates as 'the girl from the last century' (*La ragazza del secolo scorso*). Rossanda, therefore, places her autobiography in a double past that is by now irretrievable: that of her lost youth and that of the Bolshevik revolution that ultimately failed – the twentieth century.
6. Macaluso, *50 anni nel PCI*, p. 3.
7. Erving Goffman, *Behaviour in Public Places* (New York, 1966), p. 89.
8. Ingrao, *Volevo la luna*, p. 2.
9. As Ben Yagoda observes in *When You Catch an Adjective, Kill It: The Parts of Speech for Better and/or Worse* (New York, 2007), p. 23, the use of too many adjectives by writers has the effect 'of being flowery or obscure for no other reason than to call attention to themselves'.
10. Armando Cossutta (1926–2015 – communist leader and member of parliament from 1972 to 2008), *Una storia comunista* (Milan, 2004), p. 28.
11. In truth, a reasonably similar declaration of intent appears before the *Preface*, as an exergue, preceded by a dedication to his grandchildren: 'this is not a history. It is a chronicle, a little chronicle that forms part of a great history.' In a certain sense, however, this statement occupies the same position in the book that the passage I transcribed previously occupies in the *Preface*: just as the latter concludes the introduction, the former is a sort of postscript to the title, passing comment on it, serving one of the functions of the epigraph that Gérard Genette refers to in *Paratexts*, p. 156. The exergue, then, states that *Una storia comunista* is simply a chronicle, and a little chronicle at that.
12. As Simone Neri Serneri observes in 'A past to be thrown away? Politics and history in the Italian Resistance', *Contemporary European History* 4/3 (1995), p. 367. 'During the first decades, the experience and values of the Resistance provided the ideological basis of the Italian Republic.'

13 The idea of sacrifice as a condition that makes society possible naturally comes from René Girard, *Violence and the Sacred* (London, 2005).
14 Max Weber, *Economy and Society: An Outline of Interpretive Sociology*, ed. Guenther Roth and Claus Wittich (Berkeley, 1978), Vol. I, p. 213.
15 The master narrator is the supreme narrator figure who manages the master narrative by way of which the party autobiographies take form. For a discussion of the concept of master narrative or grand narrative, see Jean-François Lyotard, *The Postmodern Condition: A Report on Knowledge* (Manchester, 1984).
16 Giuseppe Chiarante (1929–2012 – joined the PCI in 1958, member of the Chamber of Deputies between 1972 and 1979, a member of the Senate between 1979 and 1994), *Tra De Gasperi e Togliatti. Memorie degli anni Cinquanta* (Rome, 2006), p. 94.
17 Lucio Magri who walked the same political path as Giuseppe Chiarante – moving from the DC to the PCI in 1956 – penned a memoir that has a lot in common with Chiarante's. In his work *The Tailor of Ulm* (London, 2011), he opts for a non-autobiographical first-person narrative – stating that 'autobiography will only feature below when it is strictly necessary' – and expresses a certain scepticism regarding the value of his personal experience – 'I don't find my own personal experience very interesting, and even if it were I would not know how to communicate it.' Unlike Chiarante, Magri clearly defines the reasons that inspired him to write an autobiography that is not an autobiography: precisely because he did not become a communist to fight Fascism and because he was aware of the weight of Stalinism, he has 'to clarify, first of all to myself, whether this was the right decision' (ibid., p. 15) to join the PCI.
18 Ibid., p. 9.
19 We might say that in Chiarante's work, as is typically the case with political memoirs, 'history and politics are narrated in a personalized form' (in George Eagerton, 'Introduction', in G. Eagerton (ed.), *Political Memoir: Essays in the Politics of Memory* (London, 1994), p. XI), but the statement would not be entirely true. Rather, in his case, the situation is reversed: the personal is narrated in a historicized and political form.
20 Chiarante, *Tra De Gasperi e Togliatti*, p. 13.
21 As observed by Herrero De Jáuregui in '*Pathein* and *mathein* in the descents to Hades', in G. Ekroth and I. Nilsson (eds), *Round Trip to Hades in the Eastern Mediterranean Tradition: Visit to Underworld from Antiquity to Byzantium* (Leiden, 2018), p. 115, 'after all, obtaining specific knowledge was a fundamental reason to go to Hades'.
22 Ingrao, *Volevo la luna*, p. 81.
23 Ibid., p. 79.
24 Ingrao attempts to circumscribe his passion for the material bodily stratum through infelicitous recourse to lyrical writing: 'I lived through the obscure pollution of puberty, on which neither parents nor school shone any light. And yet sexuality burst forth in my body, and I naturally abandoned myself to masturbation' (ibid. p. 21). Worse still is his description of his carnal relations with his future wife Laura Lombardo Radice: 'And so began for us that euphoric moment in which our bodies fused together in their secret, profound language' (ibid. 126).
25 Friedrich Nietzsche, *On the Advantage and Disadvantage of History for Life*, trans. Peter Preuss (Indianapolis, 1980), p. 3.
26 Diego Novelli (born 1931 – Mayor of Turin from 1975 until 1985, elected to the European Parliament in 1984, member of the Chamber of Deputies from 1987 until 2001), *Com' era bello il mio PCI* (Milan, 2006), pp. 23–4.

27 Diego Novelli is not just an antiquarian historian of his own life. Before *Com' era bello il mio PCI*, he published *Per coerenza: Stralci di vita di un militante non pentito* (Turin, 2004), the underlying style of which is closer to Macaluso, who I will discuss later in this paragraph.
28 Luciana Castellina (born 1929 – joined the PCI in 1947, expelled in 1970 because, alongside Rossana Rossanda, she was a member of the *il Manifesto* group. Rejoined the PCI in the 1980s), *Discovery of the World: A Political Awakening in the Shadow of Mussolini*, trans. Patrick Camiller (London, 2014).
29 Luciana Reichlin, 'Foreword', in L. Castellina, *Discovery of the World: A Political Awakening in the Shadow of Mussolini*, trans. Patrick Camiller (London, 2014), pp. IX–X.
30 It is that sense of reverie towards childhood that Gaston Bachelard describes in *The Poetics of Reverie: Childhood, Language and the Cosmos*, trans. Daniel Russell (Boston, 1969), pp. 97–142.
31 Nietzsche, *On the Advantage and Disadvantage of History for Life*, p. 22.
32 Rossanda, *The Comrade from Milan*, p. 202.
33 Nietzsche, *On the Advantage and Disadvantage of History for Life*, p. 15.
34 Macaluso, *50 anni nel PCI*, p. 144.
35 Nietzsche, *On the Advantage and Disadvantage of History for Life*, p. 16.
36 I describe them as elegies because, ultimately, these works are elements of a sort of ritual of public commemoration, in which each of the authors discussed here mourns the loss of his or her communist youth. For a definition of the funeral elegy and the differences between this and the epitaph, see Joshua Scodel, *The English Poetic Epitaph: Commemoration and Conflict from Jonson to Wordsworth* (Ithaca, 1991), pp. 86–109.
37 Luisa Passerini, *Autobiography of a Generation: Italy, 1968*, trans. Lisa Erdberg (Middletown, 2004).
38 The scholar's research itinerary is discussed in Ioanna Laliotou, 'On Luisa Passerini: subjectivity, Europe, affective historiography', *Women's History Review* 25/3 (2016), pp. 408–26.
39 On this matter, see Passerini, *Autobiography of a Generation*, p. 165.
40 The new Italian edition of the book – Luisa Passerini, *Autoritratto di gruppo* (Florence, 2008) – was published on the fortieth anniversary of 1968. Likewise, the 1988 edition celebrated twenty years from the relevant events.
41 Passerini, *Autobiography of a Generation*, p. 1.
42 On the idea of *mise an abyme*, see Lucien Dällenbach, *The Mirror in the Text*, trans. Jeremy Whiteley and Emma Hughes (Chicago, 1989).
43 In other words, the autobiographical account is enabled by the author's historiographical undertaking. Applicable, here, is the observation made by Goffman – in *Encounters*, p. 115 – regarding the role distance of surgeons in the operating theatre: 'Charm and colourful little informalities are thus usually the prerogatives of those in higher office, leading us mistakenly to assume that an individual's social graces helped bring him to his high position, instead of what is perhaps more likely, that the graces become possible for anyone who attains the office.' And so, it is the role of historian that authorizes the autobiographical act as an authorized break from the impersonal austerity of historiographical writing.
44 Passerini, *Autobiography of a Generation*, p. 16.

45 Lonzi, *Taci, anzi parla*, p. 364.
46 Ibid., p. 1300.
47 Passerini, *Autobiography of a Generation*, p. 164.
48 Passerini discovers the world as a stage in a sociological sense. The reference, clearly, is to Erwing Goffman, *The Presentation of Self in Everyday Life* (New York, 1959).
49 As Passerini herself says (in *Autobiography of a Generation*, p. 113): 'Once I experienced the need to be against every authority as a continual challenge. Now I have begun to accept a relationship of derivation, of paternity, from some, with their imperfections: one of my professors; my current superior. I renounce rebellion at all costs.'
50 Rosi Braidotti, Roberta Mazzanti, Serena Sapegno and Annamaria Tagliavini, *Baby Boomers: Vite parallele dagli anni Cinquanta ai cinquant'anni* (Florence, 2003).
51 In fact, the choice of title also requires a certain courage. The baby boomer generation had become a somewhat controversial subject, in the English-speaking world more so than in Italy. In this regard, the title of the following texts leave little room for doubt: Paul Begala, 'The worst generation: or how I learned to stop worrying and hate the boomers', *Esquire*, 3 March 2017. Available at https://www.esquire.com/news-politics/a1451/worst-generation-0400/ (accessed 23 May 2019); Bruce C. Gibney, *A Generation of Sociopaths: How the Baby Boomers Betrayed America* (New York, 2017). Much more nuanced, but equally critical, is the opinion of the *New York Times* columnist Bill Keller, in 'The entitled generation', *New York Times*, 29 July 2012. Available at https://www.nytimes.com/2012/07/30/opinion/keller-the-entitled-generation.html (accessed 23 May 2019). Beyond such articles, and from an academic perspective, see David Garland, *The Culture of Control: Crime and Social Order in Contemporary Society* (Chicago, 2001). Garland does not use the term baby boomers, but is strongly critical of that generation's contribution to shaping and disseminating contemporary repressive policies.
52 On Plutarch, see Timothy E. Duff, *Plutarch's Lives: Exploring Virtue and Vice* (Oxford, 1999).
53 Braidotti, Mazzanti, Sapegno and Tagliavini, *Baby Boomers*, p. 5.
54 On this matter, see Genette, *Narrative Discourse*, pp. 161–75.
55 Braidotti, Mazzanti, Sapegno and Tagliavini, *Baby Boomers*, p. 6.
56 The Merry Pranksters revolved around the figure of Ken Kesy, author of *One Flew Over the Cuckoo's Nest*, and they organized LSD-based parties in San Francisco in the second half of the 1970s. The photo is available on Getty Images, at the following url: https://www.gettyimages.com/detail/news-photo/young-couple-sits-on-the-floor-and-smoke-at-the-merry-news-photo/576842208?adppopup=true (accessed 23 May 2019).
57 Susan Sontag describes this sentiment well in *On Photography* (New York, 1977), p. 71, when she observes that 'as the fascination that photographs exercise is a reminder of death, it is also an invitation to sentimentality. Photographs turn the past into an object of tender regard, scrambling moral distinctions and disarming historical judgments by the generalized pathos of looking at time past.'
58 This is broadly reminiscent of Emmanuel Levinas's observations in *Totality and Infinity: An Essay on Exteriority*, trans. Alphonso Lingis (Dodrecht, 1991).
59 On Warhol and repetition, see Jennifer Dyer's interesting essay, 'The metaphysics of the mundane: understanding Andy Wahrol's serial imagery', *Artibus et Historiae* 25/49 (2004), pp. 33–47.
60 Braidotti, Mazzanti, Sapegno and Tagliavini, *Baby Boomers*, p. 6. The four authors refer here to a book by Marina Piazza, *Le ragazze di cinquant'anni* (Milan, 2000).

61 This descent of autobiographical writing into the realm of marketing language seems to be another manifestation of the recovery of 'artistic critique' within the language of capitalism. Embryonic traces of this tendency were evident in Carla Lonzi's writing and here, in the wake of the heroic season of protest, it emerges fully formed, albeit not on a conscious level. The reference here is to the previously cited Boltanski and Chiappello, *The New Spirit of Capitalism*.
62 Braidotti, Mazzanti, Sapegno and Tagliavini, *Baby Boomers*, p. 182.
63 Ibid. p. 183.
64 Ibid. p. 185.
65 This choice of feminism over immigration echoes an earlier choice in favour of philosophy over sociology. While carrying out research in Melbourne involving documenting the rates of illness and occupational accidents among emigrant families, Rosi Braidotti discovered the squalor of that condition and chose to abandon empirical research. She explains that she felt 'too close to the people's suffering' and that the work 'cost her too much, emotionally' (ibid. p. 180). This is a rather curious move, which sees the author being drawn to philosophy not – as in Kant's case – to plunge herself into 'das fruchtbare Bathos der Erfahrung' (the fruitful bathos of experience) – in our case immersion in social horrors – but rather to distance herself from it.
66 See Abdelmalek Sayad, *The Suffering of the Immigrant*, trans. David Macey (Cambridge, 2004).
67 Braidotti, Mazzanti, Sapegno and Tagliavini, *Baby Boomers*, pp. 187–8.
68 Braidotti defines the Australian school system as 'effectively meritocratic' (ibid., p. 182). Whereas ethnic profiling of the workforce and racism are a stabilizing tool applied to the lower tiers of the workforce – who must suffer inequality as a consequence of their racial origins – meritocracy and equality of opportunity are the mechanisms used to control the middle-management figures tasked with the technical administration of capitalist accumulation. The latter have a small, but real possibility of social ascent – for a discussion of this see Immanuel Wallerstein, *Historical Capitalism with Capitalist Civilization* (London, 1996), pp. 75–85. From this perspective, Rosi Braidotti's autobiography is the story of her transition from authoritarian discipline to voluntary compliance with norms, mediated through a form of feminism.
69 Braidotti, Mazzanti, Sapegno and Tagliavini, *Baby Boomers*, p. 174.
70 See Frank Brinkley, 'To the audacious swell below', *Literary Review*. Available at https://literaryreview.co.uk/to-the-audacious-swell-below (accessed 24 May 2019).
71 A description of the award and the full list of winners is available here: https://literaryreview.co.uk/bad-sex-in-fiction-award (accessed 24 May 2019).
72 Brinkley, 'To the audacious swell below'.
73 Braidotti, Mazzanti, Sapegno and Tagliavini, *Baby Boomers*, p. 163.
74 Ibid., p. 164.
75 Ibid., p. 167.
76 Maria Schiavo, *Movimento a più voci: il femminismo degli anni Settanta attraverso il racconto di una protagonista* (Milan, 2006).
77 An introduction to Maria Schiavo in the context of the literary activities of women in Italy can be found in Carol Lazzaro-Weis, *From Margins to Mainstream: Feminism and Fictional Modes in Italian Women's Writing, 1968–1990* (Philadelphia, 1993), pp. 83–6.
78 Braidotti, Mazzanti, Sapegno and Tagliavini, *Baby Boomers*, p. 5.
79 Schiavo, *Movimento a più voci*, p. 24.

80 Ibid. p. 28.
81 If Maria Schiavo, even indirectly, credits herself as a character with the ability to distinguish between sexual consumption and revolutionary politics, Rosi Braidotti denies such capacity to herself as a narrator: 'Our older friends had warned us to be wary of that old satrap Sartre, who consumed young people with great passion. [...] Basically, days of intense study were followed by wild nights, which left us incredibly rested, albeit with bodies marked by the delicious exhaustion that results from pleasure. And above all, with the feeling that we could always go further, of wanting it ever more' – in Braidotti, Mazzanti, Sapegno and Tagliavini, *Baby Boomers*, p. 169. The only difference between the events in Aarhus and the nights in Paris is the more chic nature of the latter. It is, however, a conventional sort of chic: if Las Vegas is the city of gambling, Rome is the home of the cardinals and Paris is the site of small, inconsequential perversities, like those portrayed in a Bernardo Bertolucci film.
82 Schiavo, *Movimento a più voci*, p. 225. Feltrinelli is a leading Italian publisher.
83 See Goffman, *Behaviour in Public Places*, p. 84.
84 Schiavo, *Movimento a più voci*, p. 227.
85 Daniela Pellegrini, *Una donna di troppo: Storia di una vita politica 'singolare'* (Milan, 2012), pp. 12–13.
86 Ibid. p. 211.
87 On the election of Giorgio Napolitano as President of the Republic of Italy, see Gianfranco Pasquino, 'The election of the eleventh President of the Italian Republic', *Journal of Modern Italian Studies* 11/4 (2006), pp. 532–42. On his strategies of communication and his interpretation of that role, meanwhile, see Francesco Amoretti and Diego Giannone, 'The power of words: the changing role of the Italian head of state during the Second Republic', *Modern Italy* 19/4 (2014), pp. 439–55.
88 Giorgio Napolitano, *Dal PCI al socialismo: un'autobiografia politica* (Rome–Bari, 2005), p. 15.
89 Ibid., p. 6.
90 Moretti, *The Way of the World*, p. 193.
91 Napolitano, *Dal PCI al socialismo*, p. 12.
92 Ibid. p. 13.
93 On this, of course, see Erving Goffman, *Stigma: Notes on the Management of Spoiled Identity* (New York, 1963).
94 Napolitano, *Dal PCI al socialismo*, p. 5.
95 Ibid., p. 23. The account of his experience of the working class and the opportunity this represented are contained on this page.
96 Following Pajetta's introduction, which I quoted above, Macaluso proceeds with his account by recalling a conversation between Pajetta and Vittorio Strada in Moscow in the 1970s, in which the former bitterly reprimands the latter for his criticism of the USSR. The anecdote ends as follows: 'When we were alone, I pointed out to him that his reaction was unfair and incomprehensible, given that, on more than one occasion with me, he himself had used much stronger words to describe the events and the men that Strada had criticised. He was somewhat embarrassed, but replied: "I can, he can't." Just as though an outsider had said that his mother was a whore, and even though he knew it, he could only whisper it to a relative like me' (Macaluso, *50 anni nel PCI*, p. 145).
97 Napolitano, *Dal PCI al socialismo*, p. VIII.
98 Paul Veyne, *Writing History: Essays on Epistemology*, trans. Mina Moore-Rinvolucri (Middletown, 1984), p. 218.

99 Weber, *Economy and Society* Vol. I, p. 225.
100 On this see Michel Crozier, *The Bureaucratic Phenomenon* (Chicago, 1964).
101 Claude Pennetier and Bernard Pudal, 'Les autobiographies des «fils du people»': de l'autobiographie édifiante à l'autobiographie auto-analytique', in C. Pennetier and B. Pudal (eds), Autobiographies, autocritiques, aveux dans le monde communiste (Paris, 2002), p. 223.
102 Laura Lepetit describes her meeting with Carla Lonzi, emphasizing its importance in *Autobiografia di una femminista distratta* (Rome, 2016), pp. 58–63.
103 Ibid., p. 6.
104 Arthur Schopenhauer, *Counsels and Maxims*, trans. Thomas Bailey Saunders (Pennsylvania, 2004), Vol. I, p. 115.
105 Laura Lepetit entitles one of her chapters *Quando ho conosciuto Virginia Woolf* (*When I Met Virginia Woolf*) – in *Autobiografia*, p. 30 – but then announces, in the first paragraph that 'it's not true, I didn't meet Virginia Woolf, I met her niece, Angelica Garnett'.
106 Ibid. pp. 120–1.
107 Ibid., pp. 36–7.
108 Ibid. pp. 12–13.
109 The same elegantly carefree attitude is applied, even more clearly, to US history: 'I know that it was later discovered that [the Americans] had massacred the Indians and their bison, burned the Vietnamese, caused disasters in Afghanistan, etc., but what can you do – heroes they were, and heroes they remain' (ibid., p. 86).
110 Laura Lepetit's fetish for commercial exchange leads her to prefer the exchange of goods to money, and money to electronic currency: 'Holding [money] in your hand and counting it has a certain impact. You see it gradually diminishing, and you're left with little. The impact of a debit card is very different, the money is invisible and you don't feel that you're spending it. It is very dangerous because you don't notice the money going' (ibid., p. 52).
111 Ibid., p. 15.
112 Georg W.F. Hegel, *Elements of the Philosophy of Right*, trans. Hugh B. Nisbet (Cambridge, 2003), p. 182.
113 Lepetit, *Autobiografia*, p. 13.
114 The countryside is the intermediary space between technological civilization that produces stress and wild nature – which never appears in Lepetit's narrative universe: 'The telephone gave up with the flood, the hole where the cable goes can't be found, nobody remembers where it is any more and the grass has grown over it. These are the joys of being in the countryside' (ibid., p. 46), because in the end, technology is an addiction, even outside of the city.
115 Ibid., pp. 21–2.
116 Ibid., p. 35.

Conclusions

1 I refer here, obviously, to Georg Lukács, *Soul and Form*, trans. Anna Bostock (Cambridge, MA, 1974).
2 As Braidotti herself puts it – in *Nomadic Subjects: Embodiment and Sexual Difference in Contemporary Feminist Theory* (New York, 1994), p. 1 – her nomadic perspective

'refers to a figurative style of thinking, occasionally autobiographical'. She also adds that 'the autobiographical tone that will emerge in the course of this, as other essays, is my way of making myself accountable for the nomadic performances that I enact in the text' (p. 6).
3   Ibid., p. 14.
4   In a certain sense, however, Laura Lepetit surpasses Rosi Braidotti in terms of nomadism. The former, in fact, is so nomadic that she is even willing to abandon feminism itself without any particular regrets.
5   Nevertheless, in her philosophical works and her autobiography, Rosi Braidotti declares herself a feminist. How is this possible? As Harold Garfinkel observes, in *Studies in Ethnometodology* (Englewood Cliffs, 1967), pp. 112–13, on the subject of jurors' decision-making in a similar situation – and not only – one's major preoccupation is with ascribing 'legitimate history' to deliberations, more so than ensuring that the latter are produced by legitimate means, according to the instructions imparted by the judge. The issue of legitimizing one's story – by adopting the label of feminist – is, therefore, completely different to the way in which that story is recounted, and its contents.
6   On continuity and discontinuity, see Michel Foucault, *The Archaeology of Knowledge*, trans. Alan M. Sheridan Smith (New York, 1972).
7   Paul Veyne, *Did the Greeks Believe in Their Myths? An Essay on the Constitutive Imagination*, trans. Paula Wissing (Chicago, 1988), p. 45.
8   The journey is similar to that described by Pierre Hadot in 'Forms of life and forms of discourse in ancient philosophy', in P. Hadot, *Philosophy as a Form of Life*, trans. Michael Chase (Oxford, 1995), p. 67, when he observes that 'the traditional myths become the objects of scholarship or of philosophical and moral interpretation'.
9   Braidotti, *Nomadic Subjects*, p. 20.
10 Rosi Braidotti's emphasis on her migratory journey, her travels, her meeting with students and scholars of all nationalities and her polyglottism can easily be read through the lens of a revived form of ancient Hellenistic cosmopolitanism. On this last point see Eric Brown, 'Hellenistic cosmopolitanism', in M. L. Gill and P. Pellegrin (eds), *A Companion to Ancient Philosophy* (West Sussex, 2009), pp. 549–58.
11 Teresa de Lauretis, 'Eccentric subjects: feminist theory and historical consciousness', *Feminist Studies* 16/1 (1990), pp. 115–50.
12 Judith Butler, *Gender Troubles: Feminism and the Subversion of Identity* (New York, 1999).
13 The DeLeuzean reference to repetition conceals the much more trivial forms of historical repetition. The old Marxist idea according to which it was communism that enabled the development of productive forces by breaking down the barriers of capitalist production is thus repeated in the form of new contemporary Deleuzean feminism, according to which the liberated subject would emerge, bringing an end to a series of features of globalized capitalism. The response to capitalist displacement is even more displacement, and this is the path to liberation. This is more or less the same perspective adopted by the accelerationists – see, for example, Nick Srnicek and Alex Williams, '#Accelerate: manifesto for an Accelerationist Politics', in J. Johnson (ed.), *Dark Trajectories: Politics of the Outside* (Hong Kong, 2013), pp. 135–55. An idea that failed the first time round and that it is hard to see why it should work now, unless its second failure is to be interpreted as a parody of the first and a success for the Deleuzean concept of repetition.

14 Carla Lonzi's pathos of authenticity derives from the fact that the Tuscan feminist, by rejecting the institutions available to her – the art and academic worlds, respectively – needed to find herself to survive the world. Rosi Braidotti's pathos of difference is rooted in a very different motivation. Having accepted the institutions that characterize this world – the academic system, in her case – the subject can become nomadic without difficulty, provided that she complies with the relevant institutional rules. The gap between autobiographical narrator and philosophical author derives from this decision. A choice that is not emphasized, just as the rather troubling origin of the feminist pathos of difference – specifically Nietzsche's pathos of distance – is not addressed. On this see Jan Rehmann, *Postmoderner Links-Nietzscheanismus: Deleuze & Foucault, eine Dekonstruktion* (Hamburg, 2004).
15 Ernesto Laclau, *On Populist Reason* (London, 2005).
16 Ibid., p. 67.
17 Direct reference to Sorel and to the political myth as a generator of revolutionary identity can be found in Ernesto Laclau and Chantal Mouffe, *Hegemony and Socialist Strategy: Towards a Radical Democratic Politics* (London, 1987), pp. 36–42. For a discussion on the use of the notions of myth and violence, described by Sorel, in contemporary political theory, see Mark Antliff, 'Bad anarchism: aesthecized mythmaking and the legacy of George Sorel', *Anarchist Developments in Cultural Studies* 2 (2011), pp. 155–87.
18 The most interesting points of Beppe Grillo's movement, on which the observations presented here draw, are presented by Alessandro Dal Lago in *Clic! Grillo, Casaleggio e la demagogia elettronica* (Naples, 2013) and in *Populismo Digitale. La crisi, la rete e la nuova destra* (Milan, 2017).
19 I am thinking, as I write this, above all, about the Italian university professors who, in 1931, refused to swear their allegiance to Fascism and lost their jobs: around fifteen out of approximately 1,200 teachers. These men came from a range of political and cultural backgrounds, and they made a decision that radically changed their lives, not on the basis of theoretical concepts or abstract political decisions. They did what they did because the world around them had become intolerable to them. On this point, see Alessandro Dal Lago, *I benpensanti: contro i tutori dell'ordine filosofico* (Genoa, 2014), pp. 197–203. And so, the decision to write one's life – in a metaphorical and also in a literal sense, by producing one's autobiography – in non-conformist terms is, in my opinion, what politics is based on. Such an act, furthermore, is essentially anarchic: it cannot be attributed to any principle or theory. The decision to act, then, does not depend on one's political perspective, be that communist or feminist.

BIBLIOGRAPHY

Agosti, Aldo, *Palmiro Togliatti: A Biography* (London: I.B. Tauris, 2008).

Althusser, Louis, 'The object of capital', in L. Althusser and E. Balibar (eds), *Reading Capital*, trans. Ben Brewster (London: New Left Books, 1970), pp. 71–193.

Amoretti, Francesco and Giannone, Diego, 'The power of words: the changing role of the Italian head of state during the Second Republic', *Modern Italy* 19/4 (2014), pp. 439–55.

Anders, Günther, *Die Antiquartheit des Menschen: Über die Seele im Zeitalter der zweiten industriellen Revolution* (Munich: Verlag C. H. Beck, 1961).

Anonymous A, 'Un anno di esperienza tra autocoscienza e lotta di fabbrica', *Sottosopra. Esperienze di gruppi femministi in Italia* (1974), pp. 187–8.

Anonymous B, 'Vedrai che dopo cambierà', *Sottosopra. Esperienze di gruppi femministi* (1974), pp. 34–5.

Anonymous C, 'Storia d'ufficio', *Sottosopra. Esperienze di gruppi femministi in Italia* (1974), pp. 32–3.

Anonymous D, 'E continuavamo a chiamarci femministe', *Sottosopra. Esperienze di gruppi femministi in Italia* (1974), pp. 227–44.

Anonymous E, "Il corpo politico", *Sottosopra. Fascicolo speciale* (1975), pp. 7–42.

Anonymous F, 'Viaggio attraverso un'esperienza', in *Differenze* 2 (1976), cit. in F. Paoli, *Pratiche di scrittura femminista* (Milan: Franco Angeli, 2011), pp. 162–7.

Anonymous G, 'La radia', in *L'Almanacco:. Luoghi, nomi, incontri, fatti, lavori in corso del movimento femminista italiano dal 1972* (Rome: Edizioni delle donne, 1978), pp. 130–1.

Auerbach, Erich, 'Figura', in E. Auerbach (ed.), *Scenes from the Drama of European Literature*, trans. Ralph Manheim (Minneapolis: University of Minnesota, 1984), pp. 11–71.

Bachelard, Gaston, *The Poetics of Reverie: Childhood, Language and the Cosmos*, trans. Daniel Russell (Boston: Beacon Press, 1969).

Bakhtin, Mikhail, *The Dialogic Imagination: Four Essays*, trans. Caryl Emerson and Michael Holquist (Austin, TX: University of Texas Press, 1981).

Bakhtin, Mikhail, *Problems of Dostoevsky's Poetics*, trans. Caryl Emerson (Minneapolis: University of Minnesota Press, 1984).

Bargaglio, Cecilia, '"Sono comunista dall'età della ragione." Il PCI a Novi Ligure attraverso i questionari biografici dei militanti. 1945-1946', in *Quaderno di storia contemporanea* 55 (2014), pp. 31–49.

Barthes, Roland, *A Lover's Discourse: Fragments*, trans. Richard Howard (New York: Wang and Hill, 2001).

Beccalli, Bianca, 'The modern women's movement in Italy', *New Left Review* I/204 (1994), pp. 86–112. Available at https://newleftreview.org/I/204/bianca-beccalli-the-modern-women-s-movement-in-italy (accessed 20 February 2019).

Becker, Howard S., *Arts World* (Berkeley: University of California Press, 1982).

Becker, Howard S., *Tricks of the Trade: How to Think about Your Research While You're Doing It* (Chicago: University of Chicago Press, 1998).

Begala, Paul, 'The worst generation: or how I learned to stop worrying and hate the boomers', *Esquire*, 3 March 2017. Available at https://www.esquire.com/news-politics/a1451/worst-generation-0400/ (accessed 23 May 2019).

Benjamin, Walter, 'Theses on the philosophy of history', in W. Benjamin (ed.), *Illuminations: Essays and Reflections*, trans. Harry Zhon (New York: Schocken Books, 2007), pp. 253–64.

Bernardelli, Giuseppe, *Il testo lirico: Logica e forma di un tipo letterario* (Milan: Vita e Pensiero, 2002).

Boarelli, Mauro, *La fabbrica del passato: Autobiografie di militanti comunisti (1945–1956)* (Milan: Feltrinelli, 2007).

Boccia, Maria Luisa, *L'io in rivolta: Vissuto e pensiero di Carla Lonzi* (Milan: La Tartaruga, 1990).

Boccia, Maria Luisa, *Con Carla Lonzi: La mia opera è la mia vita* (Rome: Ediesse, 2014).

Boer, Ronald, *Stalin: From Theology to the Philosophy of Socialism in Power* (Singapore: Springer, 2017).

Boltanski, Luc, *Distant Suffering: Morality, Media and Politics*, trans. Graham Burchell (Cambridge: Cambridge University Press, 2004).

Boltanski, Luc, and Chiappello, Ève, *The New Spirit of Capitalism*, trans. Gregory Elliott (London: Verso, 2007).

Boarelli, Mauro, *La fabbrica del passato: Autobiografie di militanti comunisti (1945–1956)* (Milan: Feltrinelli, 2007).

Bono, Paola, and Kemp, Sandra, 'Introduction: coming from the South', in P. Bono and S. Kemp (eds), *Italian Feminist Thought* (Oxford: Basil Blackwell, 1991) pp. 1–29.

Bourdieu, Pierre, *The Weight of the World. Social Suffering in Contemporary Society*, trans. Priscilla Parkhurst Ferguson, Joe Johnson and Shaggy T. Waryn (Stanford: Stanford University Press, 1999).

Bracke, Maud A., *Women and the Reinvention of the Political: Feminism in Italy, 1968–1983* (London and New York: Routledge 2014).

Braidotti, Rosi, *Nomadic Subjects: Embodiment and Sexual Difference in Contemporary Feminist Theory* (New York: Columbia University Press, 1994).

Braidotti, Rosi, Roberta Mazzanti, Serena Sapegno and Annamaria Tagliavini, *Baby Boomers: Vite parallele dagli anni Cinquanta ai cinquant'anni* (Florence: Giunti, 2003).

Brinkley, Frank, 'To the audacious swell below', *Literary Review*. Available at https://literaryreview.co.uk/to-the-audacious-swell-below (accessed 24 May 2019).

Brooks, Peter, *Reading for the Plot: Design and Intention in Narrative* (Cambridge MA and London: Harvard University Press, 1984).

Brooks, Peter, *Reading for the Plot: Design and Intention in Narrative* (Cambridge MA: Harvard University Press, 1992).

Brooks, Peter, *The Melodramatic Imagination: Balzac, Henry James, and the Mode of Excess* (New Haven and London: Yale University Press, 1995).

Brooks, Peter, *Troubling Confessions: Speaking Guilt in Law and Literature* (Chicago: University of Chicago Press, 2001).

Brown, Eric, 'Hellenistic cosmopolitanism', in M.L. Gill and P. Pellegrin (eds), *A Companion to Ancient Philosophy* (West Sussex: Blackwell, 2009), pp. 549–58.

Brückner, Margrit, 'On Carla Lonzi: the victory of the clitoris over the vagina as an act of women's liberation', *European Journal of Women's Studies* 21/3 (2014), pp. 278–82.

Butler, Judith, *Gender Troubles: Feminism and the Subversion of Identity* (New York: Routledge, 1999).

Cadinas, Pia, '"Ode" a Paestum', in *Effe* 5/2. Available at http://efferivistafemminista.it/2014/11/ode-a-paestum (accessed 8 February 2018).
Carnap, Rudolf, 'On protocol sentences', *Noûs* 21 (1987), pp. 457–70.
Carver, Raymond, 'Feathers', in R. Carver (ed.), *Cathedral* (New York: Knopf, 1983), pp. 3–26.
Castellina, Luciana, *Discovery of the World: A Political Awakening in the Shadow of Mussolini*, trans. Patrick Camiller (London: Verso, 2014).
Cavarero, Adriana, *Relating Narratives: Storytelling and Selfhood*, trans. Paul A. Kottman (London and New York: Routledge, 2000).
Chiarante, Giuseppe, *Tra De Gasperi e Togliatti: Memorie degli anni Cinquanta* (Rome: Carocci, 2006).
Collettivo della Pratica dell'Inconscio, 'Viaggio attraverso un'esperienza', in *Differenze* 2 (1976), eBook. Available at http://ebook.women.it/prodotto/differenze-collezione-completa/ (accessed 20 February 2019).
Collettivo femminista fiorentino, 'A un anno di distanza', *Sottosopra. Esperienze dei gruppi femministi in Italia* (1974), pp. 16–18.
Crozier, Michel, *The Bureaucratic Phenomenon* (Chicago: University of Chicago Press, 1964).
Dal Lago, Alessandro, 'L'infanzia interminabile', *aut aut* 191–192 (1982), pp. 27–48.
Dal Lago, Alessandro, *Clic! Grillo, Casaleggio e la demagogia elettronica* (Naples: Cronopio, 2013).
Dal Lago, Alessandro, *I benpensanti: contro i tutori dell'ordine filosofico* (Genoa: il Melangolo, 2014).
Dal Lago, Alessandro, *Populismo Digitale: La crisi, la rete e la nuova destra* (Milan: Raffaello Cortina, 2017).
Dal Lago, Alessandro and Giordano, Serena, *Mercanti d'aura: Logiche dell'arte contemporanea* (Bologna: il Mulino, 2006).
Dal Lago, Alessandro and Quadrelli, Emilio, *La città e le ombre: Crimini, criminali, cittadini* (Milan: Feltrinelli, 2003).
Dällenbach, Lucien, *The Mirror in the Text*, trans. Jeremy Whiteley and Emma Hughes (Chicago: University of Chicago Press, 1989).
De Clementi, Andreina, *Amadeo Bordiga* (Turin: Einaudi, 1971).
De Jáuregui, Herrero, '*Pathein* and *mathein* in the descents to Hades', in G. Ekroth and I. Nilsson (eds), *Round Trip to Hades in the Eastern Mediterranean Tradition: Visit to Underworld from Antiquity to Byzantium* (Leiden: Brill, 2018), pp. 103–23.
de Lauretis, Teresa, 'Eccentric subjects: feminist theory and historical consciousness', *Feminist Studies* 16/1 (1990), pp. 115–50.
Della Torre, Elena, 'The clitoris diaries: *La donna clitoridea*, feminine authenticity, and the phallic allegory of Carla Lonzi's Radical feminism', *European Journal of Women's Studies* 21/3 (2014), pp. 219–32.
Descombe, Vincent, *Le parler de soi* (Paris: Gallimard, 2014).
Detienne, Marcel, *Comparing the Incomparable*, trans. Janet Lloyd (Stanford, CA: Stanford University Press, 2008).
Duff, Timothy E., *Plutarch's Lives: Exploring Virtue and Vice* (Oxford: Oxford University Press, 1999).
Durkheim, Émile, *The Division in Social Labor*, trans. George Simpson (Glencoe: Free Press, 1960).

Durkheim, Émile, 'Two laws of penal evolution', *Economy and Society* 2/3 (1973), pp. 285–308.
Dyer, Jennifer, 'The metaphysics of the mundane: understanding Andy Wahrol's serial imagery', *Artibus et Historiae* 25/49 (2004), pp. 33–47.
Eagerton, George, 'Introduction', in G. Eagerton (ed.), *Political Memoir: Essays in the Politics of Memory* (London: Frank Cass, 1994) pp. XI–XIX.
Edwards, Rosalind and Holland, Janet, *What Is Qualitative Interviewing?* (London: Bloomsbury, 2013).
Eliana, 'Andare alle radici', *Sottosopra* (1976), pp. 120–4.
Fallaci, Oriana, *Intervista con il potere* (Milan: Rizzoli, 2009).
Ferrara, Alessandro, *La forza dell'esempio: Il paradigma del giudizio* (Milan: Feltrinelli, 2008).
Fitzpatrick, Sheila, *Tear Off the Mask! Identity and Imposture in Twentieth Century Russia* (Princeton: Princeton University Press, 2005).
Fitzpatrick, Sheila, 'Revisionism in Soviet history', *History & Theory* 26/4 (2007), pp. 77–91.
Flores, Marcello and Gallerano, Nicola, *Sul PCI: Un'interpretazione storica* (Bologna: il Mulino, 1992).
Fortini, Franco, *Dieci inverni. 1947–1957: Contributi a un discorso socialista* (Macerata: Quodlibet, 2018).
Foucault, Michel, *The Archeology of Knowledge*, trans. Alan M. Sheridan Smith (New York: Pantheon Books, 1972).
Foucault, Michel, 'The subject and power', in H.L. Dreyfus and P. Rabinow (eds), *Michel Foucault: Beyond Structuralism and Hermeneutics* (Chicago: University of Chicago Press, 1983), pp. 208–26.
Foucault, Michel, 'Technologies of the self', in Luther H. Martin, Huck Gutman and Patrick H. Hutton (eds), *Technologies of the Self: A Seminar with Michel Foucault* (Amherst: University of Massachusetts Press, 1988), pp. 16–49.
Foucault, Michel, *Security, Territory, Population: Lectures at the Collège De France, 1977–78*, trans. Graham Burchell (London: Palgrave Macmillan, 2007).
Foucault, Michel, *On the Government of the Living: Lectures at the Collège de France (1979–1980)*, trans. Graham Burchell (London: Palgrave Macmillan, 2014).
Fraire, Manuela, *Lessico politico delle donne: Teorie del femminismo* (Milan: Franco Angeli, 2002).
Fulbrook, Mary and Ulinka Rublack, 'In relation: the "social self" and ego-documents', *German History* 28/3 (2010), pp. 263–72.
Garfinkel, Harold, *Studies in Ethnomethodology* (Englewood Cliffs: Prentice-Hall, 1967).
Garland, David, *The Culture of Control: Crime and Social Order in Contemporary Society* (Chicago: University of Chicago Press, 2001).
Geary, Daniel, '"Becoming International Again". C. Wright Mills and the emergence of a new global left', *The Journal of American History* 95/3 (2008), pp. 710–36.
Genette, Gérard, *Narrative Discourse: An Essay in Method*, trans. Jane E. Lewin (Ithaca: Cornell University Press, 1980).
Genette, Gérard, *Paratexts: Thresholds of Interpretation*, trans. Jane E. Lewin. (Cambridge: Cambridge University Press, 1997).
Getty, John A., *Origins of the Great Purges: The Soviet Communist Party Reconsidered. 1933–1938* (Cambridge: Cambridge University Press, 1985).
Getty, John A., '*Samokritika* rituals in the Stalinist Central Committee', *The Russian Review* 58/1 (1999), pp. 49–70.

Giani Gallino, Tilde, 'L'amore materno è …', in *Effe* 5/9 (1977). Available at http://efferivistafemminista.it/2014/11/lamore-materno-e/ (accessed 8 January 2019).
Gibney, Bruce C., *A Generation of Sociopaths: How the Baby Boomers Betrayed America* (New York: Hachette, 2017).
Gilmore, Leigh, *The Limits of Autobiography: Trauma and Testimony* (Ithaca: Cornell University Press, 2001).
Ginsborg, Paul, *A History of Contemporary Italy: Society and Politics 1943–1988* (Basingstoke: Palgrave Macmillan, 2003).
Girard, René, *Violence and the Sacred*, trans. Patrick Gregory (London: Continuum, 2005).
Goffman, Erving, *The Presentation of Self in Everyday Life* (New York: Anchor Books, 1959).
Goffman, Erving, *Stigma: Notes on the Management of Spoiled Identity* (New York: Simon & Schuster, 1963).
Goffman, Erving, *Behaviour in Public Places* (New York: Free Press, 1966).
Goffman, Erving, *Encounters: Two Studies in the Sociology of Interaction* (Harmondsworth: Penguin Books, 1972).
Hadot Pierre, 'Forms of life and forms of discourse in ancient philosophy', in P. Hadot, *Philosophy as a Form of Life*, trans. Michael Chase (Oxford: Blackwell, 1995), pp. 49–70.
Halfin, Igal, 'Looking into oppositionist's soul: inquisition communist style', *The Russian Review* 60/3 (2001), pp. 316–39.
Halfin, Igal, *Stalinist Confessions: Messianism and Terror at the Leningrad Communist University* (Pittsburgh: University of Pittsburgh Press, 2009).
Halfin, Igal, *Red Autobiographies: Initiating the Bolshevik Self* (Seattle: University of Washington Press, 2011).
Haupt, Georges and Marie, Jean-Jacques (eds), *Makers of the Russian Revolution: Biographies of Bolshevik Leaders*, trans. C.I.P. Ferdinand and D.M. Idenos (New York and London: Routledge, 2017).
Hegel, Georg W.F., *Elements of the Philosophy of Right*, trans. Hugh B. Nisbet (Cambridge: Cambridge University Press, 2003).
Hellman, Judith A., *Journeys among Women: Feminism in Five Italian Cities* (Cambridge: Polity Press, 1987).
Ingrao, Pietro, *Volevo la luna* (Turin: Einaudi, 2007).
Jakobson, Roman, 'Closing statement: linguistics and poetics', in Thomas A. Sebeok (ed.), *Style in Language* (Cambridge MA: MIT Press, 1960), pp. 350–77.
James, Lisa M., Vo, Hoa T., 'Hawthorne effect', in *Encyclopedia of Research Design* (Thousand Oaks: Sage, 2010), pp. 561–7.
Just, Daniel, 'Is less more? A reinvention of realism in Raymond Carver's minimalist short stories', *Critiques: Studies in Contemporary Fiction* 49/3 (2008), pp. 303–17.
Keller, Bill, 'The entitled generation', *New York Times*, 29 July 2012. Available at https://www.nytimes.com/2012/07/30/opinion/keller-the-entitled-generation.html (accessed 23 May 2019).
Kharkhordin, Oleg, *The Collective and the Individual in Russia: A Study of Practices* (Berkeley: University of California Press, 1999).
Kharkhordin, Oleg, 'By deeds alone: origins of individualization in Soviet Russia', in B. Studer and B. Unfried (eds), *Parler de soi sous Staline: La construction identitaire dans le communism des années trente* (Paris: Éditions de la Maison de science de l'homme, 2002), pp. 125–45.
Kilito, Abdelfattah, *L'oeil et l'aiguille: Essais sur Les Milles et Une Nuits* (Paris: La Découverte, 1994).

Laliotou, Ioanna, 'On Luisa Passerini: subjectivity, Europe, affective historiography', *Women's History Review* 25/3 (2016), pp. 408–26.
Laplanche, Jean, *Après-coup*, trans. Jonathan House and Luke Thurston (New York: The Unconscious in Translation, 2017).
Lazzaro-Weis, Carol, *From Margins to Mainstream: Feminism and Fictional Modes in Italian Women's Writing, 1968–1990* (Philadelphia: University of Pennsylvania Press, 1993).
Leary, David E., 'William James on the self and personality: clearing the ground for subsequent theorists, researchers, and practitioners', in W. James, M.G. Johnson and T.B. Henley (eds), *Reflections on The Principles of Psychology: William James after a Century* (Hillsdale: Erlbaum Associates, 1990), pp. 101–37.
Lee, Nan-Nan, 'Sublimated or castrated psychoanalysis? Adorno's critique of the revisionist psychoanalysis: an introduction to "The Revisionist Psychoanalysis"', *Philosophy and Social Criticism* 40/3 (2014), pp. 309–38.
Lejeune, Philippe, *On Autobiography*, trans. Katherine Leary (Minneapolis: University of Minnesota Press, 1989).
Lepetit, Laura, *Autobiografia di una femminista distratta* (Rome: Nottetempo, 2016).
Levinas, Emmanuel, 'Phenomenon and enigma', in E. Levinas, *Collected Philosophical Papers*, trans. Alphonso Lingis (Dordrecht: Martinus Nijhoff Publishers, 1987), pp. 61–73.
Levinas, Emmanuel, *Totality and Infinity: An Essay on Exteriority*, trans. Alphonso Lingis (Dodrecht: Kluwer Academic Publishers, 1991).
Liliana, 'Capi e segretarie: ovvero il sesso in azienda', *Sottosopra. Esperienze di gruppi femministi* (1974), pp. 37–9.
Lonzi, Carla, *Sputiamo su Hegel. La donna clitoridea e la donna vaginale e altri scritti* (Milan: Scritti di Rivolta Femminile, 1974a), pp. 141–7.
Lonzi, Carla, 'Significato dell'autocoscienza nei gruppi femministi', in C. Lonzi (ed.), *Sputiamo su Hegel. La donna clitoridea e la donna vaginale e altri scritti* (Milan: Scritti di Rivolta Femminile, 1974b), pp. 141–7.
Lonzi, Carla, *Taci, anzi parla. Diario di una femminista* (Milan: Scritti di Rivolta Femminile, 1978).
Lonzi, Carla, *Vai Pure: Dialogo con Pietro Consagra* (Milan: Scritti di Rivolta Femminile, 1980).
Lukács, Georg, *Soul and Form*, trans. Anna Bostock (Cambridge MA: MIT Press, 1974).
Lyotard, Jean-François, *The Postmodern Condition: A Report on Knowledge* (Manchester: University of Manchester Press, 1984).
Maddalena Libri, 'Sulla comunicazione', *Differenze* 3 (1977), eBook. Available at http://ebook.women.it/prodotto/differenze-collezione-completa (accessed 20 Februaty 2019).
Magri, Lucio, *The Tailor of Ulm. Communism in the Twentieth Century*, trans. Patrick Camiller (London: Verso, 2011).
Malti-Douglas, Fedwa, 'Shahrazād feminist', in R.G. Hovannisian and G. Sabagh (eds), *The Thousand and One Nights in Arabic Literature and Society* (Cambridge: Cambridge University Press, 1997), pp. 40–55.
Marcuse, Herbert, *The New Left and the 1960s: Collected Papers*, Vol. 3, trans. Douglas Kellner (London and New York: Routledge, 2005).
Marino, Giuseppe C., *Autoritratto del PCI staliniano, 1946–1953* (Rome: Editori Riuniti, 1991).

Marti, Urs, 'Techniques de soi, techniques de domination et pratiques identitaires dans la culture stalinienne. Remarques sur la valeur analytique d'un concept de Foucault', in B. Studer and B. Unfried (eds), *Parler de soi sous Staline: La construction identitaire dans le communism des années trente* (Paris: Éditions de la maison de sciences de l'homme, 2002), pp. 35–45.

Martinelli, Alice, *Autocoscienza* (Milan: Scritti di Rivolta Femminile, 1975).

Martucci, Chiara, *La libreria delle donne a Milano. Un laboratorio di pratica politica* (Milan: Franco Angeli, 2008).

Mazur, Krystyna, 'Repetition', in R. Greene and S. Cushman (eds), *The Princeton Encyclopedia of Poetry and Poetics* 4th edition (Princenton: Princenton University Press, 2012), pp. 1167–71.

Melandri, Lea, *Una visceralità indicibile: La pratica dell'inconscio nel movimento delle donne degli anni Settanta* (Milan: Franco Angeli, 2000).

Milan Women's Bookstore Collective, *Sexual Difference: A Theory of Social-Symbolic Practice*, trans. Patricia Cicogna and Teresa de Lauretis (Bloomington: Indiana University Press, 1990).

Montale, Eugenio, *Collected Poems. 1920–1954*, trans. Jonathan Galassi (New York: Farrar, Straus and Giroux, 1998).

Moretti, Franco, *The Way of the World: The Bildungsroman in European Culture*. New edition, trans. Albert Sbragia (London: Verso, 2000).

Morgan, Kevin, 'Comparative communist history and the "biographical turn"', *History Compass* 10/6 (2012), pp. 455–66.

Morgan, Kevin, Cohen, Gidon and Flinn, Andrew (eds), *Agents of Revolution: New Biographical Approaches to the History of International Communism in the Age of Lenin and Stalin* (Oxford: Peter Lang, 2005).

Neri Serneri, Simone, 'A past to be thrown away? Politics and history in the Italian Resistance', *Contemporary European History* 4/3 (1995), pp. 367–81.

Nietzsche, Friedrich *On the Advantage and Disadvantage of History for Life*, trans. Peter Preuss (Indianapolis: Hackett, 1980).

Novelli, Diego, *Per coerenza: Stralci di vita di un militante non pentito* (Turin: Daniela Piazza Editore, 2004).

Novelli, Diego, *Com'era bello il mio PCI* (Milan: Melampo, 2006).

Onnis, Gian Carlo, 'La gioia di essere e il sacrificio da vivere. Autobiografie di comunisti savonesi 1945–1956', *Ventesimo Secolo* 3/7–8 (1993), pp. 101–37.

Parati, Graziella and West, Rebecca, 'Introduction', in G. Parati and R. West (eds), *Italian Feminist Theory and Practice: Equality and Sexual Difference* (Madison: Fairleigh Dickinson University Press, 2002), pp. 13–28.

Passerini, Luisa, *Storie di donne e di femministe* (Turin: Rosenberg&Sellier, 1991).

Passerini, Luisa, *Autobiography of a Generation: Italy, 1968*, trans. Lisa Erdberg (Middletown: Wesleyan University Press, 2004).

Passerini, Luisa, *Autoritratto di gruppo* (Florence: Giunti, 2008).

Pellegrini, Daniela, *Una donna di troppo: Storia di una vita politica 'singolare'* (Milan: FrancoAngeli, 2012).

Pennetier, Claude and Pudal, Bernard, 'La "verification" (l'encadrement biographique communiste dans l'entre-deux guerre)', *Genèses. Sciences sociales et histoire* 23 (1996), pp. 145–63.

Pennetier, Claude and Pudal, Bernard, 'Les autobiographies des «fils du people»: de l'autobiographie édifiante à l'autobiographie auto-analytique', in C. Pennetier and B. Pudal (eds), *Autobiographies, autocritiques, aveux dans le monde communiste* (Paris: Belin, 2002), pp. 217–46.

Pennetier, Claude and Pudal, Bernard, 'La volonté d'emprise. Le réferentiel biographique stalinien et ses usages dans l'univers communiste (éléments de problematique)', in C. Pennetier and B. Pudal (eds), *Autobiographies, autocritiques, aveux dans le monde communiste* (Paris: Belin, 2002a), pp. 15–39.

Pennetier, Claude and Pudal, Bernard, 'Le questionnement biographique en France (1931–1974), in C. Pennetier and B. Pudal (eds), *Autobiographies, autocritiques, aveux dans le monde communiste* (Paris: Belin, 2002b), pp. 117–56.

Piazza, Marina, *Le ragazze di cinquant'anni* (Milan: Mondadori, 2000).

Poggi, Gianfranco (ed.), *L'organizzazione partitica del PCI e della DC* (Bologna: il Mulino, 1968).

Portis, Larry, 'Les fondements politico-idéologiques de la sociologie durkheimienne', *L'homme et la societé* 84 (1987), pp. 95–110.

Possieri, Andrea, *Il peso della storia: Memoria, identità, rimozione dal Pci al Pds (1970–1991)* (Bologna: il Mulino, 2007).

Pozzetta, Andrea, 'Italian Communist Party Schools: Writing Practices and Linguistic Analysis' [1st Conference of the European Labour History Network – Workshop: Workers' Writing in Europe. A Contribution to the Cultural History of the Worlds of Work. Turin, 14–16 December 2015].

Pudal, Bernard, *Prendre parti: Pour une sociologie historique du PCF* (Paris: Presses de la Fondation national de science politiques, 1989).

Rehmann, Jan, *Postmoderner Links-Nietzscheanismus: Deleuze & Foucault, eine Dekonstruktion* (Hamburg: Argument, 2004).

Reichlin, Luciana, 'Foreword', in L. Castellina (ed.), *Discovery of the World: A Political Awakening in the Shadow of Mussolini*, trans. Patrick Camiller (London: Verso, 2014), pp. IX–XIII.

Reid, Alastair J., 'The dialectics of liberation: the old left, the new left and the counter culture', in D. Feldman and J. Lawrence (eds), *Structures and Transformations in Modern British History* (Cambridge: Cambridge University Press, 2011), pp. 261–80.

Ricoeur, Paul, 'L'hermeneutique du témoignage', in P. Ricoeur (ed.), *Lectures 3* (Paris: Seuil, 1994), pp. 105–37.

Rochester, Sherry and Martin, James R., *Crazy Talk: A Study of the Discourse of Schizophrenic Speakers* (New York and London: Plenum Press, 1979).

Rossanda, Rossana, *The Comrade from Milan*, trans. Romy C. Giuliani (London: Verso, 2010).

Rossi-Doria, Anna, 'Ipotesi per una storia del neo-femminismo italiano', in A. Rossi-Doria (ed.), *Dare forma al silenzio: Scritti di storia politica delle donne* (Rome: Viella, 2007), pp. 243–65.

Sabatini, Alma 'Il piccolo gruppo. Struttura di base del movimento femminista', in *Effe* (January 1974). Available at http://efferivistafemminista.it/2014/07/struttura-di-base-del-movimento-femminista/ (accessed 3 December 2018).

Sadri, Ahmad, *Max Weber's Sociology of Intellectuals* (New York: Oxford University Press, 1992).

Salvetti, Patrizia, 'Il Partito Comunista Italiano', in C. Vallauri (ed.), *La ricostituzione dei partiti democratici (1943–1948)* (Rome: Bulzoni, 1977), pp. 683–1087.

Sayad, Abdelmalek, *The Suffering of the Immigrant*, trans. David Macey (Cambridge: Polity Press, 2004).

Schiavo, Maria, *Movimento a più voci: il femminismo degli anni Settanta attraverso il racconto di una protagonista* (Milan: Franco Angeli, 2006).
Schmidt, Arnaud, 'From autobiographical act to autobiography', *Life Writing* 15 (2018), pp. 469–86.
Schmitt, Carl, *Political Theology: Four Chapters on the Concept of Sovereignty*, trans. George Schwab (Chicago and London: University of Chicago Press, 2005).
Schopenhauer, Arthur, *Counsels and Maxims*, trans. Thomas Bailey Saunders, Vol. I (Pennsylvania: Pennsylvania State University, 2004).
Scodel, Joshua, *The English Poetic Epitaph: Commemoration and Conflict from Jonson to Wordsworth* (Ithaca: Cornell University Press, 1991).
Sebastiani, Chiara, 'I funzionari', in A. Accornero, R. Mannheimer and C. Sebastiani (eds), *L'identità comunista. I militanti, la struttura, la cultura del PCI* (Rome: Editori Riuniti, 1983), pp. 79–178.
Secchia, Pietro, *Più forti i quadri, migliore l'organizzazione* (Rome: La Stampa Moderna, n. d).
Secchia, Pietro, 'L'arte dell'organizzazione', *Rinascita* 12 (December 1945), pp. 267–69.
Secchia, Pietro, 'La democrazia nel partito', *Quaderno dell'attivista* 2 (October 1946), pp. 43–4.
Secchia, Pietro, *Il partito della rinascita: Rapporto alla conferenza nazionale di organizzazione del Partito Comunista Italiano* (Rome: Tipografia UESISA, 1947).
Secchia, Pietro, 'Rafforzare le organizzazioni di massa, rafforzare il partito', *Quaderno dell'attivista* 6 (15 marzo 1951), p. 178.
Secchia, Pietro, 'L'operosità nel lavoro e la democrazia nel partito', *Quaderno dell'attivista* 16 (15 agosto 1952), pp. 482–3.
Simmel Georg, *The Sociology of Georg Simmel*, trans. Kurt H. Wolff (Glencoe: The Free Press, 1950).
Sontag, Susan, *On Photography* (New York: Farrar, Straus and Giroux, 1977).
Soranzo, Matteo, 'Franco (Fortini FrancoLattes)', in G. Marrone, P. Puppa and L. Simigli (eds), *Encyclopedia of Italian Literary Studies* (London and New York: Routledge, 2007), pp. 759–62.
Spitzer, Leo, *La enumeraciòn caótica en la poesía moderna* (Buenos Aires: Coni, 1945).
Spriano, Paolo, *Storia del Partito Comunista Italiano. La resistenza. Togliatti e il partito nuovo*, Vol. V (Turin: Einaudi, 1976).
Srnicek, Nick and Williams, Alex, '#Accelerate: manifesto for an Accelerationist Politics', in J. Johnson (ed.), *Dark Trajectories: Politics of the Outside* (Hong Kong, 2013), pp. 135–55.
Staiger, Emil, *Basic Concepts of Poetics*, trans. Janette C. Hudson and Luanne T. Frank (University Park: Pennsylvania State University Press, 1991).
Stalin, Joseph V., 'The foundations of Leninism', in J.V. Stalin (ed.), *Works*, Vol. 6 (Moscow: Foreign Languages Publishing House, 1953), pp. 71–196.
Stalin, Joseph V., 'Against vulgarising the slogan of self-criticism', in J.V. Stalin (ed.), *Works*, Vol. 11 (Moscow: Foreign Languages Publishing House, 1954), pp. 133–44.
Starobinsky, Jean, *Jean-Jacques Rousseau: Transparency and Obstruction*, trans. Arthur Goldhammer (Chicago: University of Chicago Press, 1988)
Studer, Brigitte, 'L'être perfectible. La formation du cadre stalinien par le "travail sur soi"', *Genèses. Sciences sociales et histoire* 51 (2003), pp. 92–113.
Studer, Brigitte, *The Transnational Word of the Cominternians* (Basingstoke: Palgrave Macmillan, 2015).

Todorov, Tzvetan, 'Le discours psychotique', in T. Todorov (ed.), *Les genres du discourse* (Paris: Seuil, 1978), pp. 78–85.

Todorov, Tzvetan, *The Genres in Discourse*, trans. Catherine Porter (Cambridge: Cambridge University Press, 1990).

Togliatti, Palmiro, 'I compiti del partito nella situazione attuale', in P. Togliatti, Opere Scelte, ed. Luciano Gruppi (Rome: Editori Riuniti, 1984), pp. 81–108.

Ventrella, Francesco, 'Carla Lonzi's artwriting and the resonance of separatism', *European Journal of Women's Studies* 21/3 (2014), pp. 282–7.

Veyne, Paul, *Writing History: Essays on Epistemology*, trans. Mina Moore-Rinvolucri (Middletown: Wesleyan University Press, 1984).

Veyne, Paul, *Did the Greeks Believe in their Myths? An Essay on the Constitutive Imagination*, trans. Paula Wissing (Chicago: University of Chicago Press, 1988).

Wallerstein, Immanuel, *Historical Capitalism with Capitalist Civilization* (London: Verso, 1996).

Watzlawick, Paul, Beavin, Jeanet H. and Jackson, Don D., *Pragmatics of Human Communication: A Study of Interactional Patterns, Pathologies, and Paradoxes* (New York: Norton, 1967).

Weber, Max, *Economy and Society: An Outline of Interpretive Sociology*, ed. Guenther Roth and Claus Wittich (Berkeley: University of California, 1978).

Wolikow, Serge and Vigreux, Jean, 'L'École Léniniste Internationale de Mouscou: une pépinière de cadres communiste', *Cahiers d'histoire* 79 (2000), pp. 45–56.

Wright Mills, Charles 'Situated actions and vocabularies of motive', *American Sociological Review* 5/6 (1940), pp. 904–13.

Yagoda, Ben, *When You Catch an Adjective, Kill It: The Parts of Speech, for Better and/or Worse* (New York: Broadway Books, 2007).

Zappaterra, Paola, 'Autobiografia e tensione alla politica nelle comuniste bolognesi', in *Storia e problemi contemporanei* 20 (1997), pp. 49–62.

Žižek, Slavoj, 'Introduction: the spectre of ideology', in S. Žižek (ed.), *Mapping Ideology* (London: Verso, 1997), pp. 1–33.

INDEX

absolute past 91, 106, 158 n.5
Augustine (Saint) 5, 6
autobiographical pact 3–6, 52
autobiographical politics 141

Benjamin, W. 37, 150 n.88, 154 n.36
Biografia del militante 21–4, 34
Braidotti, R.
    as a migrant 111, 112, 165 n.10
    Alexandrian feminism 137–40
    in *Baby Boomers* 108
    and Carla Lonzi 166 n.14
    feminist professionalism and snob feminism 133 (*see also* late feminist autobiography)
    and meritocracy 162 n.68
    Nomadic Subjects 137, 139
    and psychoanalysis 115, 116
    and sex 113–14, 163 n.81
Brooks, P. 32, 37, 71

Castellina, L. 100
Carver, R. 69–71
Chiarante, G. 95–7, 99, 102
communist autobiographical tradition 136, 137
confession 14, 17, 31–4, 55
Cossutta, A. 93, 96, 99, 102, 121
criticism and self-criticism 14, 17, 32

difference between communist and feminist self-enunciation 51, 52, 54, 56, 57, 61, 74, 135, 136, 154 n.42, 104
difference between original and later communist autobiographies 89, 90, 94, 95, 98, 103, 137
difference between original and later feminist autobiographies 104, 108, 109, 132, 133, 137, 138
Differenze (feminist journal) 87

Five Star Movement 140, 141
Foucault, M.
    pastoral power 26, 27, 29, 148 n.60
    technologies of the self 3
French Communist Party 18, 19, 126

Garfinkel, H. 3, 165 n.5
Goffman, E. 2, 106, 160 n.43

Hegel, G. W. F. 130, 131

Ingrao, P. 91, 92, 96–8, 99–101, 103, 114, 121, 137, 159 n.24
Ishmael (*Moby-Dick*'s character) 92, 102
Italian Communist Party 2, 8, 20, 89

Kharkhordin, O. 12, 37, 144 n.11

late communist autobiography
    as a *Bildungsroman* 90, 96, 100
    antiquarian self-narrative 98–100
    critical self-narrative 101
    epistemic foundation of 95, 96
    existential foundation of 95, 97
    legitimacy of 94–5, 97–100, 103, 121, 136
    monumental self-narrative 102, 103, 125
    and the working class 124
late feminist autobiography
    as a success story 138
    aphasia in 118, 119
    dream-like materials 107
    hellenistic feminism 139, 165 n.10
    legitimacy of 104, 116–17, 120, 121
    legitimate illegitimacy of 113
    normalization of 104, 109, 116, 127, 136
    paranoid strategy 106, 115
    pop-art style 110, 115

professional feminism 113, 118, 120, 139
and psychoanalysis 107, 109, 115, 132
self-marketing strategy 111, 162 n.61
schizophrenic strategy 119, 120
Lejeune, P. 3–5, 36, 37
Lepetit, L.
  as an unreliable narrator 128
  and Carla Lonzi 131, 132
  and feminist romanticism 121
  and money 129, 132, 164 n.110
  and psychoanalysis 132
  and Rosi Braidotti 165 n.4 (*see also* late feminist autobiography)
  and the violence in history 129, 130, 164 n.109
Lonzi, C.
consciousness-raising (definition) 48
dream transcripts 4, 81–2
elimination of the referent 69–71
infinite discourse in *Taci, anzi parla* 60–5
and late feminist autobiographies 137, 138
and Luisa Passerini 106–8
and Maria Schiavo 118, 119
meta-diaristic acts 67, 68, 155 n.50
Vai pure 75, 76
tears 72, 155 n.63

Macaluso, E. 91, 92, 96, 99, 102, 103, 125
Magri, L. 159 n.17
Martinelli, A. 84, 85
master narrator 94, 159 n.15
Melandri, L.
  and Carla Lonzi 85, 86, 157 n.91
  dream transcripts 84, 85
  narrative agenda of 1970s 53, 54

Napolitano, G.
  as a Weberian ideal official 126
  impersonal self-narrative 126, 137
  his political career 121, 127
neo-feminism 2, 47
  consciousness-raising groups 48–50, 53, 55, 118, 151 n.4, 151 n.10, 152 n.20
  and psychoanalysis 48, 49
  and the secret 55, 56, 71
Novelli, D. 98, 99

old and new left 1, 135
original communist autobiography
  as a *Bildungsroman* 42, 43, 61, 135
  autobiographical 'degree zero' 35–7
  in Bolshevism 11–14
  chaotic and nonchaotic enumeration 35, 36, 149 n.78
  character as *figura* 44–6
  emergence of the character 38–40
  Italian militant's self-narratives 31, 34, 35, 38–45
  plot and story 37, 38, 41
  subordination of the character to the narrator 40–4
original feminist autobiography
  catatonic strategy 59, 86–88
  degree zero of narration 66
  difference between catatonic, paranoid and schizophrenic strategy 88
  difference between paranoid and schizophrenic strategy 85, 86
  dream-like account 4, 5, 8, 81–4
  elimination of the referent 68–71, 75, 79, 85, 86
  lyrical voice 77–80
  melodrama of the self 71–3
  paranoid strategy 59, 62–4, 68, 71–3, 81–4
  schizophrenic autobiography 80, 81, 86
  schizophrenic strategy 59, 74, 80–5

Paietta, G. 30, 102, 163 n.96
paradoxical injunction (definition) 7, 8, 28, 143 n.25
paradoxical injunction in communist organization 28–30, 33, 34, 43
paradoxical injunction in feminist movement
  'be yourself!' 54, 74
  'speak the unspeakable!' 54–7, 61, 72–4, 76, 80, 83, 85, 88, 119
Passerini, L. 8, 104–10, 116, 127, 137
PCI (*see* Italian Communist Party)
PCF (*see* French Communist Party)
Pellegrini, D. 119, 120, 127, 137
Plutarch 108, 109, 111
On Populist Reason (Laclau, E.) 140, 141
protocol sentence 14, 145 n.13

revelation by deeds 12–14, 18, 37, 144 n.11
Rivolta Femminile (feminist group) 8, 60, 61, 63, 84, 153 n.32, 153 n.35, 157 n.90 (*see also* Lonzi, C.)
Rossanda, R. 90–2, 96, 99, 101, 103

Schiavo, M. 116–20, 127, 137
Schmitt, C. 29, 30
Schopenhauer, A. 128
Secchia, P.
    activation of party members 24–7, 28, 29
    party as a school 26, 27
Sottosopra (feminist journal) 8, 50, 66, 75, 76, 87, 105, 109
Staiger, E. 156 n.79
Stalin, J. V. 13–15, 17

On the Advantage and Disadvantage of History for Life (Nietzsche, F.) 98–100, 102

The Division of Labour in Society (Durkheim, É.) 15–17
The Sociology of George Simmel (Simmel, G.) 55
Todorov, T.
    catatonic discourse 58
    paranoid discourse 57, 58, 64, 65, 68, 106 (*see also* original feminist autobiography)
    schizophrenic discourse 58, 74, 79, 80, 84
Togliatti, P.
    new party 2, 19, 20, 24
    political strategy 19, 146 n.40
Thorez, M. 19, 126

Veyne, P. 136, 138, 139

Weber, M. 94, 125
Weberian ideal type 30
Wilhelm Meister's Apprenticeship (Goethe, J. W.) 150 n.96

www.ingramcontent.com/pod-product-compliance
Lightning Source LLC
Chambersburg PA
CBHW070641300426
44111CB00013B/2200